COASTAL
SOUTHEAST

Formerly Mobil Travel Guide

ACKNOWLEDGMENTS

We gratefully acknowledge the help of our representatives for their efficient and perceptive inspections of the lodgings listed. Forbes Travel Guide is also grateful to the talented writers who contributed to this book.

Some of the information contained herein is derived from a variety of third-party sources. Although every effort has been made to verify the information obtained from such sources, the publisher assumes no responsibility for inconsistencies or inaccuracies in the data or liability for any damages of any type arising from errors or omissions.

Neither the editors nor the publisher assume responsibility for the services provided by any business listed in this guide or for any loss, damage or disruption in your travel for any reason.

ISBN: 9-780841-61415-4   Manufactured in the USA

10 9 8 7 6 5 4 3 2 1

TABLE OF CONTENTS

STAR ATTRACTIONS

If you've been a reader of Mobil Travel Guide, you will have heard that this historic brand partnered with another storied media name, Forbes, in 2009 to create a new entity, Forbes Travel Guide. For more than 50 years, Mobil Travel Guide assisted travelers in making smart decisions about where to stay and dine when traveling. With this new partnership, our mission has not changed: We're committed to the same rigorous inspections of hotels, restaurants and spas—the most comprehensive in the industry with more than 500 standards tested at each property we visit—to help you cut through the clutter and make easy and informed decisions on where to spend your time and travel budget. Our team of anonymous inspectors are constantly on the road, sleeping in hotels, eating in restaurants and making spa appointments, evaluating those exacting standards to determine a property's rating.

What kind of standards are we looking for when we visit a proprety? We're looking for more than just high-thread count sheets, pristine spa treatment rooms and white linen-topped tables. We look for service that's attentive, individualized and unforgettable. We note how long it takes to be greeted when you sit down at your table, or to be served when you order room service, or whether the hotel staff can confidently help you when you've forgotten that one essential item that will make or break your trip. Unlike other travel ratings entities, we visit the places we rate, testing hundreds of attributes to compile our ratings, and our ratings cannot be bought or influenced. The Forbes Five Star rating is the most prestigious achievement in hospitality—while we rate more than 8,000 properties in the U.S., Canada, Hong Kong, Macau and Beijing, for 2010, we have awarded Five Star designations to only 53 hotels, 21 restaurants and 18 spas. When you travel with Forbes, you can travel with confidence, knowing that you'll get the very best experience, no matter who you are.

We understand the importance of making the most of your time. That's why the most trusted name in travel is now Forbes Travel Guide.

STAR RATED HOTELS

Whether you're looking for the ultimate in luxury or the best value for your travel budget, we have a hotel recommendation for you. To help you pinpoint properties that meet your needs, Forbes Travel Guide classifies each lodging by type according to the following characteristics:

★★★★★These exceptional properties provide a memorable experience through virtually flawless service and the finest of amenities. Staff are intuitive, engaging and passionate, and eagerly deliver service above and beyond the guests' expectations. The hotel was designed with the guest's comfort in mind, with particular attention paid to craftsmanship and quality of product. A Five Star property is a destination unto itself.

★★★★These properties provide a distinctive setting, and a guest will find many interesting and inviting elements to enjoy throughout the property. Attention to detail is prominent throughout the property, from design concept to quality of products provided. Staff are accommodating and take pride in catering to the guest's specific needs throughout their stay.

★★★These well-appointed establishments have enhanced amenities that provide travelers with a strong sense of location, whether for style or function. They may have a distinguishing style and ambience in both the public spaces and guest rooms; or they may be more focused on functionality, providing guests with easy access to local events, meetings or tourism highlights.

★★The Two Star hotel is considered a clean, comfortable and reliable establishment that has expanded amenities, such as a full-service restaurant.

★The One Star lodging is a limited-service hotel or inn that is considered a clean, comfortable and reliable establishment.

For every property, we also provide pricing information. All prices quoted are accurate at the time of publication; however, prices cannot be guaranteed.

STAR RATED RESTAURANTS

Every restaurant in this book comes highly recommended as an outstanding dining experience.

★★★★★Forbes Five Star restaurants deliver a truly unique and distinctive dining experience. A Five Star restaurant consistently provides exceptional food, superlative service and elegant décor. An emphasis is placed on originality and personalized, attentive and discreet service. Every detail that surrounds the experience is attended to by a warm and gracious dining room team.

★★★★These are exciting restaurants with often well-known chefs that feature creative and complex foods and emphasize various culinary techniques and a focus on seasonality. A highly-trained dining room staff provides refined personal service and attention.

★★★Three Star restaurants offer skillfully-prepared food with a focus on a specific style or cuisine. The dining room staff provides warm and professional service in a comfortable atmosphere. The décor is well-coordinated with quality fixtures and decorative items, and promotes a comfortable ambience.

★★The Two Star restaurant serves fresh food in a clean setting with efficient service. Value is considered in this category, as is family friendliness.

★The One Star restaurant provides a distinctive experience through culinary specialty, local flair or individual atmosphere.

Because menu prices can fluctuate, we list a pricing range rather than specific prices. The pricing ranges are per diner, and assume that you order an appetizer or dessert, an entrée and one drink.

STAR RATED SPAS

Forbes Travel Guide's spa ratings are based on objective evaluations of more than 450 attributes. About half of these criteria assess basic expectations, such as staff courtesy, the technical proficiency and skill of the employees and whether the facility is clean and maintained properly. Several standards address issues that impact a guest's physical comfort and convenience, as well as the staff's ability to impart a sense of personalized service. Additional criteria measure the spa's ability to create a completely calming ambience.

★★★★★Stepping foot in a Five Star spa will result in an exceptional experience with no detail overlooked. These properties wow their guests with extraordinary design and facilities, and uncompromising service. Expert staff cater to your every whim and pamper you with the most advanced treatments and skin care lines available. These spas often offer exclusive treatments and may emphasize local elements.

★★★★Four Star spas provide a wonderful experience in an inviting and serene environment. A sense of personalized service is evident from the moment you check in and receive your robe and slippers. The guest's comfort is always of utmost concern to the well-trained staff.

★★★These spas offer well-appointed facilities with a full complement of staff to ensure that guests' needs are met. The spa facilities include clean and appealing treatment rooms, changing areas and a welcoming reception desk.

GEORGIA

THINK SWEET TEA AND PEACHES. THINK CIVIL WAR AND CIVIL RIGHTS HISTORY. THINK MILES of golf, fishing, hiking and hunting…and antebellum gentility. With Georgia on your mind (and a tip of the hat to Ray Charles), there's no limit to the travel experiences offered up by the Peach State.

Tourism is one of Georgia's primary industries, and the state boasts many wonders, from its Blue Ridge vacation lands in the north—where Brasstown Bald Mountain rises 4,784 feet—to the deep "trembling earth" of the ancient Okefenokee Swamp bordering Florida. Stone Mountain, a giant hunk of rock that rises from the plain near Atlanta, is the world's largest granite exposure. The coastal Golden Isles, set off by the Marshes of Glynn, feature moss-festooned oaks that grow down to the white sandy beaches.

Historical attractions also abound, from the world's largest brick fort near Savannah to the Martin Luther King Jr. Historical District in Atlanta. There is the infamous Confederate prison at Andersonville and the still lavish splendor of the cottage colony of 60 millionaires of the Jekyll Island Club, now a state-owned resort. Most towns in the state have historical homes and museums offering perspective on Native Americans as well as Revolutionary and Civil War efforts and artifacts.

The state of Georgia holds a storied place in America's past, beginning with the founding of the Georgia Colony in the early 1700s by James Oglethorpe and named for King George II of England. Georgia's barrier islands not only sheltered the fledgling colony, they provided a bulwark on the Spanish Main for English forts to oppose Spanish Florida and help end the centuries-old struggle for domination among the Spanish, French and English along the South Atlantic Coast.

The state was one of the country's original 13 colonies and the fourth state to join the Union (January 2, 1788), but the fifth of the 11 Confederate states to secede during the Civil War. Georgia's lot in the Civil War was a harsh one from the time Sherman opened his campaign on May 4, 1864, until he achieved the Union objective of splitting the South from the Mississippi to the sea. Reconstruction ushered in a long, slow recovery, but today Georgia's capital city, Atlanta, is the center of the New South, alive with culture and history and teeming with business—the city boasts headquarters for Coca-Cola, Delta Airlines and Home Depot, among others. The state is the nation's largest producer of peanuts, pecans and peaches and is also heavy in paper and wood pulp production.

ALBANY

See also Americus

Southwestern Georgia is home to the Plantation Trace region, famous for its woodlands, rivers and its rich farm and history. Albany and surrounding Dougherty County are no exception. Known as the "Pecan Capital of the World," the area is renowned for its quail hunting and is home to a massive 800-acre animal park. The town was founded by Colonel Nelson Tift, a Connecticut Yankee who led a party up the Flint River from Apalachicola,

Florida and constructed the first log buildings. Settlers followed when the Native Americans were moved to western lands.

WHAT TO SEE
ALBANY MUSEUM OF ART
311 Meadowlark Drive, Albany, 229-439-8400; www.albanymuseum.com
The museum's collection of sub-Saharan African art is particularly strong. About 15 other permanent and changing exhibits feature both local and regional artists.
Tuesday-Friday 10 a.m.-5 p.m.

THE PARKS AT CHEHAW
105 Chehaw Park Road, Albany, 229-430-5275; www.parksatchehaw.org
The creeks, streams and cypress swamps of this 800-acre park are home to all sorts of wildlife, including deer, beavers, tortoises, alligators and a variety of birds. Nature trails allow visitors to see the animals up close, and an old-style locomotive takes visitors on a 20-minute train ride through a restored area. Don't miss the fantastic children's park and farm or the wild animal park, designed by famed naturalist Jim Fowler, which features rhinos and the only cheetah population in Georgia.
Admission: adults $2, children under 12 $1, seniors adults over 62 and military $1. Daily 9 a.m.-5 p.m. Zoo hours: 9:30 a.m.-5 p.m. Admission: adults $7.75, children under 12 $4, senior adults over 62 and military $4 (includes park pass).

WHERE TO STAY
★COMFORT SUITES
1400 Dawson Road, Albany, 229-888-3939, 888-726-3939; www.comfortsuites.com
62 rooms. Complimentary breakfast. Fitness center. Pool. $61-150

★HAMPTON INN AT ALBANY MALL
806 N. Westover Blvd., Albany, 229-883-3300, 800-426-7866; www.hamptoninn.com
82 rooms. Complimentary breakfast. Bar. Business center. Fitness center. Pool. $61-150

★★QUALITY INN
1500 Dawson Road, Albany, 229-435-7721, 888-462-7721; www.merryacres.com
110 rooms. Restaurant, bar. Complimentary breakfast. Fitness center. Pool. $61-150

★REGENCY INN
911 E. Oglethorpe Expressway, Albany, 229-883-1650
151 rooms. Restaurant, bar. Complimentary breakfast. Pool. $61-150

AMERICUS
See also Albany
Americus is at the center of an area once known as the "granary of the Creek nations," so called because Native Americans living in the area were known for their agriculture, particularly corn. The town was supposedly named for

either new world explorer Amerigo Vespucci or for the settlers themselves, who were referred to as "merry cusses" because of their reputed happy-go-lucky ways. The town flourished in the 1890s and many Victorian and Gothic Revival buildings remain from that period. Today the town has the headquarters for International Habitat for Humanity, which has built more than 225,000 homes around the world for those in need.

WHAT TO SEE
HABITAT FOR HUMANITY-GLOBAL VILLAGE AND DISCOVERY CENTER
121 Habitat South, Americus, 229-924-6935, 800-422-4828; www.habitat.org
See life-size replicas of houses around the world and exhibits on poverty. Learn about the organization's impact globally and experience hands-on what it's like to construct compressed earth blocks and clay roof tiles just as Habitat volunteers do in Asia and Africa.

WHERE TO STAY
★★WINDSOR HOTEL
125 W. Lamar St., Americus, 229-924-1555, 888-297-9567;
www.windsor-americus.com
53 rooms. Restaurant, bar. Spa. $61-150

ALSO RECOMMENDED
1906 PATHWAY INN BED & BREAKFAST
501 S. Lee St., Americus, 229-928-2078, 800-889-1466; www.1906pathwayinn.com
For a small-town getaway, this English Colonial bed and breakfast offers guests Old South charm.
6 rooms. Complimentary breakfast. $61-150

WHERE TO EAT
★★★GRAND DINING ROOM
125 W. Lamar St., Americus, 229-924-1555; www.windsor-americus.com
Located in the Windsor Hotel, this restaurant offers traditional Southern favorites along with cuisine from different regions of the country. A quaint Victorian setting completes the dining experience.
American. Dinner. Bar. $151-250

ATHENS
This ultimate college town is the site of the University of Georgia, which was chartered in 1785. The landscape here is stunning—set on a hill beside the Oconee River—enhanced by towering oaks and elms, white-blossomed magnolias, old-fashioned boxwood gardens and many well-preserved and still-occupied antebellum houses. But what makes Athens worth mentioning is the university's claim as one of the best college experiences in America and the town's lively (some lists even rank it among the top 10) music scene. Bands like REM, the B-52s and the Indigo Girls among others all got their start here. Whether you're looking for music festivals, college sports or antebellum history, the home of the Georgia Bulldogs offers up an active mix.

WHAT TO SEE
CHURCH-WADDEL-BRUMBY HOUSE
280 E. Dougherty St., Athens, 706-353-1820

This restored 1820 Federal-style house is thought to be the oldest residence in Athens. It houses the Athens Welcome Center, which has information on self-guided tours of other historic houses and buildings.
Monday-Saturday 10 a.m.-6 p.m., Sunday noon-6 p.m.

STATE BOTANICAL GARDEN
2450 S. Milledge Ave., Athens, 706-542-1244; www.uga.edu/botgarden

Occupying 300 acres, the botanical garden features natural trails, wildlife and special collections.
Gardens October-March daily 8 a.m.-6 p.m.; April-September daily 8 a.m.-8 p.m. Visitor Center & Conservatory Tuesday-Saturday 9 a.m.-4:30 p.m., Sunday 11:30 a.m.-4:30 p.m.

TAYLOR-GRADY HOUSE
634 Prince Ave., Athens, 706-549-8688; www.taylorgradyhouse.com

Pefectly restored in the Greek Revival style, this 1844 mansion is surrounded by 13 columns, which are said to symbolize the 13 original states. The home contains period furniture throughout.
Monday-Friday 9 a.m.-1 p.m., 2-5 p.m.

THE UNIVERSITY OF GEORGIA
College Station and East Campus Roads, Athens, 706-542-0842; www.uga.edu

Consisting of 16 schools and colleges, the main campus extends more than two miles south from the Arch, College Avenue and Broad Street. Nearby are farms managed by the College of Agriculture, a forestry preserve and University Research Park. Historic buildings from the 1800s include Demosthenian Hall; chapel; Old College, the oldest building, designed after Connecticut Hall at Yale; Waddel Hall and Phi Kappa Hall.

SPECIAL EVENTS
NORTH GEORGIA FOLK FESTIVAL
Sandy Creek Park, 400 Bob Holman Road, Athens, 706-208-0985; www.athensfolk.org

This annual festival showcases music that has roots in the region. Genres include bluegrass, gospel and more.
Early October.

SPRING TOUR OF HOMES
489 Prince Ave., Athens, 706-353-1801, www.achfonline.org

The tour celebrates Athens architecture and is held by the Athens-Clarke Heritage Foundation.
May.

WHERE TO STAY
★BEST WESTERN COLONIAL INN
170 N. Milledge Ave., Athens, 706-546-7311, 800-592-9401; www.bestwestern.com

70 rooms. Complimentary breakfast. Pool. $61-150

★★HOLIDAY INN ATHENS

197 E. Broad St., Athens, 706-549-4433, 800-465-4329; www.holidayinn.com
307 rooms. Fitness center. Spa. Pool. $61-150

★HOLIDAY INN EXPRESS ATHENS

513 W. Broad St., Athens, 706-546-8122, 800-465-4329; www.holidayinn.com
160 rooms. Complimentary breakfast. Fitness center. $61-150

WHERE TO EAT
★★HARRY BISSETT'S NEW ORLEANS CAFÉ AND OYSTER BAR

279 E. Broad St., Athens, 706-353-7065; www.harrybissetts.net
Cajun, Creole. Lunch, dinner, brunch, bar. Reservations recommended. Outdoor seating. *$16-35*

★THE VARSITY

1000 W. Broad St., Athens, 706-548-6325; www.thevarsity.com
American. Lunch, dinner. Outdoor seating. $15 and under

ATLANTA
See also Buford, Cartersville, Marietta

"An old city that feels new," is how one traveler describes this capital of the New South. Indeed, the real story of Atlanta is not its Civil War past but its present. While Atlanta proper has a population of only 429,500 due to policies that prevent annexation, the metro area is closer to 5 million. And those millions have supported the growth of Atlanta into a world-class city that offers culture (the famed Alliance Theatre), sports (four professional teams, a NASCAR speedway, numerous golf courses and an Olympic Park), 19 colleges and universities (from the Georgia Institute of Technology to Emory University to Spelman and Morehouse Colleges) and yes, some pretty spectacular history.

Atlanta began as "Standing Pitch Tree," a Native American Creek settlement until 1813 when the military built a fort and white settlers followed, making it an important trading post. After Georgia's secession from the Union on January 19, 1861, the city became a manufacturing, storage, supply and transportation center for the Confederate forces, and the last real barrier on General William Tecumseh Sherman's "March to the Sea." Although Atlanta had quartered 60,000 Confederate wounded, it was untouched by actual battle until Sherman began the fierce fighting of the Atlanta Campaign on May 7, 1864. When Union forces seized the railroad 20 miles south at Jonesboro on September 1, General Hood evacuated Atlanta, and the mayor surrendered the city the next day. The 117-day siege razed 90 percent of its buildings and homes. Many citizens returned to the city by early 1865, and Atlanta became the federal headquarters for Reconstruction. Railroad lines led the way; by 1872, Atlanta was on its way to becoming an expanded rail center for the country. Georgia is still a center for paper and wood pulp, peaches, peanuts and pecans and some mining, but Atlanta's role as the business hub of the South has really launched the region. From Coca-Cola, developed in response to Prohibition and first served at Jacob's Pharmacy on May 8, 1886, to Home Depot and Delta Airlines, Atlanta is home to many international corporate giants.

Atlanta has also been a historical center for black enterprise and culture.

Martin Luther King Jr. was born here, the annual National Black Arts Festival is the largest of its kind and the city is home to more than five historically black colleges and universities.

Cultural and historical attractions thrive on Peachtree Street, Atlanta's equivalent to New York's Broadway. Peach blossoms are few. Instead, the busy thoroughfare is lined with the city's most important skyscrapers, luxury shops and hotels.

WHAT TO SEE
ATLANTA BOTANICAL GARDEN
1345 Piedmont Ave., Atlanta, 404-876-5859; www.atlantabotanicalgarden.org
Come stroll through the 15 acres of blooming outdoor gardens: Japanese, rose, perennial and others. The Fuqua Conservatory has tropical, desert and rare plants from around the world. There's also a special exhibit area for carnivorous plants.
Tuesday-Sunday, April-October, 9 a.m.-7 p.m.; May-October, Thursdays until 10 p.m.; November-March 9 a.m.-5 p.m. Closed Mondays.

ATLANTA BRAVES (MLB)
Turner Field, 775 Hank Aaron Drive, Atlanta, 404-522-7630; www.atlantabraves.com
The Atlanta Braves are Georgia's Major League Baseball team.
April-September.

ATLANTA CYCLORAMA
Grant Park, 800 Cherokee Ave. S.E., Atlanta, 404-658-7625; www.atlantacyclorama.org
This theater in the round tells the story of the 1864 Battle for Atlanta as the studio revolves around a massive painting and diorama completed in 1885.
Tuesday-Sunday 9 a.m.-4:30 p.m.

ATLANTA HISTORY CENTER
130 W. Paces Ferry Road, Atlanta, 404-814-4000; www.atlantahistorycenter.com
The center consists of five major structures and 33 acres of woodlands and gardens. Exhibits range from basic state history to regional folk art to Georgia golf legend Bobby Jones.
Monday-Saturday 10 a.m.-5:30 p.m., Sunday noon-5:30 p.m. (gardens and grounds close at 5:15 p.m.).

CENTENNIAL OLYMPIC PARK
265 Park Ave., West, Atlanta, 404-223-4412; www.centennialpark.com
This 21-acre park was constructed for the 1996 Summer Olympics and serves as Atlanta's downtown centerpiece. It features the Fountain of Rings (where water shoots up in the shape of Olympic rings), an amphitheater and Great Lawn for festivals and concerts, a visitor center and a memorial to the two people killed in the bombing here during the Games.
Daily 7 a.m.-11 p.m.

CNN STUDIO TOUR
1 CNN Center, Atlanta, 404-827-2300, 877-426-6868; www.cnn.com
Tour the studio, view a recreation of the main control room, visit an interac-

tive exhibit of top news stories or learn the secrets of working a weather map. The 45-minute tours leave every 20 minutes; reservations recommended. Daily 9 a.m.-5 p.m.

FERNBANK MUSEUM OF NATURAL HISTORY

767 Clifton Road N.E., Atlanta, 404-929-6300; www.fernbank.edu
Exhibits at this monumental four-story museum include the Earth's formation, the dinosaur era, the first European settlers in North America and more. An IMAX theater shows nature-themed films on its giant screen and hosts "Martinis & IMAX" every Friday night.
Monday-Saturday 10 a.m.-5 p.m., Sunday noon-5 p.m.

FERNBANK SCIENCE CENTER

156 Heaton Park Drive N.E., Atlanta, 678-874-7102; www.fernbank.edu
The center includes an exhibit hall, an observatory, a planetarium and a science library. The grounds also contain a 65-acre forest area with marked trails.
Monday-Wednesday 8:30 a.m.-5 p.m., Thursday-Friday 8:30 a.m.-10 p.m., Saturday 10 a.m.-5 p.m., Sunday 1-5 p.m.

FOX THEATRE

660 Peachtree St. N.E., Atlanta, 404-881-2100; www.foxtheatre.org
One of the most lavish movie theaters in the world, the Fox was conceived as a Shriners' temple with a more than 4,000-seat auditorium, and hosts performances by the Atlanta Ballet, Broadway shows, a summer film festival, a full spectrum of concerts, theatrical events, plus trade shows and conventions. Guests in the theater (built in 1929) sit in an Arabian courtyard under an azure-painted sky with hundreds of 11-watt bulbs fixed in crystals, twinkling like stars. With 3,622 pipes, the colossal organ is the second-largest theater organ in the United States.
Tours Monday, Wednesday-Thursday 10 a.m., Saturday 10 a.m. and 11 a.m.

GEORGIA AQUARIUM

225 Baker St., Atlanta, 404-581-4000; www.georgiaaquarium.org
This three-year-old aquarium is the world's largest and most up-to-date. The site holds more than 8 million gallons of fresh and salt water and more animals than any other aquarium in existence. On display are rare whale sharks, beluga whales, penguins, eels, seals and just about any kind of fish imaginable.
Sunday-Friday 10 a.m.-5 p.m., Saturday 9 a.m.-6 p.m.

GEORGIA STATE FARMERS' MARKET

16 Forest Parkway, Forest Park, 404-675-1782; www.agr.state.ga.us
Owned and operated by the state and covering 150 acres, this is one of the largest farmers' markets of its kind in the Southeast.
Tuesday-Saturday.

HIGH MUSEUM OF ART

1280 Peachtree St. N.E., Atlanta, 404-733-4444; www.high.org
The High Museum features African sculpture; European, American and

contemporary painting and sculpture; decorative art; and photography. They have rotating exhibits.

Tuesday-Saturday 10 a.m.-5 p.m., Thursday 10 a.m.-8 p.m., Sunday noon-5 p.m.

JIMMY CARTER LIBRARY AND MUSEUM

441 Freedom Parkway, Atlanta, 404-865-7100; www.jimmycarterlibrary.org

This museum has exhibits on life in the White House, major events during the Carter administration and the life of President Carter. It includes a full-scale replica of the Oval Office.

Museum: Monday-Saturday 9 a.m.-4:45 p.m., Sunday noon-4:45 p.m.

Library: Monday-Friday 8:30 a.m.-4:30 p.m.

MARGARET MITCHELL HOUSE

990 Peachtree St., Northeast, Atlanta, 404-249-7015; www.gwtw.org

Home of the famous Atlanta native and author of *Gone with the Wind*, which was written here in a cramped basement apartment. The museum displays a portrait of Scarlett O'Hara from the movie, the original door from Tara, Scarlett's home and a great collection of movie posters. There are hour-long guided tours.

Monday-Saturday 9:30 a.m.-5:30 p.m., Sunday noon-5 p.m.

MARTIN LUTHER KING, JR. NATIONAL HISTORIC SITE

450 Auburn Ave., Atlanta, 404-331-5190; www.nps.gov/malu

This two-block area memorializes of the famed leader of the Civil Rights movement and winner of the Nobel Peace Prize. Features include the Freedom Hall Complex, Chapel of All Faiths, King Library and Archives and the reflecting pool. Films and slides on Dr. King's life and work may be viewed in the screening room. The National Park Service operates an information center. Guided tours of King's boyhood home are conducted by park rangers.

Daily 9 a.m.-5 p.m.

SIX FLAGS OVER GEORGIA

7561 Six Flags Parkway, Austell, 770-739-3400; www.sixflags.com/parks/overgeorgia

The whole family will love this theme park featuring Georgia's history under the flags of England, France, Spain, the Confederacy, Georgia and the U.S. There are more than 100 rides, shows and attractions, including the Georgia Cyclone roller coaster.

Mid-May-early September daily; early March-mid-May and early September-October weekends only.

STATE CAPITOL

214 State Capitol, Atlanta, 404-656-2844; www.sos.state.ga.us

The dome, topped with native gold, is 237 feet high. Inside are historical flags, statues and portraits.

Monday-Friday 8 a.m.-5:30 p.m. Tours 10 a.m., 11 a.m., 1 p.m. and 2 p.m.

STONE MOUNTAIN PARK

Highway 78 E., Stone Mountain, 770-498-5690; www.stonemountainpark.com

This 3,200-acre park surrounds the world's largest granite monolith, which rises 825 feet from the plain. The top of the mountain is accessible by foot or cable car. Surrounding the sculpture are Memorial Hall, a Civil War museum, an antebellum plantation featuring 19 buildings restored and furnished with 18th- and 19th-century heirlooms. An antique Auto and Music Museum houses cars dating from 1899 and an antique mechanical music collection; riverboat *Scarlett O'Hara* provides scenic trips around a 363-acre lake, while full-size replicas of Civil War trains make a 5-mile trip around the base of the mountain. Also, a 45-minute laser show is projected onto the north face of the mountain.

Attractions daily 10 a.m.-5 p.m.

SYMPHONY HALL

1280 Peachtree St., Atlanta, 404-733-4900; www.atlantasymphony.org

This stunning building is the permanent home of the Atlanta Symphony Orchestra, Chorus and Youth Orchestra. Check the Web site for performance dates. September-May and mid-June-mid-August.

UNDERGROUND ATLANTA

50 Upper Alabama St. S.W., Atlanta, 404-523-2311; www.underground-atlanta.com

This underground mall features shops, pushcart peddlers, restaurants and nightclubs, street entertainers and various attractions. The six-block area was created in the 1920s when several viaducts were built over existing streets at second-story level to move traffic above multiple rail crossings. Merchants moved their shops to the second floors, relegating the first floors to oblivion for nearly half a century. Today, visitors descend onto the cobblestone streets of a Victorian city in perpetual night. On lower Alabama Street, the shops are housed in the original, once-forgotten storefronts.

Monday-Saturday 10 a.m.-9 p.m., Sunday 11 a.m.-6 p.m.

THE WORLD OF COCA-COLA

101 Baker St., Atlanta, 404-676-5151; www.wocacatlanta.com

This recently renovated and expanded tribute to the world's most popular soft drinks has a 4-D theater and interactive displays and exhibits that trace the history of Coca-Cola from its introduction in 1886 at Jacob's Pharmacy Soda Fountain on Atlanta's Peachtree Street to the present. The tasting room of more than 70 different Coke products is the main draw.

September-May, Monday-Saturday 9 a.m.-5 p.m., Sunday 11 a.m.-5 p.m.; June-August, Monday-Saturday 9 a.m.-6 p.m., Sunday 11 a.m.-5 p.m.

WREN'S NEST

1050 Ralph D. Abernathy Blvd., Southwest, Atlanta, 404-753-7735

It is hard to miss this eccentric Victorian house of Joel Chandler Harris, journalist and transcriber of the Uncle Remus stories. The home features original family furnishings, books and photographs.

Tours Tuesday-Saturday 10 a.m.-2:30 p.m.

ZOO ATLANTA

Grant Park, 800 Cherokee Ave. S.E., Atlanta, 404-624-5600; www.zooatlanta.org

Located in picturesque Grant Park, the zoo features natural habitat settings and is known for its primate center, aviary and representative Southeastern habitats exhibits. The giant panda exhibit is a major draw.
Daily 9:30 a.m.-5:30 p.m., ticket booths close at 4:30 p.m.

SPECIAL EVENTS
ATLANTA DOGWOOD FESTIVAL

887 W. Marietta St., Atlanta, 404-817-6642; www.dogwood.org

This springtime festival in celebration of the blooming of Atlanta's dogwood trees features an artists' market, a kids' village full of activities and live music.
Early April.

WHERE TO STAY
★★★ATLANTA MARRIOTT MARQUIS

265 N.E. Peachtree Center Ave., Atlanta, 404-521-0000, 888-855-5701;
www.marriott.com

This polished convention hotel has a 50-story atrium and unlimited views of the city. The guest rooms are elegantly appointed, and the hotel has 120,000 square feet of meeting space.
1,663 rooms. Restaurant, bar. Spa. $151-250

★★EMBASSY SUITES BUCKHEAD

3285 Peachtree Road N.E., Atlanta, 404-261-7733, 800-362-2779;
www.atlantabuckhead.embassysuites.com
316 rooms. Restaurant, bar, Complimentary breakfast. Spa. $151-250

★★EMBASSY SUITES HOTEL AT CENTENNIAL OLYMPIC PARK

267 Marietta St., Atlanta, 404-223-2300, 800-362-2779; www.embassysuites.com
321 rooms. Restaurant, bar, Complimentary breakfast. Fitness center. Pool.
$151-250

★★EMORY INN

1641 Clifton Road, Atlanta, 404-712-6000, 800-933-6679;
www.emoryconferencecenter.com
107 rooms. Restaurant. Spa. $61-150

★★★★★FOUR SEASONS HOTEL ATLANTA

75 14th St., Atlanta, 404-881-9898, 800-332-3442; www.fourseasons.com

This Neo-classical tower rises over Atlanta's Midtown, where world-class culture, flourishing businesses and enticing stores line the streets. Well-suited for both business and leisure travelers, this hotel offers its guests fine accommodations and flawless, intuitive service. Earth tones and polished woods set a relaxed elegance in the rooms and suites. The state-of-the-art fitness center is complete with an indoor pool and sun terrace. Park 75's fresh approach to American cuisine earns praise from locals and hotel guests alike.
244 rooms. Restaurant, bar. Business center. Fitness center. Pool. Spa. $351 and up

★★★GEORGIA TECH HOTEL AND CONFERENCE CENTER

800 Spring St. N.W., Atlanta, 404-347-9440, 800-706-2899; www.gatechhotel.com

This Midtown hotel offers state-of-the-art conveniences such as flat-screen TVs to the business travelers who frequent it. The contemporary guest rooms are comfortable and feature marble bathrooms.

252 rooms. Restaurant, bar. Fitness center. Pool. $151-250

★★★THE GLENN HOTEL

110 Marietta St. N.W., Atlanta, 404-521-2250, 866-404-5366; www.glennhotel.com

Situated at the intersection of Marietta and Spring streets, the Glenn Hotel has a convenient downtown location. The Philips Arena and CNN Center are nearby, and restaurants, shops and businesses are within walking distance. The hotel is modern and cozy at the same time. Rooms have plasma TVs, large work desks with Herman Miller Aeron chairs, rain showers and Gilchrist & Soames bath amenities.

110 rooms. Restaurant, bar. $251-350

★★★GRAND HYATT ATLANTA

3300 Peachtree Road N.E., Atlanta, 404-237-1234, 888-591-1234;
www.atlanta.hyatt.com

Handsomely appointed accommodations, impeccable service and access to fashionable Buckhead dining and shopping make this city hotel a popular choice.

438 rooms. Restaurant, bar. Fitness center. $251-350

★HAMPTON INN

3398 Piedmont Road N.E., Atlanta, 404-233-5656, 888-537-1091;
www.hamptoninn.com

154 rooms. Bar. Complimentary breakfast. Pool. $151-250

★★★HILTON ATLANTA AIRPORT AND TOWERS

1031 Virginia Ave., Atlanta, 404-767-9000, 800-445-8667; www.hilton.com

Conveniently located near the airport as well as the zoo, Stone Mountain and Six Flags, this chain property is a step above with amenities that include an Olympus Gym, Jacuzzi and 24-hour room service.

504 rooms. Restaurant, bar. Pool. $151-250

★★★HILTON ATLANTA AND TOWERS

255 Courtland St. N.E., Atlanta, 404-659-2000, 800-445-8667; www.hilton.com

With five restaurants, three bars, a fitness center with a jogging track, tennis courts and billiard rooms, guests don't need to leave. The contemporary rooms feature comfortable working areas and large bathrooms.

1,226 rooms. Restaurant, bar. Fitness center. $151-250

★HOLIDAY INN EXPRESS

505 Pharr Road, Atlanta, 404-262-7880, 800-465-4329; www.hiexpress.com

87 rooms. Complimentary breakfast. Fitness center. Spa. Pool. $61-150

★★HOTEL INDIGO

683 Peachtree St. N.E., Atlanta, 404-874-9200; www.hotelindigo.com
140 rooms. Restaurant, bar. $151-250

★★★HYATT REGENCY ATLANTA

265 Peachtree St. N.E., Atlanta, 404-577-1234, 800-591-1234; www.hyatt.com
Located downtown, this 23-story atrium hotel successfully combines convenience with superb accommodations and first-class amenities, including a state-of-the-art fitness center. Minutes away are the Atlanta Market Center, Georgia Dome, Underground Atlanta and Centennial Olympic Park.
1,260 rooms. Restaurant, bar. Fitness center. Pool. $151-250

★★★★INTERCONTINENTAL BUCKHEAD

3315 Peachtree Road N.E., Atlanta, 404-946-9000, 800-972-2404;
www.intercontinental.com
Recognized as one of the leading business hotels in the area, the InterContinental Buckhead is also great for leisure travelers. Lenox Square, the largest shopping mall in the Southeast, and the upscale Phipps Plaza are within walking distance. It also boasts the only day spa in an Atlanta hotel. Vast and lovely grounds add to the experience.
422 rooms. Restaurant, bar. Complimentary breakfast. Fitness center. Spa. $251-350

★★★JW MARRIOTT HOTEL BUCKHEAD ATLANTA

3300 Lenox Road N.E., Atlanta, 404-262-3344, 800-613-2051; www.marriott.com
The upscale JW Marriott Hotel Buckhead has a prime location near the city's top shopping malls and best restaurants. Rooms have luxury bedding and pillow top mattresses, as well as marble bathrooms and soaking tubs.
367 rooms. Restaurant, bar. $251-350

★★★★THE MANSION ON PEACHTREE, A ROSEWOOD HOTEL

3376 Peachtree Road, Atlanta, 404-995-7500; www.rwmansiononpeachtree.com
Opened in May 2008, this 127-room luxury spot in the heart of Buckhead is the tallest hotel in the neighborhood. Made from limestone and cast stone, the structure soars 580 feet over the traffic on Peachtree Road. Guests are catered to by a staff of professionally trained butlers, each of whom is assigned to guests in their comfortably appointed rooms full of mirrors, modern furnishings and marble bathrooms. With daily fresh flowers and housekeeping service twice a day, this hotel is the newest destination for travelers with the most discriminating tastes. A 15,000-square-foot spa is onsite and the Tom Colicchio-owned restaurant Craft serves his brand of upscale sustainable fare to diners.
127 rooms. Restaurant, bar. Business center. Fitness center. Spa. Pool. $351 and up

★★★MARRIOTT DOWNTOWN ATLANTA

160 Spring St. N.W., Atlanta, 404-688-8600, 866-316-5959; www.marriott.com
Ideal for business travelers, this contemporary hotel has ample meeting space, a friendly staff and a location near Olympic Park, CNN Center and the

Georgia World Congress Center.

312 rooms. Restaurant, bar. $151-250

★★★OMNI HOTEL AT CNN CENTER

100 CNN Center N.W., Atlanta, 404-659-0000, 888-444-6664; www.omnihotels.com

Located in downtown Atlanta and conveniently connected to the CNN Center and the Georgia World Congress Center, this hotel offers guests spacious rooms and good service. Take a stroll through Centennial Olympic Park located across the street or enjoy the 50,000-square-foot, state-of-the-art Turner Athletic Club.

1,067 rooms. Restaurant, bar. Spa. $151-250

★★REGENCY SUITES HOTEL

975 W. Peachtree St. N.E., Atlanta, 404-876-5003, 800-642-3629;
www.regencysuites.com

96 rooms. Complimentary breakfast. $151-250

★★★THE RITZ-CARLTON, ATLANTA

181 Peachtree St. N.E., Atlanta, 404-659-0400, 800-241-3333; www.ritzcarlton.com

Its prime downtown location makes this cosmopolitan hotel convenient to businesses, government offices and sporting arenas. The rooms are handsomely decorated and offer views of the city skyline. Many suites have kitchenettes, and some feature baby grand pianos. Twice-daily housekeeping and a technology butler service are available. The clubby Atlanta Grill serves updated Southern cooking.

444 rooms. Restaurant, bar. $251-350

★★★★THE RITZ-CARLTON, BUCKHEAD

3434 Peachtree Road N.E., Atlanta, 404-237-2700, 800-241-3333; www.ritzcarlton.com

This hotel is in one of the city's most fashionable neighborhoods and offers a warm and luxurious experience. The hotel underwent a complete renovation in 2008. Rooms have antique furnishings and sublime amenities like pillow-top mattresses and flat-screen TVs. Bay windows showcase views of the downtown skyline. The fitness center appeals to athletic-minded visitors, as does the indoor pool and sundeck. Afternoon tea in the Lobby Lounge is a Georgia tradition, especially after a day of perusing the area's shops. The Café is a popular gathering place for casual fare.

517 rooms. Restaurant, bar. Business center. Fitness center. Pool. $351 and up

★★★SHERATON ATLANTA HOTEL

165 Courtland St., Atlanta, 404-659-6500, 800-325-3535;
www.sheratonatlantahotel.com

Three restaurants, business conveniences and a full range of amenities make this hotel a good option for business travelers. It is close to CNN Center, the Georgia Dome and Centennial Park.

760 rooms. Restaurant, bar. $151-250

★★★★THE ST. REGIS ATLANTA

88 West Paces Ferry Road, Atlanta 404-563-7900; www.starwoodhotels.com/stregis

The sweeping grounds alone are enough to convince you never to leave this elegant Buckhead property. Wait until you set your sights on the guest rooms. Floor to ceiling windows, original art work and ebony finishes provide a sense of upscale luxury, while state-of-the-art flat-screen TVs and iPod sound docks keep rooms in line with the newest tech trends. Butler service ensures that you won't want for anything. Rejuvinate at the Remede Spa or wallow away an afternoon in the 40,000-square-foot pool piazza. Dining options run the gamut from casual bistro fare to elegant afternoon tea in the Long Gallery.

151 rooms. Restaurant, bar. Fitness center. Business center. Spa. Pool. $351 and up.

★★★TWELVE HOTEL & RESIDENCES

361 17th St. N.W., Atlanta, 404-961-1212;www.twelvehotels.com

The 26-story Twelve Hotel & Residences is located in Atlanta's recently constructed Midtown at Atlantic Station. Many shops, restaurants, a grocery store and a movie theater are just steps away. The large lobby is modern and relaxed, with floor-to-ceiling windows. Guest suites feature full kitchens, walls adorned with local artwork and LCD TVs.

101 rooms. Restaurant, bar. $151-250

★★★W ATLANTA AT PERIMETER CENTER

111 Perimeter Center West, Atlanta, 770-396-6800, 888-625-5144;www.whotels.com

Located near the Perimeter mall, this hotel has contemporary guest rooms and a lively lounge scene in the downstairs bar.

275 rooms. Restaurant, bar. $251-350

★★★THE WESTIN BUCKHEAD ATLANTA

3391 Peachtree Road N.E., Atlanta, 404-365-0065, 800-937-8461;
www.westin.com/buckhead

Located in Buckhead and adjacent to the city's best shopping malls, this 22-story hotel is a landmark. All guest rooms are spacious and decorated with Biedermeier-style furnishings. Nearby attractions include Zoo Atlanta and the Fernbank-Museum of Natural History.

376 rooms. Restaurant, bar. Fitness center. Spa. $351 and up

★★★THE WESTIN PEACHTREE PLAZA

210 Peachtree St. N.W., Atlanta, 404-659-1400, 800-937-8461;
www.westin.com/peachtree

As if the gracious service and spacious guest rooms with views of downtown weren't enough, this hotel also offers special touches such as signature luxury bedding and bath products. Dine at either of the two restaurants, enjoy a workout in the fitness center or just relax at the indoor pool.

1,068 rooms. Restaurants, bar. Fitness center. Spa. Pool. $151-250

★★★WYNDHAM PEACHTREE CONFERENCE CENTER HOTEL

2443 Highway 54 W., Peachtree City, 770-487-2000, 877-999-3223;
www.wyndham.com

Surrounded by 19 wooden acres this comfy hotel provides large rooms with pillow-top mattresses. You can also enjoy an array of activities onsite, including racquetball, tennis and volleyball. Or get in a game of golf at the adjacent course. Casual dining is available at the Terrace Restaurant.

250 rooms. Restaurant, bar. Tennis. $61-150

ALSO RECOMMENDED
GASLIGHT INN BED & BREAKFAST

1001 St., Charles Ave., N.E., Atlanta, 404-875-1001; www.gaslightinn.com

Located in the Virginia Highlands area, with easy access to rapid transit, the freeway, shopping and dining, this bed and breakfast is popular for its cozy guest rooms and great location.

Eight rooms. Restaurant. Complimentary breakfast. $151-250

LAUREL HILL BED & BREAKFAST

1992 McLendon Ave., Atlanta, 404-377-3217; www.laurelhillbandb.com

Six rooms. Complimentary breakfast. No children under age 12. $61-150

SERENBE BED & BREAKFAST

10950 Hutcheson Ferry Road, Palmetto, 770-463-2610; www.serenbe.com

This inn, built in 1901, is located on a farm where guests can feed animals, go on hayrides, have marshmallow roasts or paddle canoes and view nearby waterfalls.

Seven rooms. Complimentary breakfast. $61-150

SHELLMONT INN

821 Piedmont Ave. N.E., Atlanta, 404-872-9290; www.shellmont.com

This beautifully restored Victorian masterpiece is filled with antiques; some are original to the house.

Five rooms, one carriage house. Children under 12 in carriage house only. Complimentary breakfast. $151-250

WHERE TO EAT
★★★ANTHONY'S

3109 Piedmont Road N.E., Atlanta, 404-262-7379; www.anthonysfinedining.com

Set back from the road on a three-acre wooded lot, Anthony's is housed in a plantation house built in 1797. The 12 different dining rooms and seven working fireplaces in the main dining room make for an intimate experience, perfect for special occasion and group dining. The New American menu offers classics, like veal Anthony (scallopine stuffed with lobster) and pumpkin seed and coriander-crusted grouper.

American. Lunch, dinner. Closed Sunday. Bar. Reservations recommended. $36-85

★★★ARIA

490 E. Paces Ferry Road, Atlanta, 404-233-7673; www.aria-atl.com

Once a private library in upscale Buckhead, Aria has been transformed into a contemporary restaurant. Leather walls, metal curtains and an eclectic chandelier all help to lure sophisticated diners in for chef Gerry Klaskala's Southern-inspired American cuisine. There is also a private table in the wine cellar downstairs, but you'll have to call ahead (those in-the-know book three months in advance).

American. Dinner. Closed Sunday. Bar. Reservations recommended. Outdoor seating. $36-85

★★★ATLANTA FISH MARKET

265 Pharr Road, Atlanta, 404-262-3165; www.buckheadrestaurants.com

Tucked away from the bustle of Buckhead (but hard to miss with its giant outdoor fish statue), this large, family-friendly seafood restaurant is a favorite among locals. The restaurant features several airy, comfortable dining rooms and menus printed twice daily to update customers with the freshest seafood choices. The open kitchen showcases the chefs at work.

Seafood. Lunch, dinner. Bar. Children's menu. Reservations recommended. Outdoor seating. $16-35

★★★AU PIED DE COCHON

3315 Peachtree Road N.W., Atlanta, 404-946-9070, 888-424-6835;
www.aupieddecochonatlanta.com

This popular, 24-hour French brasserie is located in the Intercontinental Buckhead
hotel. The American-French menu is available around the clock. A raw bar features fish flown in daily. Jazz five nights a week up the ante on Au Pied's offerings.

American, French. Breakfast, lunch, dinner, late-night, brunch. Bar. Children's menu. Outdoor seating. $36-85

★★BABETTE'S CAFÉ

573 N. Highland Ave., Atlanta, 404-523-9121; www.babettescafe.com

International. Dinner, Sunday brunch. Closed Monday. Bar. Children's menu. Reservations recommended. Outdoor seating. $16-35

★★★★BACCHANALIA

1198 Howell Mill Road, Atlanta, 404-365-0410; www.starprovisions.com

Set in a renovated factory complex, this urban dining room has a sleek, industrial feel. The dramatic vaulted ceiling and exposed brick-trimmed factory windows of the dining room nicely contrast the long, low-lit, sexy bar of this former meat-packing plant. Chefs Anne Quatrano and Clifford Harrison create vibrant, seasonal American menus that change daily based on whatever organic and small-farm produce is available. Plates are presented with little fuss but lots of flavor.

American. Dinner. Closed Sunday. Bar. Reservations recommended. Outdoor seating. $36-85

★BASIL'S MEDITERRANEAN CAFÉ

2985 Grandview Ave., Atlanta, 404-233-9755; www.basilsinbuckhead.com

Mediterranean. Lunch, dinner, brunch. Bar. Reservations recommended. Outdoor seating. $16-35

★★★BLUEPOINTE

3455 Peachtree Road, Atlanta, 404-237-9070; www.buckheadrestaurants.com

This popular restaurant is located in the Pennacle office building next to Lenox Square Mall. The modern décor, featuring chrome railings, eclectic tile floors, an open display kitchen, oversized windows and blue velvet and leather booths, perfectly complements the inventive Pacific Rim-Pan-Asian cuisine prepared by executive chef Doug Turbush.

Pacific-Rim/Pan-Asian. Lunch, dinner. Bar. Sushi bar. Reservations recommended. $36-85

★★★BONE'S RESTAURANT

3130 Piedmont Road N.E., Atlanta, 404-237-2663; www.bonesrestaurant.com

The masculine décor matches the juicy steaks and sides. Huge portions and high prices attract a power lunch, cigar-loving crowd. The homemade steak sauce and shortbread cookies are worth a return trip.

Steak. Lunch, dinner (Monday-Friday). Bar. Reservations recommended. $36-85

★★★THE CAFÉ

3434 Peachtree Road N.E., Atlanta, 404-237-2700, 800-241-3333; www.ritzcarlton.com

Chef Christophe LeMetayer takes his cue from his native France for the menu of this all-day restaurant in the Ritz-Carlton, Buckhead hotel. Sunday brunch is a particular treat, with more than 100 dishes offered.

American. Breakfast, lunch, Sunday brunch. Bar. Children's menu. Reservations recommended. Outdoor seating. $16-35

★★★CANOE

4199 Paces Ferry Road N.W., Atlanta, 770-432-2663; www.canoeatl.com

Right on the banks of the Chattahoochee River, this casual but sophisticated restaurant serves delicious American cuisine prepared by executive chef and seventh generation Atlantan Carvel Grant Gould. The eclectic menu ranges from slow-roasted beef short ribs to seared Georgia Mountain Trout. A canoe-like ceiling, wrought iron paddle table legs, overstuffed chairs, art by local artists and a brick display kitchen with a copper hood add to the experience.

American. Lunch, dinner, Sunday brunch. Bar. Outdoor seating. $36-85

★★★CHOPS

70 W. Paces Ferry Road, Atlanta, 404-262-2675; www.buckheadrestaurants.com

Chops is really two restaurants in one. Upstairs, power diners chomp on delicious prime-aged beef in a clubby steakhouse atmosphere (dark mahogany paneling, black leather booths with burgundy seats and an open display kitchen). Downstairs in the Lobster Bar, diners sit in white stucco grottos and savor delicate seafood creations.

Steak, seafood. Lunch, dinner. Bar. Reservations recommended. $36-85

★★★CITY GRILL
50 Hurt Plaza, Atlanta, 404-524-2489; www.citygrillatlanta.com

Located in a office building that once housed the Federal Reserve Bank, this sophisticated restaurant features regional American cuisine in an elegant environment.

American. Lunch, dinner. Closed Sunday. Bar. Children's menu. Reservations recommended. $36-85

★THE COLONNADE
1879 Cheshire Bridge Road, Atlanta, 404-874-5642

American. Lunch, dinner. Bar. Outdoor seating. No credit cards accepted. $16-35

★COWTIPPERS
1600 Piedmont Ave., Atlanta, 404-874-3751; www.cowtippersatlanta.com

Tex-Mex. Lunch, dinner. Bar. Children's menu. Outdoor seating. $16-35

★★DAILEY'S
17 International Blvd., Atlanta, 404-681-3303; www.daileysrestaurant.com

American. Lunch, dinner. Bar. $16-35

★DUSTY'S BARBECUE
1815 Briarcliff Road, Atlanta, 404-320-6264; www.dustys.com

Barbecue. Lunch, dinner. Children's menu. $15 and under

★★★ECCO
40 Seventh St., Atlanta, 404-347-9555; www.ecco-restaurant.com

Ecco, located in Midtown Atlanta, offers fresh selections of meats and cheeses, abundant small plates and main courses. The seasonal European cuisine—with Spanish, Italian and French influences—includes dishes such as roasted chicken breast with rapini, olives, lemon and sage or fig-glazed lamb loin with warm potatoes and chicory. Enhance the experience with any of the unique cocktails served.

International. Dinner. Bar. Reservations recommended. Outdoor seating. $16-35

★★FIRE OF BRAZIL CHURRASCARIA
118 Perimeter Center West, Atlanta, 770-551-4367; www.fireofbrazil.com

Brazilian. Lunch, dinner. Bar. Reservations recommended. Outdoor seating. $36-85

★FLYING BISCUIT CAFÉ
1655 McLendon Ave., Atlanta, 404-687-8888; www.flyingbiscuit.com

American. Breakfast, lunch, dinner. Children's menu. Reservations recommended. $16-35

★★★THE FOOD STUDIO
887 W. Marietta St., Studio K 102, Atlanta, 404-815-1178; www.thefoodstudio.com

Inside a century-old renovated factory lies this hidden gem of a restaurant. With dishes such as seared sea scallops with edamame succotash and smoked tomato vinaigrette, and an organic heirloom tomato salad with grilled corn-bread and lemon mayonnaise, this restaurant celebrates the wide array of regional flavors found across America.

American. Dinner. Bar. Reservations recommended. Outdoor seating. $36-85

★★FRITTI
309 N. Highland Ave., Atlanta, 404-880-9559; www.frittirestaurant.com

Italian. Lunch, dinner. Bar. Children's menu. Reservations recommended. Outdoor seating. $16-35

★GEORGIA GRILLE
2290 Peachtree Road, Atlanta, 404-352-3517; www.georgiagrille.com

Southwestern. Dinner. Closed Monday. Bar. Reservations recommended. $36-85

★HAVELI
225 Spring St., Atlanta, 404-522-4545

Indian. Lunch, dinner. Bar. Reservations recommended. $16-35

★★HORSERADISH GRILL
4320 Powers Ferry Road, Atlanta, 404-255-7277; www.horseradishgrill.com

American, Southern. Lunch, dinner, Sunday brunch. Bar. Children's menu. Reservations recommended. Outdoor seating. $16-35

★★HSU'S GOURMET CHINESE
192 Peachtree Center Ave., Atlanta, 404-659-2788; www.hsus.com

Chinese. Lunch, dinner. Bar. Children's menu. Reservations recommended. $16-35

★★IMPERIAL FEZ
2285 Peachtree Road N.E., Atlanta, 404-351-0870; www.imperialfez.com

Mediterranean, Moroccan. Dinner. Children's menu. Reservations recommended. $16-35

★★★JOËL
3290 Northside Parkway, Atlanta, 404-233-3500; www.joelrestaurant.com

Executive chef and owner Joël Antunes was the former executive chef at the Ritz-Carlton, Buckhead restaurant. In 2005 he won the James Beard award for best chef Southeast, so one can likely count on the fare at Joël to be delicious. And it is. Sample dishes include lobster risotto with asparagus and artichokes and braised beef short ribs in red wine sauce.

American. Lunch, dinner. Closed Sunday. Bar. Reservations recommended. Outdoor seating. $36-85

★★★KYMA
3085 Piedmont Road, Atlanta, 404-262-0702; www.buckheadrestaurants.com

True to its name, the atmosphere at Kyma ("wave" in Greek) brings to mind the crisp, clean seascape colors of the Greek Islands. The restaurant specializes in classic Greek dishes, especially fresh seafood.

Greek. Dinner. Closed Sunday. Bar. Reservations recommended. Outdoor seating. $36-85

★★★LA GROTTA

2637 Peachtree Road N.E., Atlanta, 404-231-1368; www.lagrottaatlanta.com

There are two outposts of this upscale Italian restaurant (this one in Buckhead and a sister property in Dunwoody), both of which are decorated in traditional Italian décor. The menu includes homemade pastas such as goat cheese ravioli and entrées like grilled salmon.

Italian. Dinner. Closed Sunday. Bar. Reservations recommended. Outdoor seating. $36-85

★MARY MAC'S TEA ROOM

224 Ponce de Leon Ave. N.E., Atlanta, 404-876-1800; www.marymacs.com

Southern. Lunch, dinner. Bar. Children's menu. Reservations recommended. $15 and under

★★★MCKENDRICK'S

4505 Ashford Dunwoody Ave., Atlanta, 770-512-8888; www.mckendricks.com

This upscale steakhouse restaurant is located near the Perimeter shopping mall and is a great place for business dinners. The atmosphere is clubby, the steaks thick and the seafood fresh (try the lobster). The 350-strong wine list has won critical acclaim. Steak. Lunch, dinner. Bar. Reservations recommended. $36-85

★★MCKINNON'S LOUISIANE

3209 Maple Drive, Atlanta, 404-237-1313; www.mckinnons.com

Cajun/Creole. Dinner. Bar. Live music. Reservations recommended. $16-35

★★NAKATO JAPANESE RESTAURANT

1776 Cheshire Bridge Road N.E., Atlanta, 404-873-6582; www.nakatorestaurant.com

Japanese. Dinner. Bar. Children's menu. Reservations recommended. $16-35

★★★NAVA

3060 Peachtree Road, Atlanta, 404-240-1984; www.buckheadrestaurants.com

The Southwestern décor (terra cotta stone floor, log-beamed ceilings, cow hide-covered bar seats) complements the food, which is full of bold flavors, vibrant colors and exotic textures. Signature margaritas, Ancho chili grilled flatiron steak, jalapeno grilled shrimp, garlic chipotle mashed potatoes and Serrano roasted lamb rack are just some of the authentic offerings from chef Jesse Perez.

Southwestern. Lunch, dinner. Bar. Reservations recommended. Outdoor seating. $36-85

★★NICKIEMOTO'S

990 Piedmont Ave., Atlanta, 404-253-2010; www.nickiemotosmidtown.com

Sushi/Pan-Asian. Lunch, dinner. Bar. Reservations recommended. Outdoor seating. $16-35

★★★NIKOLAI'S ROOF

255 Courtland St., Atlanta, 404-221-6362, 800-445-8667; www.nikolaisroof.com

Located at the Hilton in downtown Atlanta, this French-Russian restaurant delivers a panoramic view along with chilled vodka and Russian classics like borscht and piroshkis, foie gras and boar tenderloin. The restaurant also offers the largest single malt collection in the city. Choose from an eight-course prix fixe dinner or an à la carte menu. Wine pairings from the award-winning wine list are also offered.

International. Dinner. Closed Sunday. Bar. Children's menu. Reservations recommended. $36-85

★★★ONE MIDTOWN KITCHEN

559 Dutch Valley Road, Atlanta, 404-892-4111; www.onemidtownkitchen.com

Located off the beaten path near Piedmont Park, this Midtown restaurant serves a changing menu of small plates and dishes such as pork dumplings with hominy, braised lamb shank with red pepper grits and port-anise poached pear. Wines can be enjoyed four ways from five price tiers. This list changes nightly, too. Dessert by noted pastry chef Jonathan St. Hilaire should not be skipped.

American. Dinner. Bar. Reservations recommended. Outdoor seating. $16-35

★★★PANO'S & PAUL'S

1232 W. Paces Ferry Road, Atlanta, 404-261-3662; www.buckheadrestaurants.com

Don't let the strip mall location of this restaurant fool you. Locals say this upscale restaurant defines Buckhead fine dining. Executive chef Gary Donlick's American-Continental menu includes fried lobster tail and other contemporary specialties. An extensive wine list, weekend piano music and friendly service complete the experience.

American, Continental. Dinner. Closed Sunday. Bar. Reservations recommended. $36-85

★★★★PARK 75

75 14th St. N.E., Atlanta, 404-253-3840, 800-332-3442; www.fourseasons.com

Located in the Four Seasons Hotel, Park 75 is a classic choice for tranquil and comfortable fine dining. The serene, pale-yellow dining room is warmed by iron candelabras, custom lighting and oversized watercolor murals. The cross-cultural menu offers seasonal local vegetables, meats and fish. The signature Park 75 surf and turf, for example, puts a twist on the classic by combining butter-braised Maine lobster with milk-fed veal filet and foie gras. The wine list is mostly American, with some boutique and international selections. For a special treat, reserve the chef's table and enjoy an eight-course menu with wines to match.

American. Breakfast, lunch, dinner, Sunday brunch. Bar. Children's menu. Reservations recommended. $36-85

★★PETITE AUBERGE

2935 N. Druid Hill Road, Atlanta, 404-634-6268; www.petiteauberge.com

Continental, French. Lunch, dinner. Closed Sunday. Bar. Reservations recommended. Outdoor seating. $16-35

★PITTYPAT'S PORCH

25 International Blvd., Atlanta, 404-525-8228; www.pittypatsrestaurant.com

Southern. Dinner. Bar. Children's menu. Reservations recommended. $36-85

★★★PRICCI

500 Pharr Road, Atlanta, 404-237-2941; www.buckheadrestaurants.com

This ultra-modern upscale Italian restaurant is the place to see and be seen. Among the menu highlights are pastas like beef short rib ravioli and osso bucco. The wine list has an extensive selection of regional Italian labels. Italian. Lunch, dinner. Bar. Reservations recommended. $36-85

★★★PRIME

3393 Peachtree Road N.E., Atlanta, 404-812-0555; www.heretoserverestaurants.com

Prime redefines the term "surf and turf" by including sushi. Floor-to-ceiling windows, an open kitchen that displays chef Tom Catherall in action and a location in the upscale Lenox Square Mall make this an exciting alternative to the traditional steakhouse.

Seafood, steak, sushi. Lunch, dinner. Bar. Children's menu. Reservations recommended. $16-35

★★★★QUINONES AT BACCHANALIA

1198 Howell Mill Road, Atlanta, 404-365-0410; www.starprovisions.com

Quinones at Bacchanalia has an intimate dining area—11 tables, with room for only 38 guests—and a subdued atmosphere with pressed Irish linens and oil lamps on the tables. A 10-course prix-fixe contemporary American menu features new creations daily. Sample inspired Southern-influenced dishes such as squab with turnip greens and butter beans, or flounder with local pecans, apples and butternut squash. Desserts are elegant takes on Southern classics, like pecan tart with vanilla bean ice cream.

Contemporary American. Dinner. Closed Sunday-Tuesday. Reservations recommended. $86 and up

★★★RATHBUN

112 Krog St., Atlanta, 404-524-8280; www.rathbunsrestaurant.com

This polished restaurant serves American cuisine in Inman Park on Atlanta's east side. The building, which was a potbelly stove factory, is nestled among rehabbed buildings and condos. Nationally acclaimed chef Kevin Rathbun is a fixture on Atlanta's restaurant scene.

American. Dinner. Closed Sunday. Bar. Reservations recommended. Outdoor seating. $36-85

★★RAY'S ON THE RIVER

6700 Powers Ferry Road, Atlanta, 770-955-1187; www.raysrestaurants.com

Seafood. Lunch, dinner, Sunday brunch. Bar. Children's menu. Outdoor seating. $16-35

★★★RESTAURANT EUGENE

2277 Peachtree Road, Atlanta, 404-355-0321; www.restauranteugene.com

Restaurant Eugene co-owner Gina Hopkins and chef/co-owner Linton Hopkins aim for a friendly, exceptional dining experience. The menu features dishes like beef rib eye with beer-battered onion rings, and Berkshire black pork belly with cabbage, granny smith apples, spiced pecans and whole grain mustard. Dessert includes cornmeal pound cake with warm spiced peaches, and an ice-cream sundae with fried plantain chips, dark chocolate sauce, homemade strawberry preserves and pineapple chunks.

American. Dinner. Bar. Reservations recommended. Outdoor seating. $36-85

★★★THE RIVER ROOM
4403 Northside Parkway, Atlanta, 404-233-5455; www.riverroom.com

Come on a Friday night to the tavern lounge and listen to some of the city's best musicians. The menu here is extensive, with dishes such as feta-stuffed free-range chicken served with couscous and chili-fried onion rings, and baked lobster with a cornbread stuffing.

American. Lunch, dinner, Sunday brunch. Bar. Reservations recommended. Outdoor seating. $16-35

★ROCK BOTTOM
3242 Peachtree Road, Atlanta, 404-264-0253; www.rockbottomsouth.com

American. Lunch, dinner. Bar. Children's menu. Reservations recommended. Outdoor seating. $16-35

★★★RUTH'S CHRIS STEAK HOUSE
5788 Roswell Road, Atlanta, 404-255-0035; www.ruthschris.com

This Atlanta outpost of the steakhouse chain is located on a busy road between Buckhead and the Perimeter area of Atlanta. The U.S. prime-aged, hand-cut, Midwestern, corn-fed beef is the main attraction.

Steak. Dinner. Bar. Reservations recommended. $36-85

★★SOHO CAFÉ
4300 Paces Ferry Road, Atlanta, 770-801-0069; www.sohoatlanta.com

American. Lunch, dinner. Bar. Children's menu. Reservations recommended. Outdoor seating. $16-35

★★★SOTTO SOTTO
313 N. Highland Ave., Atlanta, 404-523-6678; www.sottosottorestaurant.com

Located right next door to its sister restaurant Fritti, this spot serves dishes that prove simplicity is the best way to highlight the best ingredients. Diners can see and smell the magic happening in the open kitchen, which is also visible from the street.

Italian. Dinner. Bar. Reservations recommended. Outdoor seating. $16-35

★★SOUTH CITY KITCHEN
1144 Crescent Ave., Atlanta, 404-873-7358; www.southcitykitchen.com

Southern American. Lunch, dinner, Sunday brunch. Bar. Children's menu. Reservations recommended. Outdoor seating. $36-85

★TAQUERIA SUNDOWN CAFÉ
2165 Cheshire Bridge Road, Atlanta, 404-321-1118; www.sundowncafe.com

Southwestern. Lunch, dinner. Closed Sunday. Bar. Outdoor seating. $16-35

★★THAI CHILI

2169 Briarcliff Road Northeast, Atlanta, 404-315-6750; www.thaichilicuisine.com

Thai. Lunch, dinner. Children's menu. Reservations recommended. $16-35

★★TOULOUSE

2293 Peachtree Road N.E., Atlanta, 404-351-9533; www.toulouserestaurant.com

French. Dinner. Bar. Reservations recommended. Outdoor seating. $16-35

★★TWO URBAN LICKS

820 Ralph McGill Blvd., Atlanta, 404-522-4622; www.twourbanlicks.com

American. Dinner. Bar. Reservations recommended. Outdoor seating. $16-35

★THE VARSITY

61 North Ave., Atlanta, 404-881-1706; www.thevarsity.com

American. Lunch, dinner, late-night. Children's menu. Outdoor seating. No credit cards accepted. $15 and under

★★★VENI VIDI VICI

41 14th St., Atlanta, 404-875-8424; www.buckheadrestaurants.com

This upscale Midtown trattoria serves some of the best Italian food in town. The lunch and dinner menus are organized into small antipasti, perfect for tasting a variety of dishes.

Italian. Lunch, dinner. Bar. Reservations recommended. Outdoor seating. $36-85

★★★VILLA CHRISTINA

4000 Summit Blvd., Atlanta, 404-303-0133; www.villachristina.com

An unpretentiousness air is one of the reasons why this spot is one of the most popular Italian restaurants in Atlanta, welcoming families as well as those looking for a fine dining experience. The menu of creative Italian dishes includes an assortment of pastas, such as spaghetti with spicy pancetta, Parmesan, garlic, eggs and herbs.

Italian. Lunch, dinner. Closed Sunday. Bar. Reservations recommended. Outdoor seating. $36-85

★★THE VININGS INN

3011 Paces Mill Road, Atlanta, 770-438-2282; www.viningsinn.com

American. Lunch, dinner. Bar. Children's menu. Reservations recommended. Outdoor seating. $16-35

★★★WISTERIA

471 Highland Ave., Atlanta, 404-525-3363; www.wisteria-atlanta.com

Soft colors and fresh flowers make for a pleasant setting at this casual, comfortable restaurant located just two and a half blocks west of downtown Decatur. Popular dishes include fried catfish with hush puppies and Country Captain stew.

American. Dinner. Bar. Children's menu. Reservations recommended. $16-35

★ZOCALO

187 10th St., Atlanta, 404-249-7576; www.zocalocreativemex.com

Mexican. Lunch, dinner, Sunday brunch. Bar. Children's menu. Outdoor seating. $16-35

SPA

★★★★29 SPA AT THE MANSION ON PEACHTREE

The Mansion on Peachtree, 3376 Peachtree Road N.E., Atlanta, 404-995-7529;
www.rwmansiononpeachtree.com

Atlanta native Lydia Mondavi (whose name you may have seen on a bottle of cabernet or pinot noir) brings the anti-aging body benefits of wine to 29 SPA. The Mansion on Peachtree is home to the 15,000-square-foot spa where all of the most fabulous Georgia peaches get pampered in the 14 rooms, each complemented by heated waterbed tables, bathed in linen and silk and serving the signature wine. Quench your thirst head to toe with wine and grape seed-infused treatments for the scalp and body, massages and facials, or get primped to the (twenty) nines at home if you grab some goodies from Mondavi's line 29 Cosmetics.

★★★★REMÈDE SPA, ST. REGIS ATLANTA

88 West Paces Ferry Road, Atlanta 404-563-7900; www.starwoodhotels.com/stregis

Customization is key at this intimate hotel spa, where every service from a brow wax to a Buckhead escape body treatment is personalized and serene. The spa's 10 treatment rooms are comfortable and spacious, stocked with the Remède's exclusive line of amenities. After strolling around the city all day, nothing will feel better on your feet than a micro-exfoliating pedicure, which includes an amino acid peeling mask to smooth and soften tired toes. Or book a hot stone massage for the ultimate in muscle relaxation.

GREATER ATLANTA AREA

WHERE TO STAY

★★CLARION HOTEL ATLANTA AIRPORT

5010 Old National Highway, College Park, 404-768-9199, 877-424-6423;
www.choicehotels.com

Restaurant, bar. Complimentary breakfast. Business center. Fitness center. Pool. $151-250

★COMFORT INN AND SUITES

5985 Oakbrook Parkway, Norcross, 770-662-8175, 877-424-6423;
www.comfortinn.com

115 rooms. Complimentary breakfast. $61-150

★★COURTYARD BY MARRIOTT

2050 Sullivan Road, College Park, 770-997-2220, 800-321-2221; www.marriott.com

144 rooms. Restaurant, bar. $61-150

★★DOUBLETREE HOTEL

1075 Holcomb Bridge Road, Roswell, 770-992-9600;
www.atlantaroswell.doubletree.com

172 rooms. Restaurant, bar. $61-150

★★★HILTON ATLANTA NORTHEAST

5993 Peachtree Industrial Blvd., Norcross, 770-447-4747, 800-445-8667;
www.hilton.com

This hotel has spacious and recently redesigned guest rooms, as well as a warm and friendly staff.

272 rooms. Restaurant, bar. $61-150

★★HOLIDAY INN

6050 Peachtree Industrial Blvd. N.W., Norcross, 770-448-4400; www.holidayinn.com

244 rooms. Restaurant, bar. $61-150

★HOMEWOOD SUITES

10775 Davis Drive, Alpharetta, 770-998-1622, 800-225-5466; www.homewoodsuites.com

112 rooms. Complimentary breakfast. $151-250

★★★MARRIOTT ALPHARETTA

5750 Windward Parkway, Alpharetta, 770-754-9600, 800-228-9290; www.marriott.com

Chandeliers, Oriental rugs and luxurious furnishings accent the lobby of this elegant hotel located in Windward Office Park. Its corporate surroundings, business center services and upscale décor and amenities make it perfect for business travelers.

318 rooms. Restaurant, bar. $151-250

★★★MARRIOTT ATLANTA GWINNETT PLACE

1775 Pleasant Hill Road, Duluth, 770-923-1775, 800-228-9290; www.marriott.com

Located on 11 landscaped acres in Gwinnett County in a northeastern suburb of Atlanta, this hotel offers spacious guest rooms, an indoor and outdoor pool, whirlpool and health club.

426 rooms. Restaurant, bar. Business center. Fitness center. Pool. $151-250

★★★MARRIOTT ATLANTA NORCROSS-PEACHTREE CORNERS

475 Technology Parkway, Norcross, 770-263-8558, 800-228-9290; www.marriott.com

Located in Technology Park, this well-appointed 218-room hotel is great for business travelers. The hotel has a well-equipped business center and 4,000 square feet of meeting space.

218 rooms. Restaurant, bar. $61-150

WHERE TO EAT

★★★BISTRO VG

70 W. Crossville Road, Roswell, 770-993-1156; www.knowwheretogogh.com

This out-of-the-way restaurant offers a surprisingly lovely dining experience. The food is eclectic American, while the setting is old-Southern charm. The dining room, dotted with Van Gogh reproductions, serves New American creations by chef-owners Christopher and Michele Sedgwick. The wine cellar has more than 500 selections from around the world.

American. Lunch, dinner. Bar. Children's menu. Reservations recommended. $36-85

★★DOMINICK'S
95 S. Peachtree St., Norcross, 770-449-1611; www.dominicksitalian.com
Italian. Lunch (Monday-Friday), dinner (Saturday-Sunday). Bar. Children's menu. $16-35

★★★HI LIFE
3380 Holcomb Bridge Road, Roswell, 770-409-0101; www.hiliferestaurant.com
This American restaurant has a sleek, modern design. The creative food is fresh and flavorful. Of particular note is a four-course lobster tasting menu. American. Lunch (Monday-Friday), dinner. Closed Sunday. Bar. Children's menu. Reservations recommended. Outdoor seating. $16-35

★★RAY'S KILLER CREEK
1700 Mansell Road, Alpharetta, 770-649-0064; www.raysrestaurants.com
Steakhouse. Lunch, dinner. Bar. Children's menu. Reservations recommended. Outdoor seating. $36-85

★★SIA'S
10305 Medlock Bridge Road, Duluth, 770-497-9727; www.siasrestaurant.com
American, Asian, Southwestern. Lunch, dinner. Closed Sunday. Bar. Children's menu. Reservations recommended. Outdoor seating. $36-85

★★VINNY'S ON WINDWARD
5355 Windward Parkway, Alpharetta, 770-772-4644; www.knowwheretogogh.com
This restaurant serves upscale Italian fare (sausage, goat cheese and fennel pizza or black truffle seafood risotto) cooked in an open-kitchen so diners can observe the chef's every move. The wine list includes both Italian and Californian offerings and by-the-glass options.
Italian. Lunch (Monday-Saturday), dinner. Bar. Children's menu. Reservations recommended. Outdoor seating. $36-85

★ZAPATA
5975 Peachtree Parkway, Norcross, 770-248-0052;
Mexican. Lunch, dinner. Bar. $15 and under

AUGUSTA
Best known for its revered National Golf Course and the prestigious Masters tournament held here each April, Augusta lures Northerners every winter for its warmth, fairways and culture. The town of 195,000 supports a symphony and an opera as well as several museums devoted to the role Augusta played in the historical South.

Founded in 1736 at the head of the Savannah River, Augusta has served as a military outpost and upriver trading town, a leading 18th-century tobacco center, a river shipping point for cotton, the powder works for the Confederacy, an industrial center for the New South and a winter resort. During the Revolution, the town changed hands several times, but Fort Augusta, renamed Fort Cornwallis by its British captors, was finally surrendered to "Lighthorse Harry" Lee's Continentals on June 5, 1781.

The Civil War ruined many of the wealthy families who had contributed to the Confederate cause. To help revive their depleted bank accounts, some locals opened their houses to paying guests. Northerners wishing to escape chilly winters took notice and began an annual migration, first as renters and eventually as owners of winter residences. Golf courses and country clubs popped up, adding to the lure. Today the Masters Tournament is one of the world's top golf tournaments. At least 10 area clubs offer nonmembers opportunities to play. For other sports attractions, check out the appropriately named minor league baseball team, the Augusta GreenJackets or the more obscure Augusta Lynx minor league hockey team.

For those who don't play sports, Augusta has numerous boutiques and an array of sites honoring its eclectic collection of famous citizens. Where else can one day of sightseeing bring you President Woodrow Wilson's boyhood home, the only museum in the country dedicated to film comedians Laurel & Hardy and a statue honoring the Godfather of Soul, native Augustan James Brown?

WHAT TO SEE
AUGUSTA SYMPHONY ORCHESTRA
Sacred Heart Cultural Center, 1301 Greene St., Augusta, 706-826-4705;
www.augustasymphony.org
The Augusta Symphony's season is packed with concerts and events designed to please all types of audiences. Choose from traditional orchestra concerts, pops performances featuring world famous guest artists and smaller and more intimate chamber concerts.
Mid-September-mid-May.

THE BOYHOOD HOME OF PRESIDENT WOODROW WILSON
419 Seventh St., Augusta, 706-722-9828; www.wilsonboyhoodhome.org
Recently restored with authentic 1860s décor and artifacts, the era the Wilsons lived here, this home-turned-museum celebrates the 28th president.
Tuesday-Saturday 10 a.m.-4 p.m.

LAUREL AND HARDY MUSEUM
250 N. Louisville St., Harlem, 706-556-0401, 888-288-9108;
www.laurelandhardymuseum.org
Oliver Hardy was born in nearby Harlem, Georgia, and this museum of memorabilia and movies from the comedy team he formed with Stan Laurel is the only one of its kind in the country.
Daily 10 a.m.-4 p.m.

NATIONAL SCIENCE CENTER'S FORT DISCOVERY
One Seventh St., Augusta, 706-821-0211, 800-325-5445;
www.nationalsciencecenter.org
An innovative hands-on science, communications and technology center with 250 interactive exhibits. Also here are a Teacher Resource Center, traveling exhibits and a science store.
Monday-Saturday 10 a.m.-5 p.m., Sunday noon-5 p.m.

ST. PAUL'S EPISCOPAL CHURCH
605 Reynolds St., Augusta, 706-724-2485; www.saintpauls.org
A granite Celtic cross in the churchyard marks the site of a fort and the spot where Augusta began, established by James Oglethorpe in 1736 in honor of Princess Augusta. Oglethorpe Park, a recreational area on the Savannah River, is located behind the church, which was established in 1750.
Daily.

SPECIAL EVENT
MASTERS GOLF TOURNAMENT
Augusta National Golf Course, 2604 Washington Road, Augusta, 706-667-6000;
www.masters.org
The Masters is one of four major golfing tournaments held each year. In addition to a cash award, the winner is presented with the famous green sport coat.
First full week in April.

WHERE TO STAY
★★AUGUSTA MARRIOTT HOTEL & SUITES
2 10th St., Augusta, 706-722-8900, 800-228-9290; www.marriott.com
372 rooms. Restaurant, bar. Fitness center. Spa. $61-150

★★COURTYARD AUGUSTA
1045 Stevens Creek Road, Augusta, 706-737-3737, 800-321-2211;
www.courtyard.com
130 rooms. $61-150

ALSO RECOMMENDED
1810 WEST INN
254 N. Seymour Drive, Thomson, 706-595-3156, 800-515-1810;
www.1810westinn.com
11 rooms. No children under 12. Complimentary breakfast. $61-150

ROSEMARY HALL & LOOKAWAY HALL
804 Carolina Ave., North Augusta, 803-278-6222, 877-208-6222;
www.lookawayrosemaryhalls.com
This historic inn combines two restored Greek Revival houses, one that dates from 1898 and the other from 1902.
223 rooms. No children under 12. Complimentary breakfast. $61-150

WHERE TO EAT
★★★CALVERTS
475 Highland Ave., Augusta, 706-738-4514; www.calvertsrestaurant.com
Established in 1977, this restaurant in the Surrey Center maintains its position as one of the top local favorites.
American. Dinner. Closed Sunday. Bar. Children's menu. Reservations recommended. $36-85

★★★LA MAISON RESTAURANT & VERITAS WINE & TAPAS

404 Telfair St., Augusta, 706-722-4805; www.lamaisontelfair.com

This fine restaurant in a Southern Revival house epitomizes Southern hospitality. The menu features wild game specialties such as lamb, buffalo, pheasant and quail.

International. Dinner. Closed Sunday. Bar. Reservations recommended. Outdoor seating. $16-35

BAINBRIDGE

See also Thomasville

On the banks of the Flint River that runs into Lake Seminole, Bainbridge is Georgia's first inland port, founded in 1829. Today the city is a recreational resource for locals and tourists.

WHAT TO SEE
SEMINOLE STATE PARK

7870 State Park Drive, Donalsonville, 229-861-3137; www.gastateparks.org

Shallow by Georgia standards, the lake here holds a greater number of fish species than any other lake in the state. The park has swimming, a beach, boating, waterskiing, and fishing.

Daily 7 a.m.-10 p.m.

WHERE TO STAY
★★CHARTER HOUSE INN

1401 Tallahassee Highway, Bainbridge, 229-246-8550, 888-984-3466;
www.thecharterhouseinn.com

84 rooms. Restaurant, bar. $61-150

★SUPER 8

751 W. Shotwell St., Bainbridge, 229-246-0015, 800-800-8000; www.super8.com

53 rooms. Complimentary breakfast. $61-150

BLAKELY

Named for U.S. Navy Captain Johnston Blakeley, a hero of the War of 1812, this is an important peanut producing area in the region.

WHAT TO SEE
COHEELEE CREEK COVERED BRIDGE

Old River Road, Blakely

This 96-foot-long bridge, built in 1891, is the southernmost standing covered bridge in the U.S.

KOLOMOKI MOUNDS STATE HISTORIC PARK

205 Indian Mounds Road, Blakely, 229-724-2150; www.gastateparks.org

Native American mounds, temple mound and some excavation indicate a settlement here between A.D. 800 and A.D. 1200. There is a swimming pool, as well as fishing and boating on Kolomoki Lake; miniature golf, hiking trails, picnicking, camping are also available to visitors.

Daily 7 a.m.-10 p.m.

WHERE TO STAY
★★★TARRER INN

155 S. Cuthbert St., Colquitt, 229-758-2888, 888-282-7737; www.tarrerinn.com

Recently restored, this charming bed and breakfast has guest rooms exquisitely decorated with beautiful antiques, and three fine dining rooms.

17 rooms. Restaurant. Complimentary breakfast. $61-150

BRASELTON

This town north of Atlanta is home to the Chateau Elan Winery and Resort, which has a luxurious inn and full winery onsite, as well as an acclaimed equestrian center.

WHERE TO STAY
★★★CHATEAU ELAN WINERY AND RESORT

100 Rue Charlemagne, Braselton, 678-425-0900, 800-233-9463;
www.chateauelan.com

Just 40 minutes north of Atlanta, this delightful resort feels like a continent away from big-city bustle with its charming manor house and lush vineyards. Winemaking is a source of great pride, and the eight restaurants complement the property's excellent product. European influences are found throughout the resort, from the classic styling of the elegant accommodations to the tranquil spa.

275 rooms. Restaurant, bar. Golf. Tennis. $151-250

WHERE TO EAT
★★★CHATEAU ELAN'S LE CLOS

100 Rue Charlemagne Drive, Braselton, 678-425-0900, 800-233-9463;
www.chateauelan.com

One of the many elegant restaurants found in the luxurious Chateau Elan Winery & Resort, Le Clos features contemporary French cuisine. The intimate space seats just 28 diners. Fine, estate-bottled wines from Chateau Elan's vineyards, along with choices from other regions of the world, are expertly paired with the five-course prix fixe menu of haute cuisine. Dishes include truffled squab with chanterelle grit cakes, braised greens and blood orange glaze, and roasted beef tenderloin with celeriac and russet potato Dauphinoise and cabernet glace.

French. Dinner. Closed Monday-Wednesday. Reservations recommended. $36-85

BRUNSWICK

See also Darien, Jekyll Island, Sea Island, St. Simons Island

Brunswick, on the southern third of Georgia's seacoast, separated from the Golden Isles by the Marshes of Glynn and the Intracoastal Waterway, is the gateway to St. Simons Island, Jekyll Island and Sea Island. It's also a manufacturing and seafood processing town, known as one of the shrimp capitals of the world. Its harbor is a full oceangoing seaport, as well as a home port to coastal fishing and shrimping fleets. Its natural beauty is enhanced by plantings of palms and flowering shrubs along main avenues, contrasting with moss-covered ancient oaks in spacious parks.

WHAT TO SEE
MARSHES OF GLYNN

Traversed by causeways connecting with Highway 17, the vast saltwater marshes are bisected by several rivers and the Intracoastal Waterway. Pack a picnic and come to the park to enjoy an alfresco lunch amidst views of the marshes.
Daily.

WHERE TO STAY
★★BEST WESTERN BRUNSWICK INN

5323 New Jesup Highway, Brunswick, 912-264-0144; www.bestwestern.com
145 rooms. Restaurant, Complimentary breakfast. $61-150

★EMBASSY SUITES

500 Mall Blvd., Brunswick, 912-264-6100, 800-362-2779; www.embassysuites.com
130 rooms. Complimentary breakfast. $151-250

★JAMESON INN

661 Scranton Road, Brunswick, 912-267-0800, 800-526-3766; www.jamesoninns.com
62 rooms. Complimentary breakfast. $61-150

★QUALITY INN

125 Venture Drive, Brunswick, 912-265-4600, 877-424-6423; www.qualityinn.com
83 rooms. Complimentary breakfast. $61-150

WHERE TO EAT
★CAPTAIN JOE'S

I-95 & Highway 341, Brunswick, 912-264-8771
Seafood, steak. Lunch, dinner. Children's menu. $16-35

★★MATTEO'S ITALIAN RESTAURANT

5448 New Jesup Highway, Brunswick, 912-267-0248
Italian. Lunch, dinner. Closed Sunday. Children's menu. $15 and under

BUFORD

See also Atlanta
This city near Atlanta is home to Lake Lanier, a popular warm weather weekend destination for city dwellers.

WHAT TO SEE
LAKE LANIER ISLANDS

7000 Holiday Road, Buford, 770-932-7200; www.lakelanierislands.com
This 1,200-acre, year-round resort offers swimming, waterskiing, a water park with a wave pool, 10 water slides and other attractions, fishing and boating. Landlubbers can enjoy horseback riding, two 18-hole golf courses and tennis.

WHERE TO STAY
★★★EMERALD POINTE RESORT
7000 Holiday Road, Buford, 770-945-8787, 800-840-5253; www.lakelanierislands.com
Best known for its championship golf course, Emerald Pointe is set on a hillside surrounded by hardwood trees and Lake Sidney Lanier. The island-like setting has swimming, boating and more. This is a favorite Southern retreat. 224 rooms. Restaurant, bar. Beach. Golf. $61-150

★★★WHITWORTH INN
6593 McEver Road, Flowery Branch, 770-967-2386; www.whitworthinn.com
Bask in the tranquility of this beautifully landscaped bed and breakfast located 40 miles north of Atlanta.
10 rooms. Complimentary breakfast. $61-150

CALHOUN
See also Chatsworth, Dalton, Rome
Once called Oothcaloga, "place of the beaver dams," the name was changed in 1850 to honor John Caldwell Calhoun, Secretary of State to President John Tyler. Although the town was directly in the path of General Sherman's 1864 "March to the Sea," Calhoun was not destroyed. Now, Calhoun is the seat of Gordon County and center of a dairy, beef cattle and poultry raising area. The town has a major carpet industry and several manufacturing companies that provide a wide range of products.

WHAT TO SEE
NEW ECHOTA STATE HISTORIC SITE
1211 Chatsworth Highway N.E., Calhoun, 706-624-1321;
www.gastateparks.org-info-echota

The Cherokee Nation had a legislative hall, a Supreme Court house, a mission and several other buildings at New Echota. In the 1950s, the citizens of Calhoun bought the 200-acre site and donated it to the state for restoration and preservation. Missionary Samuel A. Worcester arrived from Boston in 1827 and built a house, which is the only original building still standing.
Tuesday-Saturday 9 a.m.-5 p.m., Sunday 2-5:30 p.m.

RESACA CONFEDERATE CEMETERY
300 S. Wall St., Calhoun, 800-887-3811; www.gordonchamber.org
This is the site of the Civil War battle that opened the way to Atlanta for General Sherman. Stop off at the Civil War markers and cemetery on the Civil War Discovery Trail.
Daily 8:30 a.m.-5 p.m.

WHERE TO STAY
★★★BARNSLEY GARDENS RESORT
597 Barnsley Gardens Road, Adairsville, 877-773-2447; www.barnsleyresort.com
This full-service luxury resort gets national accolades for its accommodations, grounds and top-ranking golf course. A full spa, three restaurants and a variety of suites and cottages make up the elegant interior.
70 rooms. Restaurant, bar. Golf. Spa. $151-250

★JAMESON INN

189 Jameson St. S.E., Calhoun, 706-629-8133, 800-526-3766; www.jamesoninns.com
59 rooms. Complimentary breakfast. $61-150

WHERE TO EAT
★PENGS PAVILLION

1120 S. Wall St., Calhoun, 706-629-1453
Chinese. Lunch, dinner. Closed Sunday. $15 and under

CARTERSVILLE

See also Atlanta, Marietta, Rome

Cartersville today is known as a mining center in Georgia (ocher, barite and manganese), but its ancient past is what attracts tourists. Archeologists have identified ruins from Native Americans dating back to 1000 A.D. The local state park is also a draw.

WHAT TO SEE
ETOWAH INDIAN MOUNDS HISTORIC SITE AND ARCHAEOLOGICAL AREA

813 Indian Mounds Road S.W., Cartersville, 770-387-3747; www.gastateparks.org

The most impressive of more than 100 settlements in the Etowah Valley, this village was occupied from A.D. 1000-1500. It was the home of several thousand people of a relatively advanced culture. Six earthen mounds grouped around two public squares, the largest of which occupies several acres, served as funeral mounds, bases for temples and the residences of the chiefs. A museum displays artifacts from the excavations; crafts, foods, way of life of the Etowah. Don't miss the painted white marble mortuary.
Tuesday-Saturday 9 a.m.-5 p.m., Sunday 2-5:30 p.m.

WHERE TO STAY

★COMFORT INN

28 SR 20 Spur S.E., Cartersville, 770-387-1800, 877-424-6423; www.comfortinn.com
60 rooms. Complimentary breakfast. Pool. $61-150

★DAYS INN

5618 Highway 20 S.E., Cartersville, 770-382-1824, 800-329-7466; www.daysinn.com
52 rooms. Complimentary breakfast. Pool. $61-150

★★HOLIDAY INN

2336 Highway 411 N.E., Cartersville, 770-386-0830, 800-315-2621;
www.holidayinn.com
144 rooms. Restaurant, bar. $61-150

CHATSWORTH

See also Calhoun, Dalton

Almost a third of the land in Murray County is forest and mountains. Opportunities for fishing, hunting, camping, backpacking and mountain biking abound in the surrounding Cohutta Wilderness and woodlands.

WHAT TO SEE
CHIEF VANN HOUSE STATE HISTORIC SITE

82 Highway 225 N., Chatsworth, 706-695-2598; www.gastateparks.org-info-chiefvann
This brick house was the showplace of the Cherokee Nation. James Vann was half Scottish, half Cherokee. His chief contribution to the tribe was his help in establishing the nearby Moravian Mission for the education of the young Cherokees. The three-
story house, with foot-thick brick walls, is modified Georgian in style and partly furnished.
Tuesday-Sunday.

WHERE TO STAY
★★COHUTTA LODGE & CONFERENCE CENTER

500 Cochise Trail, Chatsworth, 706-695-9601, 800-394-9790; www.cohuttalodge.com
61 rooms. Restaurant. $61-150

WHERE TO EAT
★COHUTTA DINING ROOM

500 Cochise Trail, Chatsworth, 706-695-9601; www.cohuttalodge.com/restaurant
American. Breakfast, lunch, dinner. $16-35

COLUMBUS

See also Pine Mountain
Power from the falls of the Chattahoochee River feeds the industries of this dynamic city. Originally a settlement of the Creek Indians, the city reached a peak of manufacturing and commerce between 1861 and 1864, when it supplied the Confederate Army with shoes, caps, swords and pistols. Reconstruction created havoc for a time, but by 1874 Columbus's industries were more numerous and varied than before the war. From 1880-1920, a commercial ice-making machine was produced in the town, and by the beginning of World War II, Columbus was a great iron-working center and the second-largest producer of cotton in the South.

Much of the original city plan of 1827 is still evident, with streets 99-164 feet wide flanked by magnificent trees. Dogwood and wisteria add color in the spring. The atmosphere is exemplified by the brick-lined streets and gaslights in the 28-block historic district and by the Victorian gardens, gazebos and open-air amphitheaters on the Chattahoochee Promenade along the banks of the river.

WHAT TO SEE
THE COLUMBUS MUSEUM

1251 Wynnton Road, Columbus, 706-748-2562; www.columbusmuseum.com
The museum features Chattahoochee Legacy, a regional history gallery with recreated period settings, fine and decorative arts galleries and Transformations, a youth-oriented participatory gallery.
Tuesday-Wednesday, Friday-Saturday 10 a.m.-5p.m., Thursday until 9 p.m., Sunday 1-5 p.m.

FORT BENNING

I-185, Columbus, 706-545-2011; www.benningmwr.com

The largest infantry post in the U.S. established during World War I, the fort was named for Confederate General Henry L. Benning of Columbus. There is an infantry school and demonstrations of Airborne 5000 at jump tower. Monday mornings.

WHERE TO STAY

★BEST WESTERN COLUMBUS

3443 Macon Road, Columbus, 706-568-3300, 800-780-7234; www.bestwestern.com

66 rooms. Complimentary breakfast. $61-150

★★FOUR POINTS BY SHERATON

5351 Sidney Simons Blvd., Columbus, 706-327-6868; www.fourpointscolumbus.com

178 rooms. Restaurant, bar. $61-150

★LA QUINTA INN

3201 Macon Road, Columbus, 706-568-1740, 800-642-4271; www.laquinta.com

122 rooms. Complimentary breakfast. $61-150

★★★MARRIOTT

800 Front Ave., Columbus, 706-324-1800; www.marriott.com

Situated among the scenic downtown historic business district, this hotel caters to corporate travelers and families alike.

177 rooms. Restaurant, bar. $61-150

WHERE TO EAT

★★★BLUDAU'S GOETCHIUS HOUSE

405 Broadway, Columbus, 706-324-4863; www.goetchiushouse.com

This classic Southern restaurant is situated in a restored antebellum mansion overlooking the river. A special chateaubriand is the favorite entrée. Mint juleps are served in the speakeasy downstairs.

American. Dinner. Closed Sunday. Bar. Outdoor seating. $16-35

★COUNTRY'S NORTH

6298 Veterans Parkway, Columbus, 706-660-1415; www.countrysbarbecue.com

American. Lunch, dinner. Children's menu. Outdoor seating. $15 and under

CUMBERLAND ISLAND NATIONAL SEASHORE

See also Brunswick, Jekyll Island, St. Simons Island,

Cumberland Island National Seashore, off the coast of Georgia, is accessible only by a passenger tour boat, which operates year-round. Mainland departures are from Saint Marys. A visit to the island is a walking experience, and there are no restaurants or shops. Salt marshes fringe the island's western side, while white-sand beaches decorate the Atlantic-facing east side. The interior is forested primarily by live oak. Native Americans, Spanish and English have all lived on the island; most structures date from the pre-Civil War plantation era, though there are turn-of-the-century buildings built by the Thomas Carnegie family, who used the island as their 19th-century retreat.

WHERE TO STAY
★★★GREYFIELD INN
4 N. Second St., Fernandina Beach, Cumberland Island, 904-261-6408, 866-401-8581;
www.greyfieldinn.com

Accessible by private ferry from Fernandina Beach, Fla., this inn is a tranquil place to enjoy Cumberland Island's natural beauty and abundant wildlife, including wild horses and many species of birds. Furnished with family heirlooms and antiques, the guest rooms and suites vary widely. Room rates include breakfast, a picnic lunch, gourmet dinner (jacket required) and snacks throughout the day, as well as unlimited use of the inn's sporting, fishing and beach equipment. A two-night minimum stay is required. Not all rooms have private baths.

17 rooms. Restaurant, bar. Fitness center. No children under 6. $351 and up

DAHLONEGA
See also Gainesville

Gold fever struck this area in 1828, 20 years before the Sutter's Mill discovery in California. Dahlonega, derived from the Cherokee word for the color yellow, yielded so much ore that the federal government established a local mint that produced $6,115,569 in gold coins from 1838-1861. Dahlonega is the seat of Lumpkin County, where tourism, manufacturing, higher education and agribusiness are the major sources of employment.

WHAT TO SEE
ANNA RUBY FALLS
Off Highway 356, 6 miles north of Helen, 706-878-3574

Approximately 1,600 acres of wilderness surround a double waterfall, with drops of 50 and 153 feet. The scenic area is enhanced by laurel, wild azaleas, dogwood and rhododendron.

Daily 9 a.m.-dusk.

APPALACHIAN NATIONAL SCENIC TRAIL
304-535-6278; www.nps.gov/appa

Thirteen lean-tos are maintained along 76 miles of the southern portion of the trail. Following the crest of the Blue Ridge divide, the trail begins outside Dahlonega and continues for more than 2,000 miles to Mount Katahdin, Maine.

CHATTAHOOCHEE NATIONAL FOREST
1755 Cleveland Highway, Dahlonega, 770-297-3000; www.fs.fed.us/conf

This vast forest, occupying 748,608 acres, includes Georgia's Blue Ridge Mountains toward the north, which have elevations ranging from 1,000 to nearly 5,000 feet. Because the forest ranges from the Piedmont to mountainous areas, the Chattahoochee has a diversity of trees and wildlife. There are 25 developed camping areas, 24 picnicking areas, 10 wilderness areas and six swimming beaches.

CONSOLIDATED GOLD MINES

185 Consolidated Gold Mine Road, Dahlonega, 706-864-8473;
www.consolidatedgoldmine.com

They offer an underground mine tour (40-45 minutes) through tunnel network. There are displays of original equipment used and Instructors available for gold panning.
Daily 10 a.m.-5 p.m.

DAHLONEGA COURTHOUSE GOLD MUSEUM STATE HISTORIC SITE

1 Public Square, Dahlonega, 706-864-2257; www.gastateparks.org

Located in the old Lumpkin County Courthouse, there are exhibits on the first major gold rush and display of gold coins minted in Dahlonega. Films are shown every half hour.
Monday-Saturday 9 a.m.-5 p.m., Sunday 10 a.m.-5 p.m.

WHERE TO STAY
★★FORREST HILLS MOUNTAIN RESORT

135 Forrest Hills Drive, Dahlonega, 770-534-3244, 800-654-6313; www.foresths.com
30 rooms. Restaurant. $61-150

★SUPER 8

20 Mountain Drive, Dahlonega, 706-864-4343, 800-800-8000; www.super8.com
60 rooms. Continental breakfast. Pool. $61-150

ALSO RECOMMENDED
THE SMITH HOUSE

84 S. Chestatee St., Dahlonega, 706-867-7000, 800-852-9577; www.smithhouse.com
16 rooms. Restaurant. Complimentary breakfast. $61-150

WHERE TO EAT
★★SMITH HOUSE

84 S. Chestatee St., Dahlonega, 706-867-7000, 800-852-9577; www.smithhouse.com
American. Lunch, dinner. Closed Monday. $15 and under

DALTON

See also Calhoun, Chatsworth

Once a part of the Cherokee Nation, Dalton was involved in fierce battles and skirmishes in the Civil War as Union forces advanced on Atlanta. Today, Dalton has more than 100-carpet outlets and manufactures a large portion of the world's carpets. Dalton also produces other tufted textiles, chemicals, latex, thread and yarn.

WHAT TO SEE
CROWN GARDEN & ARCHIVES

715 Chattanooga Ave., Dalton, 706-278-0217
This is the headquarters of the Whitfield-Murray Historical Society. There is a genealogical library and changing exhibits include Civil War items.
Tuesday-Friday 10 a.m.-5 p.m., Saturday 9 a.m.-1 p.m.

WHERE TO STAY
★★BEST WESTERN INN OF DALTON
2106 Chattanooga Road, Dalton, 706-226-5022, 800-780-7234; www.bestwestern.com
99 rooms. Restaurant, bar. Pool. $61-150

WHERE TO EAT
★★DALTON DEPOT
450 Housatonic St., Dalton, 413-684-1730
American. Lunch, dinner. Closed Sunday. Bar. Children's menu. $16-35

DARIEN
See also Brunswick, Jekyll Island, Sea Island, St. Simons Island
James Oglethorpe recruited Scottish Highlanders to protect Georgia's frontier on the Altamaha River in 1736. Calling their town Darien, they guarded Savannah from Spanish and native attack and carved out large plantations from the South Georgia wilderness. After 1800, Darien thrived as a great timber port until the early 20th century. Today, shrimp boats dock in the river over which Darien Scots once kept watch.

WHAT TO SEE
FORT KING GEORGE STATE HISTORIC SITE
1600 Wayne St., Darien, 912-437-4770; www.gastateparks.org
South Carolina scouts built this fort in 1721 near an abandoned Native American village and Spanish mission to block Spanish and French expansion into Georgia, thereby establishing the foundation for the later English Colony of Georgia. The fort and its blockhouse have been reconstructed to original form. The museum interprets the periods of Native American, Spanish and British occupations, the settlement of Darien and Georgia's timber industry.
Tuesday-Saturday 9 a.m.-5 p.m., Sunday 2-5:30 p.m.

HOFWYL-BROADFIELD PLANTATION STATE HISTORIC SITE
5556 Highway 17 N., Brunswick, 912-264-7333; www.gastateparks.org
The evolution of this working rice plantation, from 1807 to 1973, is depicted through tours of the plantation house, museum and trails.
Tuesday-Saturday 9 a.m.-5 p.m., Sunday 2-5:30 p.m.

DUBLIN
The seat of Laurens County, Dublin sits on land once occupied by Creek Indians. Area industries manufacture a wide range of goods, including textiles, carpeting, missile control systems and computer components. Agricultural products include soybeans, wheat, grain, peanuts, corn, cotton and tobacco.

WHAT TO SEE
DUBLIN-LAURENS MUSEUM
311 Academy Ave., Dublin, 478-272-9242
Local history museum featuring Native American artifacts, art, textiles and relics from early settlers.
Tuesday-Friday 1-4:30 p.m.

WHERE TO STAY
★HOLIDAY INN EXPRESS
2192 Highway 441 S., Dublin, 478-272-7862, 800-315-2621; www.holidayinn.com
124 rooms. Restaurant, bar. Complimentary breakfast. $61-150

FORSYTH
Forsyth is a small town near Macon in the center of the state. The nearby town of Juliette was the setting for the 1991 film *Fried Green Tomatoes*.

WHAT TO SEE
JARRELL PLANTATION STATE HISTORIC SITE
711 Jarrell Plantation Rd., Forsyth, 478-986-5172; www.gastateparks.org
This authentic plantation has 20 historic buildings dating from 1847-1940, including a plain-style plantation house, sawmill, gristmill and blacksmith shop.
Tuesday-Saturday 9 a.m.-5 p.m., Sunday 2-5:30 p.m.

WHERE TO STAY
★BEST WESTERN HILLTOP INN
951 Highway 42 N., Forsyth, 478-994-9260, 800-780-7234; www.bestwestern.com
120 rooms. Complimentary breakfast. Pool. $61-150

★★HOLIDAY INN
Juliette Road & I-75, Forsyth, 478-994-5691, 800-315-2621; www.holidayinn.com
120 rooms. Restaurant, bar. Complimentary breakfast. $61-150

WHERE TO EAT
★WHISTLE STOP CAFÉ
443 McCrackin St., Juliette, 478-992-8886; www.thewhistlestopcafe.com
This was the site where *Fried Green Tomatoes* was filmed. Of course fried green tomatoes, barbecue, and sweet tea are standouts of the menu.
American. Breakfast (Monday-Saturday), lunch. $15 and under

GAINESVILLE
See also Buford, Dahlonega
On the shore of 38,000-acre Lake Sidney Lanier, Gainesville is the headquarters for the Chattahoochee National Forest.

WHAT TO SEE
GREEN STREET HISTORICAL DISTRICT
Gainesville
Perfect for a leisurely afternoon stroll, the district is filled with broad streets and Victorian and Classical Revival houses dating from the late 19th and early 20th centuries.

WHERE TO STAY
★★HOLIDAY INN LANIER CENTRE
400 E. Butler Parkway, Gainesville, 770-531-0907, 800-780-7234;
www.laniercentrehotel.com
122 rooms. Restaurant, bar. $61-150

★★QUALITY INN & SUITES
726 Jesse Jewell Parkway, Gainesville, 770-536-4451, 877-4242-6423;
www.choicehotels.com
96 rooms. Restaurant, bar. $61-150

WHERE TO EAT
★POOR RICHARD'S
1702 Park Hill Drive, Gainesville, 770-532-0499; www.prgainesville.com
Steak. Dinner. Closed Sunday. Bar. Children's menu. $16-35

★★RUDOLPH'S
700 Green St., Gainesville, 770-534-2226; www.rudolphsdining.com
American, Continental. Lunch, dinner, Sunday brunch. Bar. Children's menu.
Reservations recommended. $$

GREENSBORO
This central Georgia town is located near Lake Oconee and set amidst rolling
hills and pine trees. The new Ritz-Carlton complex at Reynolds Plantation
has made the area a center for golf.

WHERE TO STAY
★★★★THE RITZ-CARLTON LODGE, REYNOLDS PLANTATION
1 Lake Oconee Trail, Greensboro, 706-467-0600, 800-542-8680; www.ritzcarlton.com
Located an hour from Atlanta, this resort on the 8,000-acre Reynolds Planta-
tion overlooks Lake Oconee, Georgia's second-largest lake. Fill your days
with fishing, boating or waterskiing on the lake. Golf is a major attraction,
with 99 holes designed by legends like Jack Nicklaus, Rees Jones, Tom Fazio
and Bob Cupp. Then retire to one of the comfortable guest rooms, designed
with a rich blend of American and European fabrics and furniture.
251 rooms. Restaurant, bar. Business center. Fitness center. Spa. Beach.
Pool. Golf. Tennis. $251-350

WHERE TO EAT
★★★GEORGIA'S
1 Lake Oconee Trail, Greensboro, 706-467-0600; www.ritzcarlton.com
Located on the lower level of The Ritz-Carlton Lodge Reynolds Plantation,
Georgia's offers countryside charm with a fireplace, antler chandeliers and
views of Lake Oconee. A menu of inventive regional Southern cuisine makes
any occasion special. Splurge on a bottle from the Captain's Wine List, which
features hard-to-find varietals that range from $200-$600 per bottle.
Southern. Breakfast, lunch, dinner, brunch. Closed for lunch from mid-
March to late October. Children's menu. Reservations recommended.
Outdoor seating. $36-85

SPAS
★★★★THE RITZ-CARLTON LODGE SPA, REYNOLDS PLANTATION
1 Lake Oconee Trail, Greensboro, 706-467-0600, 800-241-3333; www.ritzcarlton.com
This 26,000-square-foot spa offers an array of massages, body treatments, facials and other therapies. Massage techniques include Swedish, deep tissue and reflexology. The resort's wellness center features advanced cardiovascular equipment, an indoor lap pool, health screenings and consultations with counselors who will design an individual exercise program.

HELEN
The natural setting of the mountains and the Chattahoochee River helped create the atmosphere for this logging town. Helen was reborn in 1969 when the citizens, with the help of a local artist, decided to transform it into an Alpine, Bavarian-inspired town. Here you'll find quaint cobblestone streets, gift shops with an international flavor, crafts, restaurants and festivals—a bit of the Old World in the heart of the mountains of northeast Georgia.

SPECIAL EVENTS
HELEN TO THE ATLANTIC BALLOON RACE & FESTIVAL
Highway 75, Helen, 706-878-2271; www.helenballoon.com
The weekend begins with a Friday morning liftoff for about 25 balloons participating in the Helen to the Atlantic race, which ends anywhere along Interstate 95. After those balloons take off, several more stay in Helen for local flights and special activities.
First weekend in June.

OKTOBERFEST
726 Brucken Strasse, Helen, 706-878-1908; www.helencvb.com/oktoberfest
This German music and beer festival is one of the longest-running Oktoberfests in the country.
September-October.

WHERE TO STAY
★★CASTLE INN
8287 Main St., Helen, 706-878-0022, 800-395-3644; www.castleinn-helen.com
12 rooms. Restaurant. $61-150

★ECONO LODGE
101 Edelweiss Strasse, Helen, 706-878-8000, 877-424-6423; www.econolodge.com
56 rooms. Complimentary breakfast. $61-150

★★UNICOI LODGE AND CONFERENCE CENTER
1788 Highway 356, Helen, 706-878-2201, 800-573-9659; www.unicoilodge.com
100 rooms. Restaurant. $61-150

WHERE TO EAT
★★HOFBRAUHAUS
9001 Main St., Helen, 706-878-2184; www.riverfronthotel.com
German. Dinner. Bar. Children's menu. $16-35

HIAWASSEE

A picturesque mountain town, Hiawassee is on Lake Chatuge, surrounded by the Chattahoochee National Forest. Its backdrop is a range of the Blue Ridge Mountains topped by Brasstown Bald Mountain, Georgia's highest peak. Rock hunting, including hunting for the highly prized amethyst crystal, is a favorite activity in surrounding Towns County.

WHAT TO SEE
BRASSTOWN BALD MOUNTAIN-VISITOR INFORMATION CENTER
2941 St., Highway 180, Hiawassee, 706-896-2556; www.fs.fed.us/conf
At 4,784 feet, this is Georgia's highest peak. Observation deck affords a view of four states. The visitor center has interpretive programs presented in a mountaintop theater and exhibit hall.
June-October, daily; late April-May, weekends only, weather permitting.

SPECIAL EVENTS
GEORGIA MOUNTAIN FAIR
1311 Music Hall Road, Hiawassee, 706-896-4191; www.georgia-mountain-fair.com
Individual accomplishment is the theme of this gathering. Displays of arts and crafts, farm produce, flowers, minerals, Native American relics, board splitting, soap and hominy making and quilting are a big draw. Camping, beach and tennis courts are available at Georgia Mountain Fairgrounds and Towns County Recreation Park.
Twelve days in late July.

WHERE TO STAY
★★★BRASSTOWN VALLEY RESORT
6321 Highway 76, Young Harris, 706-379-9900, 800-201-3205;
www.brasstownvalley.com
Guests get lost in the views from this mountain lodge as they take in the beautiful Blue Ridge Mountain countryside. This resort offers a rustic feel with many modern touches. Don't miss the vast stables and opportunities for riding trails on horseback. 102 rooms. Restaurant, bar. Spa. Golf. Pool. $61-150

JEKYLL ISLAND
See also Brunswick, Darien, Sea Island, St. Simons Island
Connected to the mainland by a causeway, Jekyll Island, the smallest of Georgia's coastal islands with 5,600 acres of highlands and 10,000 acres of marshland, was favored by Native Americans for hunting and fishing. Spanish missionaries arrived in the late 16th and early 17th centuries and established a mission. In 1734, during an expedition southward, General James Oglethorpe passed by the island and named it for his friend and financial supporter, Sir Joseph Jekyll. Later, William Horton, one of Oglethorpe's officers, established a plantation on the island.
Horton's land grant passed to several owners before the island was sold to Christophe du Bignon, a Frenchman who was escaping the French Revolution. It remained in the du Bignon family as a plantation for almost a century. In 1858, the slave ship *Wanderer* arrived at the island and unloaded the last

major cargo of slaves ever to land in the U.S. In 1886, John Eugene du Bignon sold the island to a group of wealthy businessmen from the northeast, who formed the Jekyll Island Club.

Club members who wintered at Jekyll in exclusive privacy from early January to early April included J.P. Morgan, William Rockefeller, Edwin Gould, Joseph Pulitzer and R.T. Crane Jr. Some built fabulous houses they called cottages, many of which are still standing. By World War II, the club had been abandoned for economic and social reasons, and in 1947, the island was sold to the state. The Jekyll Island Authority was created to conserve beaches and manage the island while maintaining it as a year-round resort.

WHAT TO SEE
HORTON HOUSE
375 Riverview Drive, Jekyll Island, 912-635-2119
Ruins of former house of William Horton, sent from St. Simons as captain by General James Oglethorpe. On Jekyll, he established an outpost and plantation. Horton became the major of all British forces at Fort Frederica after Oglethorpe's return to England.

JEKYLL ISLAND CLUB NATIONAL HISTORIC LANDMARK DISTRICT
901 Jekyll Island Causeway, Jekyll Island, 912-635-3636; www.jekyllisland.com
Once one of the nation's most exclusive resorts, this restored district is a memorable example of turn-of-the-century wealth. Exhibition buildings and shops are open daily. Tours are available.

WHERE TO STAY
★★★JEKYLL ISLAND CLUB HOTEL
371 Riverview Drive, Jekyll Island, 912-635-2600, 800-535-9547; www.jekyllclub.com
Once a popular and exclusive retreat for the nation's wealthy elite, this gorgeous hotel on Georgia's historic Jekyll Island pampers guests and entertains with golf, fishing, water sports, shopping and more.
157 rooms. Restaurant, bar. Beach. $151-250

★★VILLAS BY THE SEA
1175 N. Beachview Drive Jekyll Island, 866-920-1263; www.jekyllislandga.com
150 rooms. Pool. Beach. $151-250

WHERE TO EAT
★★BLACKBEARD'S
200 N. Beachview Drive, Jekyll Island, 912-635-3522
American. Lunch, dinner. Bar. Children's menu. Outdoor seating. $16-35

★★★GRAND DINING ROOM
371 Riverview Drive, Jekyll Island, 912-635-2400; www.jekyllclub.com
The formal dining room of this historic resort is as grand as its name suggests. A dramatic colonnade leads to a large fireplace, lined by plushly upholstered chairs. The low country cooking features local seafood.
American. Breakfast, lunch, dinner, Sunday brunch. Children's menu. Jacket required (dinner). Reservations recommended. $36-85

★LATITUDE 31
1 Pier Road, Jekyll Island, 912-635-3800; www.crossoverjekyll.com
American. Lunch (Tuesday-Saturday), dinner. Closed Monday. Bar. Children's menu. Outdoor seating. $16-35

★★THE SURF STEAKHOUSE
1175 N. Beachview Drive, Jekyll Island, 912-635-3588
Steak. Dinner. $15 and under

★ZACHRY'S SEAFOOD
44 Beachview Drive, Jekyll Island, 912-635-3128
Seafood. Lunch, dinner. Children's menu. $16-35

MACON
See also Forsyth, Perry
One of the larger cities in Georgia, Macon stands out for its musical heritage, its cherry trees and its African-American heritage. Sure, the kazoo was invented here in the 1840s, but more notable is the number of musicians who were born here or called Macon home over the past century: Lena Horne, The Allman Brothers Band, Otis Redding and Little Richard, to name just a few. Macon is also the birthplace of poet Sidney Lanier.

Macon began as a trading post. It served as a fort and rallying point for troops in the War of 1812. Later it became a major rail center. During the Civil War, Macon manufacturers produced quartermaster supplies, harnesses, small weapons and cannons, and the city harbored $1.5 million in Confederate gold.

WHAT TO SEE
CITY HALL
700 Poplar St., Macon, 478-751-7170; www.cityofmacon.net
The main entrance of this Classical Revival building is flanked by panels depicting history of the Macon area.
Monday-Friday 8:30 a.m.-5:30 p.m.

GEORGIA MUSIC HALL OF FAME
200 Martin Luther King Jr. Blvd., Macon, 478-751-3334, 888-427-6257;
www.gamusichall.com
Exhibits such as the Soda Fountain playing songs of the 1950s, the Jazz Club, Gospel Chapel and Rhythm & Blues Revue, explore Georgia's musical heritage.
Monday-Saturday 9 a.m.-5 p.m., Sunday 1-5 p.m.

MACON HISTORIC DISTRICT
450 Martin Luther King Jr. Blvd., Macon, 800-768-3401; www.visitmacon.org
The area makes up nearly all of old Macon: 48 buildings and houses have been cited for architectural excellence and listed on the National Register of Historic Places. An additional 575 structures have been noted for architectural significance. Walking and driving tours are noted on Heritage Tour Markers.

OLD CANNONBALL HOUSE & MACON-CONFEDERATE MUSEUM

856 Mulberry St., Macon, 478-745-5982; www.cannonballhouse.org

This Greek Revival house was struck by a Union cannonball in 1864. The museum contains Civil War relics and Macon historical items.
March-December, Monday-Saturday 10 a.m.-5 p.m. January-February, Monday-Friday 11 a.m.-5 p.m., Saturday 10 a.m.-5 p.m.

TUBMAN AFRICAN-AMERICAN MUSEUM

340 Walnut St., Macon, 478-743-8544; www.tubmanmuseum.com

The Tubman Museum features African-American art, African artifacts and traveling exhibits on the history and culture of African-American people. Resource center, workshops and tours are by appointment.
Monday-Friday 9 a.m.-5 p.m., Saturday 12-4 p.m.; closed Sunday.

SPECIAL EVENTS
CHERRY BLOSSOM FESTIVAL

794 Cherry St., Macon, 478-751-7429; www.cherryblossom.com

Historic tours, concerts, fireworks, hot air balloons, sporting events and a parade are just part of the 10-day long festival, ranked among the top 100 in the country.
Mid-March.

WHERE TO STAY
★★BEST WESTERN RIVERSIDE INN

2400 Riverside Drive, Macon, 478-743-6311, 888-454-4565; www.bestwestern.com
122 rooms. Restaurant, bar. Business center. $61-150

★HOLIDAY INN EXPRESS

2720 Riverside Drive, Macon, 478-743-1482, 800-315-2621; www.holidayinn.com
94 rooms. Complimentary breakfast. $61-150

MARIETTA

See also Atlanta, Cartersville

Located just outside of Atlanta, Marietta boasts business parks, hotels for travelers and an amusement park and water park for the kids.

WHERE TO STAY
★HAMPTON INN ATLANTA-MARIETTA

455 Franklin Road S.E., Marietta, 770-425-9977, 800-426-7866;
www.hamptoninnmarietta.com
139 rooms. Complimentary breakfast. Pool. $61-150

★★★HYATT REGENCY SUITES PERIMETER NORTHWEST ATLANTA

2999 Windy Hill Road, Marietta, 770-956-1234, 800-233-1234;
www.atlantasuites.hyatt.com

Located just 15 minutes from downtown Atlanta, this suburban all-suite property offers an array of amenities for business and leisure travelers. The guest rooms have modern conveniences like flat-screen TVs and wireless Internet access.
202 rooms. Restaurant, bar. Business center. $151-250

★LA QUINTA INN ATLANTA MARIETTA

2170 Delk Road, Marietta, 770-951-0026, 800-642-4271; www.lq.com

130 rooms. Complimentary breakfast. $61-150

★★★MARIETTA CONFERENCE CENTER AND RESORT

500 Powder Springs St., Marietta, 770-427-2500, 888-685-2500;
www.mariettaresort.com

Located just a short walk from Marietta Square and overlooking a championship golf course, this resort (former site of the Georgia Military Institute) works well for business and family vacations, offering luxury suites, fine dining and first-class amenities. Along with an outdoor pool, whirlpool, tennis and golf, the resort also hosts croquet games on the lawn in the summer.

199 rooms. Restaurant, bar. Pool. Tennis. Golf. $61-150

ALSO RECOMMENDED
THE WHITLOCK

57 Whitlock Ave., Marietta, 770-428-1495; www.whitlockinn.com

Located just one block west of Marietta Square on a stately tree-lined street, this fully restored Victorian mansion with distinctively different guest rooms provides all the charm one would expect in the South.

Five rooms. No children under 12. Complimentary breakfast. $61-150

WHERE TO EAT
★LA STRADA

2930 Johnson Ferry Road N.E., Marietta, 770-640-7008; www.lastradainc.com

Italian. Dinner. Bar. Children's menu. $16-35

★SHILLING'S ON THE SQUARE

19 N. Park Square N.E., Marietta, 770-428-9520; www.shillingsonthesquare.com

American. Lunch, dinner, Sunday brunch. Bar. $15 and under

PERRY

See also Macon

Perry is known as the crossroads of Georgia because of its location near the geographic center of the state. The town is full of stately houses and historic churches.

WHAT TO SEE
THE ANDERSONVILLE TRAIL

Perry, 478-988-8000; www.perryga.com

Along the drive are American Camellia Society gardens, two state parks, antebellum houses and the Andersonville National Historic Site.

MASSEE LANE GARDENS

100 Massee Lane, Fort Valley, 478-967-2358; www.camellias-acs.com

The beautiful 10-acre Camellia garden reaches its peak blooming season between November and March. The gardens also include a large greenhouse, Japanese garden and rose garden. The Colonial-style headquarters include the Annabelle Lundy Fetterman Educational Museum and an exhibition hall

with rare books and porcelain.
Tuesday-Saturday 10 a.m.-4:30 p.m., Sunday 1-4:30 p.m. Closed Monday.

WHERE TO STAY
★COMFORT INN
1602 Sam Nunn Blvd., Perry, 478-987-7710, 800-424-6423; www.comfortinn.com
102 rooms. Complimentary breakfast. Pool. $61-150

★★HOLIDAY INN
200 Valley Drive, Perry, 478-987-3313, 800-315-2621; www.holidayinn.com
203 rooms. Restaurant. Bar. Pool. $61-150

★★NEW PERRY HOTEL
800 Main St., Perry, 478-987-1000, 800-877-3779; www.newperryhotel.com
43 rooms. Restaurant. $61-150

PINE MOUNTAIN
See also Columbus
This lush area of West Central Georgia is home to Callaway Gardens, a well-preserved vacation destination. It's less than an hour from Atlanta.

WHAT TO SEE
FRANKLIN D. ROOSEVELT STATE PARK
2970 Highway 190, Pine Mountain, 706-663-4858; www.gastateparks.org
One of the largest parks in the state, it has many historic buildings and the King's Gap Indian trail.Onsite activities include a swimming pool, fishing, hiking, bridle and nature trails, picnicking, camping and cottages.
Daily 7 a.m.-10 p.m.

THE GARDENS AT CALLAWAY

17800 U.S. Highway 27, Pine Mountain, 706-663-2281, 800-225-5292;
www.callawaygardens.com
This distinctive public garden and resort, consisting of 14,000 acres of gardens, woodlands, lakes, recreation areas and wildlife, was conceived by textile industrialist Cason J. Callaway to be "the finest garden on earth since Adam was a boy." Originally the family's weekend vacation spot in the 1930s, Callaway and his wife, Virginia, expanded the area and opened it to the public in 1952. Callaway is now home to more than 100 varieties of butterflies, 230 varieties of birds, 400 varieties of fruits and vegetables and thousands of species of plant life, including the rare planifolia azalea, which is indigenous to the area. The complex offers swimming, boating and other water recreation on its 13 lakes, including 175-acre Mountain Creek Lake and the white sand beach of Robin Lake; 23 miles of roads and paths for hiking or jogging, 63 holes of golf (a 9-hole and three 18-hole courses), 10 lighted tennis courts, two indoor racquetball courts, 10 miles of bike trails, skeet and trapshooting ranges, fishing, fly-fishing, picnicking, a country store, cottages, villas, an inn and restaurants.
Daily.

WHERE TO STAY
★★★MOUNTAIN CREEK INN AT CALLAWAY GARDENS
17800 Highway 27, Pine Mountain, 706-663-2281, 800-225-5292;
www.callawaygardens.com

Offering plenty of outdoor pursuits, including tennis and a championship golf course, this 14,000-acre property provides a relaxing venue to enjoy the entire Callaway Gardens area.

323 rooms. Restaurant, bar. Beach. Pool. $61-150

ROME

See also Calhoun, Cartersville

According to legend, five men, seven hills, three rivers and a hat were the equation that led to the founding of Rome, Ga. The seven hills spurred the five founders to suggest that "Rome" be one of the names for the town, discovered at the junction of three rivers, to be drawn from a hat.

Nobles' Foundry Lathe, one of the few that produced Confederate cannons, is on display on Civic Center Hill and is a reminder of Sherman's occupation. Rome fell despite the frantic ride of Georgia's Paul Revere, a mail carrier named John E. Wisdom, who rode 67 miles by horse from Gadsden, Alabama, in 11 hours to warn that the Yankees were coming.

WHAT TO SEE
BERRY COLLEGE
2277 Martha Berry Highway, Mt. Berry, 706-232-5374; www.berry.edu

Just 1,800 students enjoy the more than 26,000 acres of buildings and forest preserves that make this one of the largest campuses in the world.

CHIEFTAINS MUSEUM
501 Riverside Parkway, Rome, 706-291-9494; www.chieftainsmuseum.org

This is the 18th century house of prominent Cherokee leader Major Ridge featuring artifacts with an emphasis on Cherokee history.

Tuesday-Friday 9 a.m.-3 p.m., Saturday 10 a.m.-4 p.m.

OAK HILL AND THE MARTHA BERRY MUSEUM
24 Veterans Memorial Highway, Rome, 706-368-6789; www.berry.edu

This Antebellum plantation house was owned and occupied by Martha Berry, the founder of Berry College. Manicured lawns, formal gardens and nature trails abound. The museum is located on the grounds of Oak Hill and serves as reception center for visitors.

Monday-Saturday 10 a.m.-5 p.m.

WHERE TO STAY
★DAYS INN
840 Turner McCall Blvd., Rome, 706-295-0400, 800-329-7466; www.daysinn.com

107 rooms. Complimentary breakfast. Pool. Business center. $61-150

★★HOLIDAY INN
20 Highway 411 E., Rome, 706-295-1100, 800-315-2621; www.ramada.com

200 rooms. Restaurant, bar. $61-150

SAINT SIMONS ISLAND

See also Brunswick, Darien, Jekyll Island, Sea Island

One of Georgia's Golden Isles, St. Simons Island has been under five flags: Spain, France, Britain, the U.S. and Confederate States of America. Fragments of each culture remain, including Fort Frederica national monument, the fort defending the Georgia colony from the Spaniards. Cotton plantations ruled the island for a time, but today it's a thriving resort community with sandy beaches, golf courses, dolphin watches, shopping and restaurants.

WHAT TO SEE
GASCOIGNE BLUFF
Arthur J. Moore Drive (where the bridge crosses the Frederica River on the southwest side of island), St. Simons Island

This is a low-wooded, shell-covered bank named for Captain James Gascoigne, commander of *HMS Hawk*, which convoyed the two ships bringing the original settlers to the area in 1736. Great live oaks cut here were used to build the first U.S. Navy vessels, including the *U.S.S. Constitution* ("Old Ironsides") in 1794. St. Simons Marina is open to the public.

ST. SIMONS LIGHTHOUSE
101 12th St., St. Simons Island, 912-638-4666; www.saintsimonslighthouse.org

The original lighthouse, which stood 75 feet high, was destroyed by Confederate troops in 1861 to prevent it from guiding Union invaders onto the island. The present lighthouse, 104 feet high, has been in continuous operation, except during wartime, since 1872. Visitors may climb to the top.

WHERE TO STAY
★BEST WESTERN ISLAND INN
301 Main St., St. Simons Island, 912-638-7805, 800-780-7234; www.bestwestern.com

61 rooms. Complimentary breakfast. $61-150

★★★KING AND PRINCE RESORT
201 Arnold Road, St. Simons Island, 912-638-3631, 800-342-0212;
www.kingandprince.com

Located on the ocean's edge directly on the beach, the resort is within minutes of a quaint shopping village and restaurants. The property offers oceanfront rooms, a one-bedroom house and a five-bedroom house. Outdoor amenities are abundant, including biking, kayaking and sailboat rentals, pools, a beach and tennis.

186 rooms. Restaurant, bar. Beach. $151-250

★★★★★THE LODGE AT SEA ISLAND GOLF CLUB
100 Retreat Ave., St. Simons Island, 912-638-3611, 888-732-4752; www.seaisland.com

Generations of privileged travelers have made Sea Island their top vacation destination. Created in the spirit of European sporting estates, this resort features first-rate tennis and equestrian facilities, three championship golf courses and exquisite dining options. Guest rooms are tastefully decorated with hardwood floors, exposed beam ceilings and private balconies overlooking the rolling fairways of the Plantation Golf Course, St. Simons Sound or the Atlantic Ocean. Complimentary bicycles and 24-hour butler service solidify the top-notch customer service.

40 rooms. Complimentary breakfast. Restaurant, bar. Fitness center. Spa. Beach. Golf. Tennis. Business center. $351 and up

★★★THE LODGE ON LITTLE ST. SIMONS ISLAND

1000 Hampton Point Drive, St. Simons Island, 912-638-7472, 888-733-5774;
www.littlestsimonsisland.com

This small inn is a collection of five cottages and 15 rooms vested in preserving the natural wilderness. The inn offers comfortable lodging and fine restaurants, plus a great view of the surrounding flora and fauna.

15 rooms. Restaurant. $351 and up

★★SEA PALMS GOLF & TENNIS RESORT

5445 Frederica Road, St. Simons Island, 912-638-3351, 800-841-6268;
www.seapalms.com

140 rooms. Restaurant, bar. Fitness center. Pool. Tennis. $151-250

WHERE TO EAT

★BENNIE'S RED BARN

5514 Frederica Road, St. Simons Island, 912-638-2844; www.benniesredbarn.com
American. Dinner. Bar. Children's menu. $16-35

★BROGEN'S SOUTH

504 Beachview Drive, Simons Island, 912-638-1109; www.brogens.com
American. Lunch, dinner. Closed Sunday, October-April. Bar. Outdoor seating. $16-35

★★CHELSEA

1226 Ocean Blvd., St. Simons Island, 912-638-2047; www.chelsea-stsimons.com
Seafood, American. Dinner. Bar. Children's menu. $16-35

★★J. MAC'S

407 Mallory St., St. Simons Island, 912-634-0403; www.jmacsislandrestaurant.com
Seafood. Dinner. Closed Sunday. Bar. $15 and under

SAVANNAH

See also Tybee Island

Savannah has a wealth of history and architecture that few American cities can match. Savannah natives pride themselves on their Southern charm and hospitality. Famous Southern chef Paula Deen hails from Savannah, and author John Berendt gave the rest of the country a taste of the city's allure in his 1990s novel (and later movie) *Midnight in the Garden of Good and Evil.*

The city's many rich, green parks—it has 16 in the historic district alone—are blooming legacies of the brilliance of its founder, General James E. Oglethorpe, who landed at Yamacraw Bluff with 120 settlers on February 12, 1733. His plan for the colony was to make the "inner city" spacious, beautiful. Savannah quickly took its place as a leading city first in the settling of America and later in the wealth and grandeur of the Old South as the leading market and shipping point for tobacco and cotton.

Reconstruction was painful, but 20 years after the Civil War, cotton was king again. Surrounding pine forests produced lumber and resins. The Cotton and Naval Stores Exchange was launched in 1882 when financiers and brokers strode the streets with confidence. By the 20th century, Savannah turned to manufacturing. With more than 200 industries by World War II, the city's prosperity has been measured by the activity of its port, which included ship-building booms during both world wars. Today more than 1,400 historically and architecturally significant buildings have been restored in Savannah's historic district, making it one of the largest urban historic landmark districts in the country. Fountains, small gardens, intricate ironwork and other amazing architectural details decorate this town and add to its beauty. Another area, the Victorian district south of the historic district, offers some of the best examples of post-Civil War Victorian architecture in the country.

WHAT TO SEE
ANDREW LOW HOUSE

329 Abercorn St., Savannah, 912-233-6854; www.andrewlowhouse.com
Built for Andrew Low in 1848, this was later the residence of Juliette Gordon Low, founder of Girl Scouts of America. There are period furnishings throughout the residence.
Monday-Wednesday, Friday-Saturday 10 a.m.-4:30 p.m., Sunday noon-4:30 p.m. Closed Thursday.

CHRIST EPISCOPAL CHURCH

28 Bull St., Savannah, 912-234-4131; www.christchurchsavannah.org
The mother church of Georgia, the congregation dates from 1733. Among early rectors were John Wesley and George Whitfield. The present church is the third building erected on this site.
Tuesday and Friday, limited hours.

CITY HALL

Bull and Bay streets, Savannah, 912-651-6410; www.ci.savannah.ga.us
A gold dome tops the four-story neoclassic façade of this 1905 building, which replaced the original 1799 structure. A tablet outside commemorates the sailing of the *SS Savannah*. A model is displayed in the Council Chamber. Another tablet is dedicated to the *John Randolph*, the first iron-sided vessel launched in American waters.
Monday-Friday.

COLONIAL PARK CEMETERY

E. Oglethorpe Ave. and Abercorn St., Savannah, 912-651-6843; www.savannahga.gov
This was the colony's first and only burial ground for many years. Button Gwinnett, a signer of the Declaration of Independence, is buried in the cemetery, as are other distinguished Georgians. Closed since 1853, it has been a city park since 1896.

DAVENPORT HOUSE

324 E. State St., Savannah, 912-236-8097; www.davenporthousemuseum.org
Constructed by master builder Isaiah Davenport, this is one of the finest ex-

amples of Federal architecture in Savannah. Saved from demolition in 1955 by the Historic Savannah Foundation, it is now restored and furnished with period antiques.

Gardens. Monday-Saturday 10 a.m.-4 p.m., Sunday 1-4 p.m.

GREEN-MELDRIM HOUSE

1 W. Macon St., Savannah, 912-233-3845; www.stjohnssav.org

The Antebellum house used by General Sherman during the occupation of Savannah from 1864 to 1865 is now the Parish House of St. John's Church. Tours are available.

Tuesday and Thursday-Saturday, 10 a.m.-3:30 p.m.

HISTORIC SAVANNAH WATERFRONT AREA

John P. Rousakis Riverfront Plaza, Savannah

Restoration of the riverfront bluff has worked to preserve and stabilize the historic waterfront, which includes a nine-block brick concourse of parks, studios, museums, shops, restaurants and pubs.

Daily.

JULIETTE GORDON LOW BIRTHPLACE

10 E. Ogelthorpe Ave., Savannah, 912-233-4501;
www.girlscouts.org-who/we_are/birthplace

This restored Regency town house was the birthplace of the founder of Girl Scouts of America in 1860. Many original Gordon family pieces are found throughout the home. The garden was restored to how it would have appeared in the Victorian period.

Monday-Tuesday, Thursday-Saturday 10 a.m.-4 p.m., Sunday 11 a.m.-4 p.m.

LAUREL GROVE CEMETERY (SOUTH)

37th St., Ogeechee Road, Savannah, www.savannahga.gov

Possibly the oldest black cemetery currently in use, Laurel Grove houses graves of both antebellum slaves and free blacks. Andrew Bryan (1716-1812), a pioneer Baptist preacher, is buried here.

Daily 8 a.m.-5 p.m.

OWENS-THOMAS HOUSE

124 Abercorn St., Savannah, 912-233-9743; www.telfair.org

This authentically furnished Regency-style house was designed between 1816 and 1819 by William Jay. The walled garden is designed and planted in 1820s style.

Tuesday-Saturday 10 a.m.-5 p.m., Sunday 1-5 p.m., Monday noon-5 p.m. Closed January.

SAVANNAH HISTORY MUSEUM

303 Martin Luther King Jr. Blvd., Savannah, 912-651-6825; www.chsgeorgia.org/shm

This 19th-century railroad shed was renovated to house the historical orientation center. The mural in the lobby chronicles major events in Savannah's 250-year history.

Monday-Friday 8:30 a.m.-5 p.m., Saturday-Sunday 9 a.m.-5 p.m.

TRUSTEES' GARDEN SITE

10 E. Broad St., Savannah, 912-443-3277; www.trusteesgarden.com

This is the original site of a 10-acre experimental garden modeled in 1733 after the Chelsea Gardens in London. Peach trees planted in the garden launched Georgia's peach industry. The Pirates' House, a former inn for visiting seamen, has been restored and is now a restaurant. Robert Louis Stevenson referred to the inn in his book, Treasure Island.

U.S. CUSTOMS HOUSE

1-5 E. Bay St., Savannah

The U.S. Customs House was erected in 1850 on the site of the colony's first public building. The granite columns' carved capitals were modeled from tobacco leaves. A tablet on Bull Street marks the site where John Wesley preached his first Savannah sermon; a tablet on Bay Street marks the site of Oglethorpe's headquarters.

SPECIAL EVENTS
SAVANNAH SCOTTISH GAMES AND HIGHLAND GATHERING

J.F. Gregory Park, Highway 144, Richmond Hill; www.savannahscottishgames.com

Clans gather for a weekend of Highland games, piping, drumming, dancing and the traditional "Kirkin' o' the Tartans."
Early May.

SAVANNAH TOUR OF HOMES AND GARDENS

18 Abercorn St., Savannah, 912-234-8054; www.savannahtourofhomes.org

Tours are sponsored by Christ Episcopal Church with the Historic Savannah Foundation. They offer day and candlelight tours of more than 30 private houses and gardens.
March.

ST. PATRICK'S DAY PARADE

912-233-4804; www.savannahsaintpatricksday.com

This parade rivals the one in New York City in size. The route runs north of Jones Street to the river, west of East Broad Street, east of Boundary Street and the Talmadge Bridge.
March.

WHERE TO STAY
★★★17 HUNDRED 90 INN AND RESTAURANT

307 E. President St., Savannah, 912-236-7122, 800-487-1790; www.17hundred90.com

Savannah's oldest inn features 14 rooms furnished with antiques and fireplaces. The inn also has an excellent restaurant.
14 rooms. Restaurant, bar. Complimentary breakfast. $151-250

★★COURTYARD SAVANNAH MIDTOWN

6703 Abercorn St., Savannah, 912-354-7878, 888-832-0327; www.courtyard.com

144 rooms. Restaurant, bar. $61-150

★★DAYS INN

201 W. Bay St., Savannah, 912-236-4440, 800-329-7466; www.daysinn.com
257 rooms. Restaurant. Business center. Pool. $61-150

★★★EAST BAY INN

225 E. Bay St., Savannah, 912-238-1225, 800-500-1225; www.eastbayinn.com
Just steps away from the historic waterfront, this romantic inn has many beautiful rooms filled with period furnishings and antiques. The owners hold a cheese and wine reception every evening for guests.
28 rooms. Restaurant. Complimentary breakfast. $151-250

★★★HILTON SAVANNAH DE SOTO

15 E. Liberty St., Savannah, 912-232-9000, 800-774-1500; www.hilton.com
This fully equipped hotel is close to shops, sightseeing and restaurants. The hotel, built in the 1890s, has a rooftop pool and fine dining restaurant.
246 rooms. Restaurant, bar. Business center. $151-250

★★★HYATT REGENCY SAVANNAH

2 W. Bay St., Savannah, 912-238-1234; www.hyatt.com
Perched on the scenic waterfront of the Savannah River, this hotel offers superb accommodations, first-class amenities and an attentive staff.
351 rooms, Restaurant, bar. Business center. $61-150

★★★MARRIOTT SAVANNAH RIVERFRONT

100 General McIntosh Blvd., Savannah, 912-233-7722, 800-228-9200;
www.marriott.com
Adjacent to the world-renowned River Street and the historic riverfront, this hotel makes for a truly delightful stay for vacationers. A stroll along the hotel's riverwalk leads to taverns, quaint shops and great restaurants.
341 rooms. Restaurant, bar. $151-250

★★★THE PRESIDENT'S QUARTERS INN

225 E. President St., Savannah, 912-233-1600, 800-233-1776;
www.presidentsquarters.com
Once a place where diplomats and generals rested their heads, The President's Quarters now opens its doors to guests of all stripes. Feel like royalty relaxing in the elegantly appointed parlors or strolling through the renowned gardens.
16 rooms. Restaurant. Complimentary breakfast. $151-250

★★★RIVER STREET INN

124 E. Bay St., Savannah, 912-234-6400, 800-253-4229; www.riverstreetinn.com
Rooms have four-poster beds and French balconies and offer views of the Savannah River. Wine and appetizers are served in the afternoon, homemade chocolates are delivered to rooms in the evening.
86 rooms. Restaurant, bar. $151-250

★★★THE WESTIN SAVANNAH HARBOR GOLF RESORT AND SPA
1 Resort Drive, Savannah, 912-201-2000, 800-937-8461; www.westin.com
Just a water taxi ride away from the historic district, resort features include a PGA-tour quality golf course, full-service spa, waterfront pools, four tennis courts and access to fishing charter boats.
403 rooms. Restaurant, bar. Business center. Spa. Pool. $151-250

ALSO RECOMMENDED
BALLASTONE INN & TOWNHOUSE
14 E. Oglethorpe Ave., Savannah, 912-236-1484, 800-822-4553; www.ballastone.com
One of Savannah's first bed and breakfasts, the Inn is set in a 160-year-old mansion. It is voted annually by locals as the best romantic getaway in Savannah.
16 rooms. Complimentary breakfast. No children under 16. $151-250

BED & BREAKFAST INN
117 W. Gordon St., Savannah, 912-238-0518, 888-238-0518; www.savannahbnb.com
This restored 1853 Federal town house is nestled in the heart of the historic district.
15 rooms. Complimentary breakfast. $61-150

ELIZA THOMPSON HOUSE
5 W. Jones St., Savannah, 912-236-3620, 800-348-9378;
www.elizathompsonhouse.com
Elegantly restored and recently refurbished, rooms offer quiet and comfortable surroundings.
25 rooms. Complimentary breakfast. $151-250

FOLEY HOUSE INN
14 W. Hull St., Savannah, 912-232-6622, 800-647-3708; www.foleyinn.com
Located in the center of historic Savannah, this inn has been serving guests since the Civil War. It's made up of two restored mansions facing Chippewa Square.
19 rooms. Complimentary breakfast. Spa. $151-250

THE GASTONIAN
220 E. Gaston St., Savannah, 912-232-2869, 800-322-6603; www.gastonian.com
17 rooms. No children under 12. Complimentary breakfast. $251-350

OLDE HARBOUR INN
508 E. Factors Walk, Savannah, 912-234-4100, 800-553-6533;
www.oldeharbourinn.com
24 rooms. Complimentary breakfast. $151-250

WHERE TO EAT
★★17 HUNDRED 90 INN & RESTAURANT
307 E. President St., Savannah, 912-236-7122; www.17hundred90.com
International. Lunch, dinner. Bar. $36-85

★★BELFORD'S
313 W. St. Julian St., Savannah, 912-233-2626; www.belfordssavannah.com
American. Breakfast, lunch, dinner, Sunday brunch. Bar. Children's menu. Reservations recommended. Outdoor seating. $16-35

★★BISTRO SAVANNAH
309 W. Congress St., Savannah, 912-233-6266
American, seafood. Dinner. Bar. $36-85

★★CHART HOUSE
202 W. Bay St., Savannah, 912-234-6686; www.chart-house.com
Seafood, steak. Dinner. Bar. Children's menu. Outdoor seating. $16-35

★★★ELIZABETH ON 37TH
105 E. 37th St., Savannah, 912-236-5547; www.elizabethon37th.net
Opened in 1981 by chef Elizabeth Terry and her husband, Michael, this charming restaurant is the birthplace of New Southern cuisine. The interior of the 1900 Greek Revival-style mansion has a homey feel with brightly painted walls, antique chairs and warm service. Fresh and authentic cuisine (Terry extensively researched 18th- and 19th-century Savannah cooking) draws admiration from across the country.
American. Dinner. $36-85

★★GARIBALDI'S CAFÉ
315 W. Congress St., Savannah, 912-232-7118; www.garibaldisavannah.com
Seafood. Dinner. Bar. $36-85

★JOHNNY HARRIS
1651 E. Victory Drive, Savannah, 912-354-7810, 888-547-2823; www.johnnyharris.com
American. Lunch, dinner. Closed Sunday. Bar. Children's menu. $16-35

★MOON RIVER BREWING CO.
21 W. Bay St., Savannah, 912-447-0943; www.moonriverbrewing.com
American. Lunch, dinner. Bar. Children's menu. $16-35

★★MRS. WILKES' DINING ROOM
107 W. Jones St., Savannah, 912-232-5997; www.mrswilkes.com
American. Lunch. Closed Saturday-Sunday. $16-35

★★OLDE PINK HOUSE
23 Abercorn St., Savannah, 912-232-4286
American. Dinner. Bar. Children's menu. $16-35

★★RIVER HOUSE
125 W. River St., Savannah, 912-234-1900, 800-317-1912; www.riverhouseseafood.com
Seafood. Lunch, dinner. Bar. Children's menu. $16-35

SEA ISLAND

See also Brunswick, Darien, Jekyll Island, St. Simons Island

This exclusive island retreat was created in the 1920s by Hudson Motor Company magnate Howard Coffin. The first hotel to open on the island was The Cloisters, which underwent an extensive and impressive multimillion dollar renovation in 2006. The outstanding golf courses have also been renovated. The small and luxurious Lodge at Sea Island offers an intimate 40-room retreat.

WHERE TO STAY

★★★★★THE CLOISTER

100 First St., Sea Island, 912-634-3964; www.cloister.com

This 80-year-old resort recently underwent an impressive $350 million renovation, including the addition of a magnificent spa, replete with 23 elaborate treatment rooms and exclusive product lines. Wood-beamed rooms are now decorated with rich, jewel-toned Turkish rugs and plush, pillow-topped beds. Restaurants include a casual raw bar and grill, where after-beach oysters and cocktails are the specialty. The five miles of private beachfront is the ideal setting for an afternoon stroll.

212 rooms. Restaurant, bar. Complimentary breakfast. Fitness center. Spa. Golf. $351 and up

WHERE TO EAT

★★★COLT & ALISON

The Lodge at Sea Island, 100 First St., Sea Island, 800-732-4752; www.seaisland.com

After working up an appetite on Sea Island Resort's renowned 18 holes, take a seat at the steakhouse named after the golf course's creators: Colt & Alison. Nestled in the Lodge, the restaurant is a cozy backdrop for a scrumptious meal, enjoyed at the fireside tables and leather chairs. Foodies will fill their bellies with classic Caesar salads, filet mignon au poivre and bananas foster all prepared tableside. Colt & Alison stays true to its Southern roots with family style comfort food, decadent desserts and wine from the resort's extensive cellar.

American, steakhouse. Dinner, Sunday brunch. $86 and up

★★★★★GEORGIAN ROOM

100 First St., Sea Island, 800-732-4752; www.seaisland.com

The magnificent Georgian Room is tucked inside The Cloister. The décor is stunningly grand, with bas-relief details, gilded chandeliers and a carved stone fireplace. Tables are set with crisp white linens, hand-painted china and silver flatware. Dishes highlight seasonal, fresh ingredients and might include butter-poached sea bass with frog's leg confit and herb dumplings, or succulent kobe beef filet with smoked morel mushrooms. Vegetarian dishes are available as well. The staff is polished and attentive. A gorgeous private dining room for up to 10 guests makes special events even more memorable.

Continental. Dinner. Jacket and tie required. Reservations required. $86 and up

SPAS
★★★★★THE CLOISTER SPA
100 First St., Sea Island, 912-638-3611, 888-732-4752; www.seaisland.com
Recently renovated, the Spa at Sea Island focuses on customization, with 23 treatment rooms dedicated to an extensive menu of offerings. Spa guides design an experience for guests that may include anything from nutritional consultations to bodywork, baths, wraps and energy treatments. Turkish and Japanese baths personify the spa's simple approach, with the signature bathing ritual and a seven-step infusion of ginger grass and cherry blossom rice body polishes. A special KidSpa program for spagoers ages 8-15 promotes healthy skin care and includes kid-friendly massages, sports and nature hikes.

STATESBORO
This quaint town is home to Georgia Southern University, as well as a huge water park, which is popular with families.

WHAT TO SEE
GEORGIA SOUTHERN UNIVERSITY
Highway 301 S., Statesboro, 912-681-5611; www.georgiasouthern.edu
The campus has 14,000 students. For visitors there is an art department gallery.
Museum: Monday-Friday. Planetarium: by appointment. Botanical garden: daily.

WHERE TO STAY
★★★HISTORIC STATESBORO INN
106 S. Main St., Statesboro, 912-489-8628, 800-846-9466; www.statesboroinn.com
This country inn has a comfortable and stylish atmosphere and surroundings. Rich in local history, it offers elegant dining featuring a menu of seasonal favorites with Southern flavors.
17 rooms. Restaurant. Complimentary breakfast. $61-150

THOMASVILLE
See also Bainbridge
This small town near the Florida border has been a resort destination for those wishing to escape winter weather since the 1800s.

WHAT TO SEE
PEBBLE HILL PLANTATION
1251 Highway, 319 S., Thomasville, 229-226-2344; www.pebblehill.com
This historic plantation dates from the 1820s. Elaborate Greek The Revival house is furnished with art, antiques, porcelains, crystal, silver and Native American relics belonging to the Hanna family of Ohio, who rebuilt the house, guest houses, stables and garages after a fire in the 1930s.
Tuesday-Saturday 10 a.m.-5 p.m., Sunday 1-5 p.m. Must be over 6 years of age.

THOMAS COUNTY MUSEUM OF HISTORY

725 N. Dawson St., Thomasville, 229-226-7664; www.thomascountyhistory.org

The property consists of five free-standing buildings, including a log house with period furnishings, an 1877 frame house furnished in middle-class fashion of that period, an 1893 Victorian bowling alley, a garage housing historic vehicles, and a 1920s mansion, which houses the main museum.

Monday-Saturday 10 a.m.-12 p.m. and 2-4 p.m. Closed Sunday.

THOMASVILLE CULTURAL CENTER

600 E. Washington St., Thomasville, 229-226-0588; www.thomasvilleculturalcenter.com

This is a center for visual and performing arts. Facilities include art galleries with permanent and changing exhibits, a children's room and 550-seat auditorium. Concerts, musicals, children's programs, art classes and other programs are offered.

Monday-Friday 9 a.m.-5 p.m., Saturday 1-5 p.m.

WHERE TO STAY

★★★MELHANA THE GRAND PLANTATION

301 Showboat Lane, Thomasville, 229-226-2290, 888-920-3030; www.melhana.com

Built on the grounds of an historic plantation, this resort has an indoor pool, tennis courts, horseback riding and a wide assortment of leisure activities.

33 rooms. Restaurant, bar. Complimentary breakfast. $151-250

ALSO RECOMMENDED

1884 PAXTON HOUSE INN

445 Remington Ave., Thomasville, 229-226-5197; www.1884paxtonhouseinn.com

This Victorian mansion is a great base for exploring the history and beauty of Thomasville.

Nine rooms. Complimentary breakfast. No children under 12. $151-250

SERENDIPITY COTTAGE

339 E. Jefferson St., Thomasville, 229-225-8394, 800-383-7377;
www.serendipitycottage.com

Four rooms. Complimentary breakfast. No children under 12. $61-150

WHERE TO EAT

★★PLAZA RESTAURANT

217 S. Broad St., Thomasville, 229-226-5153; www.thomasvilleplaza.com

Greek, American. Breakfast, lunch, dinner, Sunday Brunch. Bar. Children's menu. $16-35

TYBEE ISLAND

See also Savannah

This popular year-round Georgia resort is essentially a V-shaped sandbar fronting the Atlantic for nearly four miles and the Savannah River for more than two miles. The beach runs the entire length of the island. Its north end is marked by old coastal defenses, a museum and a lighthouse at the tip. Reached by a causeway from Savannah and Highway 80, the beach has a boardwalk, fishing pier, amusements, hotels, motels and vacation cottages.

WHAT TO SEE
TYBEE MUSEUM AND LIGHTHOUSE
30 Meddin Drive, Tybee Island, 912-786-5801; www.tybeelighthouse.org

The lighthouse is one of the oldest active lighthouses in the U.S. Visitors may climb to the top for a scenic view of Tybee and historic Fort Reven. A museum tracing the history of Tybee from colonial times to 1845 is housed in a coastal artillery battery built in 1898. Exhibits and a gift shop are located in an 1880s lighthouse keeper's cottage.

Wednesday-Monday 9 a.m.-5:30 p.m.

VALDOSTA
When local citizens discovered that surveyors had left the town off the railroad right-of-way, they lost no time moving the town four miles east of the original community (then called Troupville), and the town developed into a rail center with seven branch lines. Such industrious enterprise still defines the area—Valdosta is one of Georgia's most prosperous small cities. Today products include timber, tobacco and cattle. Tourism is also a big industry given the large wooded area and numerous lakes nearby. Moody Air Force Base is 12 miles to the north.

WHAT TO SEE
BARBER HOUSE
416 N. Ashley St., Valdosta, 229-247-8100; www.valdostachamber.com

This restored 1915 neoclassical house serves as offices for the Valdosta-Lowndes County Chamber of Commerce. The home has elaborate woodwork, original light fixtures and furniture. Self-guided tours are available.

Monday-Friday 8:30 a.m.-5 p.m.

CONVERSE DALTON FERRELL HOUSE
305 N Patterson St., Valdosta, 229-244-8575; www.vjsl.org/house.asp

This 1902 neoclassical house has a wide two-story porch that wraps around the front and two sides. The interior has 20-foot ceilings, 14-foot high-pocket doors, golden-oak woodwork and some original light fixtures. By appointment only.

LOWNDES COUNTY HISTORICAL SOCIETY MUSEUM
305 W. Central Ave., Valdosta, 229-247-4780; www.valdostamuseum.org

Originally a Carnegie library, the site now contains collection of artifacts from the Civil War to present. There is also an extensive genealogical library.

Monday-Friday 10 a.m.-5 p.m. Saturday 10 a.m.-2 p.m.

WHERE TO STAY
★★BEST WESTERN KING OF THE ROAD
1403 N. St. Augustine Road, Valdosta, 229-244-7600, 800-780-7234;
www.bestwestern.com

137 rooms. Restaurant, bar. Complimentary breakfast. Pool. $61-150

★COMFORT INN
2101 W. Hill Ave., Valdosta, 229-242-1212, 877-424-6423;
www.comfortinnvaldosta.com
137 rooms. Bar. Complimentary breakfast. $61-150

★HAMPTON INN
1705 Gornto Road, Valdosta, 229-244-8800, 800-426-7866; www.hamptoninn.com
102 rooms. Complimentary breakfast. Business center. Pool. $61-150

★LA QUINTA INN AND SUITES
1800 Club House Drive, Valdosta, 229-247-7755, 800-642-4271; www.laquinta.com
121 rooms. Complimentary breakfast. Fitness center. Spa. Pool. $61-150

WHERE TO EAT
★★CHARLIE TRIPPER'S
4479 N. Valdosta Road, Valdosta, 229-247-0366; www.charlie-trippers.com
American. Dinner. Closed Sunday-Monday. Bar. $36-85

★★MOM & DAD'S
4143 N. Valdosta Road, Valdosta, 229-333-0848
Italian. Dinner. Closed Sunday-Monday. Bar. Children's menu. $16-35

WARM SPRINGS
President Franklin D. Roosevelt visited this quaint town in the 1920s after he
was stricken by polio because the area's natural mineral springs were said to
heal ailments. He built a house here and is thought to have crafted his plan
for the New Deal while staying in Warm Springs. The pools Roosevelt visited
are now part of the Roosevelt Warm Springs Institute for Rehabilitation.

WHAT TO SEE
LITTLE WHITE HOUSE HISTORIC SITE

401 Little White House Road, Warm Springs, 706-655-5870; www.gastateparks.org
President Franklin D. Roosevelt died here on April 12, 1945. Original furniture, memorabilia and the portrait on which Elizabeth Shoumatoff was working on when the president was stricken with a massive cerebral hemorrhage
are on display. A film about Roosevelt's life at Warm Springs and in Georgia
is shown at the F.D. Roosevelt Museum and Theater.
Daily 9 a.m.-4:45 p.m.

WHERE TO EAT
★★BULLOCH HOUSE
47 Bulloch St., Warm Springs, 706-655-9068; www.thebullochhouse.com
American. Lunch, dinner (Friday-Saturday). Children's menu. Outdoor seating. $15 and under

WAYCROSS
The name Waycross reflects the town's strategic location at the intersection
of nine railroads and five highways. Situated at the edge of the Okefenokee
Swamp, the town's early settlers put up blockhouses to protect themselves

from local Native Americans. The production of naval stores and the fur sales were the main industry before Okefenokee became a national wildlife refuge. Today the economy of Waycross is based on timber, railroad and tourism.

WHAT TO SEE
OKEFENOKEE HERITAGE CENTER

1460 N. Augusta Ave., Waycross, 912-285-4260; www.okefenokeeheritagecenter.org
The center features exhibits on Okefenokee area history, Native Americans of Southern Georgia and a 1912 train depot and railroad cars. There is a turn-of-the-century print shop, nature trails, Power House building and a 1840s pioneer house.
Tuesday-Saturday 10 a.m.-5 p.m.

SOUTHERN FOREST WORLD

1440 N. Augusta Ave., Waycross, 912-285-4056;
www.brantleycountychamber.org/sfworld.htm
Exhibits, with audiovisual displays, detail the development and history of forestry in the South. On display are a logging locomotive, 38-foot model of a loblolly pine andgiant cypress tree. There are also nature trails.
Tuesday-Saturday.

WHERE TO STAY
★★HOLIDAY INN

1725 Memorial Drive, Waycross, 912-283-4490, 800-315-2621; www.holidayinn.com
142 rooms. Restaurant, bar. Complimentary breakfast. Fitness center. Pool.
$61-150

NORTH CAROLINA

NORTH CAROLINA HAS THREE DISTINCTIVE REGIONS: THE COAST, THE HEARTLAND AND the mountains, each with its own regional capital and featured attractions. From bluegrass music and mountain hiking in Asheville to Atlantic beaches a quick drive from Wilmington to the cultural and business centers surrounding the capital city, Raleigh, the state is diverse.

In 1585, the first English settlement was unsuccessfully started on Roanoke Island. Another attempt at settlement was made in 1587, but the colony disappeared, leaving only the crudely scratched word "CROATOAN" on a tree—perhaps referring to the Croatan Indians living in the area. To this day historians and archaeologists are still trying to solve the mystery of "The Lost Colony." Eventually English settlers moving south from Virginia founded farms in the North Carolina territory, and even today, the state produces two-thirds of the nation's flue-cured tobacco, as well as cotton, peanuts and vegetables. Pine tar and turpentine were other early commodities produced in North Carolina and thus responsible for the "Tar Heels" moniker given to the people of North Carolina and was adopted as the mascot for the University of North Carolina. Tales of the exact origins of the nickname are varied (and not always complimentary) but North Carolinians like to say it refers to their ability to persevere. It's said North Carolina troops fighting in the Civil War would stand their ground in battle as though stuck with "tar on their heels."

Individualist and democratic from the beginning, this state refused to ratify the Constitution until the Bill of Rights had been added. In 1860, its Western citizens strongly supported the Union, and North Carolina did not join the Confederate States of America until after Fort Sumter was attacked. Tobacco helped the state recover during Reconstruction and remains a major crop, but mountain communities are also famous for their furniture-making centers. For sports fans, North Carolina delivers with two perennial basketball powerhouses, Duke University and the University of North Carolina at Chapel Hill (Michael Jordan's alma mater). Top-ranking golf courses crisscross the state, and 70 miles of the Appalachian Trail extend along North Carolina's border. For vacationers, this realism translates into a wealth of things to do.

ASHEVILLE

See also Maggie Valley, Waynesville

Asheville has gained a reputation as a charming vacation destination in the Blue Ridge Mountains. George W. Vanderbilt built his mansion here in the 1890s, and the house and winery attract scores of visitors each year. Asheville is the North Carolina city closest to the Great Smoky Mountains National Park and is also the headquarters for the Uwharrie National Forest, Pisgah National Forest, Nantahala National Forest and Croatan National Forest.

WHAT TO SEE
ASHEVILLE ART MUSEUM

Two South Pack Square, Asheville, 828-253-3227; www.ashevilleart.org

The museum houses a permanent collection of 20th and 21st century American Art, as well as numerous changing exhibits.

Tuesday-Saturday 10 a.m.-5 p.m., Friday until 8 p.m., Sunday 1-5 p.m.

BILTMORE ESTATE

1 Approach Road, Asheville, 828-255-1333, 800-411-3812; www.biltmore.com

The 8,000-acre country estate includes 75 acres of formal gardens, numerous varieties of azaleas and roses and the 250-room chateau, which is the largest house ever built in the New World. Eighty-five rooms are open for viewing. In the 1890s, George W. Vanderbilt commissioned Richard Morris Hunt to design the house, which took five years to build. Vanderbilt also employed Gifford Pinchot, later governor of Pennsylvania and famous for forestry and conservation achievements, to manage his forests. Tours of the estate include gardens, conservatory and winery facilities. There are four restaurants on the property; they offer wine tasting.
Daily.

BOTANICAL GARDENS AT ASHEVILLE

151 WT Weaver Blvd., Asheville, 828-252-5190; www.ashevillebotanicalgardens.org

This 10-acre tract of land has thousands of flowers, trees and shrubs native to southern Appalachia. There is also a 125-year-old "dog trot" log cabin.
Daily dawn-dusk.

CHIMNEY ROCK PARK

Highway 64-74A, Asheville, 828-625-9611, 800-277-9611; www.chimneyrockpark.com

The towering granite monolith Chimney Rock affords a 75-mile view. Four hiking trails lead to the 404-foot Hickory Nut Falls, Moonshiner's Cave, Devil's Head balancing rock and Nature's Showerbath. There are lots of opportunities for fun and relaxation including trails, stairs and catwalks, picnic areas, playground, nature center, and an observation lounge. Don't miss the 26-story elevator shaft through granite.
Daily 8:30 a.m.-6 p.m., weather permitting.

FOLK ART CENTER

382 Blue Ridge Parkway, Asheville, 828-298-7928; www.southernhighlandguild.org

The Folk Art Center is home of the Southern Highland Craft Guild. The stone and timber structure, and the Blue Ridge Parkway info center include craft exhibits, demonstrations, workshops and related programs.
Daily.

THOMAS WOLFE MEMORIAL

52 N. Market, Asheville, 828-253-8304; www.wolfememorial.com

The state maintains the Wolfe boardinghouse as a literary shrine, restored and furnished to appear as it did in 1916.
Tuesday-Saturday 9 a.m.-5 p.m., Sunday 1-5 p.m.

ZEBULON B. VANCE BIRTHPLACE STATE HISTORIC SITE

911 Reems Creek Road, Weaverville, 828-645-6706; www.nchistoricsites.org

Reconstructed in 1961, the log house and outbuildings mark the site where the Civil War governor of North Carolina lived during childhood. It honors the Vance family, which was deeply involved with the early history of the state. There is a visitor center with exhibits, as well as a picnic area.
April-October, Monday-Friday; rest of year, Tuesday-Friday.

SPECIAL EVENTS
MOUNTAIN DANCE AND FOLK FESTIVAL
2 S. Pack Square, Asheville, 828-257-4530; www.folkheritage.org
At the Diana Wortham Theater, folk songs and ballads are performed. This is the nation's longest running such festival and the finest of its kind for devotees of the five-string banjo, gut-string fiddle, clogging and smooth dancing. Early August.

SHAKESPEARE IN THE PARK
246 Cumberland Ave., Asheville, 828-254-5146; www.montfordparkplayers.org
Performances are weekends from early June to late August.

WHERE TO STAY
★★★CUMBERLAND FALLS BED & BREAKFAST
254 Cumberland Ave., Asheville, 828-253-4085, 888-743-2557;
www.cumberlandfalls.com
When driving up to the tree- and flower-lined house, you'll think you're returning home…if your home had freshly baked treats, a three-course breakfast and a two-person whirlpool tub always waiting for you. So basically, the Cumberland Falls Bed and Breakfast is like the home sweet home you always dreamed about, with themed rooms and an attentive staff to help plan your day and ensure you feel comfortable when you return. Besides included amenities, the innkeeper can help you set up a special surprise, like chocolate covered strawberries and champagne to accompany that Jacuzzi.
Six rooms. No Children under 10. Complimentary breakfast. $151-250

★★DOUBLETREE HOTEL BILTMORE-ASHEVILLE
115 Hendersonville Road, Asheville, 828-274-1800, 800-222-8733;
www.biltmoreasheville.doubletree.com
160 rooms. Restaurant, bar. Business center. $151-250

★★★THE GROVE PARK INN RESORT & SPA
290 Macon Ave., Asheville, 828-252-2711, 800-438-5800; www.groveparkinn.com
Set in Asheville's Blue Ridge Mountains, guest rooms are decorated in Arts and Crafts style. Choose from the 18-hole Donald Ross-designed golf course, a superb tennis facility or a 40,000-square-foot spa crafted from natural rock, which offers a range of special services from hydro bath treatments to flotation body masques.
510 rooms. Restaurant, bar. $251-350

★★★HAYWOOD PARK HOTEL & PROMENADE
1 Battery Park Ave., Asheville, 828-252-2522, 800-228-2522; www.haywoodpark.com
This all-suite hotel is decorated with polished brass, warm oak and Spanish marble. Rooms have fine furnishings, a wet bar and a bathroom that features either a garden tub or a Jacuzzi.
33 suites. Restaurants, bar. $151-250

★★★★INN ON BILTMORE ESTATE

1 Anter Hill Road, Asheville, 828-225-1660, 866-336-1240; www.biltmore.com

The Inn on Biltmore Estate provides world-class accommodations on the grounds of an American landmark, the historic Vanderbilt Biltmore Estate. Carriage rides, horseback rides and river float trips are just a few of the unique recreational activities. The hotel's distinguished character extends to its dining establishments: Bistro, Deerpark, The Dining Room and Stable Café.

213 rooms. Restaurant, bar. Spa. $251-350

★★★RENAISSANCE ASHEVILLE HOTEL

31 Woodfin St., Asheville, 828-252-8211, 800-359-7951; www.marriott.com

Centrally located around Asheville's main plaza, this comfortable hotel offers visitors shopping in the nearby mall, a farmers' market and other complexes in the area.

277 rooms. Restaurant, bar. $151-250

★★★★RICHMOND HILL INN

87 Richmond Hill Drive, Asheville, 828-252-7313, 800-549-9238;
www.richmondhillinn.com

Once the private home of an influential politician, this Queen Anne-style mansion and croquet cottages are set among nine acres of formal gardens. Rooms and suites are decorated with antiques and have either canopy or four-poster beds. The restaurant, Gabrielle's, is heralded for its continental menu.

37 rooms. Restaurant, bar. Complimentary breakfast. $251-350

ALSO RECOMMENDED

ALBEMARLE INN

86 Edgemont Road, Asheville, 828-255-0027, 800-621-7435; www.albemarleinn.com

This dramatic, majestic home, with enormous white pillars and manicured gardens, offers guests luxurious rooms, a complimentary breakfast, plus afternoon wine and hors d'oeuvres.

11 rooms. Complimentary breakfast. No children under 12. $151-250

APPLEWOOD MANOR INN

62 Cumberland Circle, Asheville, 828-254-2244, 800-442-2197;
www.applewoodmanor.com

This Colonial turn-of-the-century home was built in 1910. Rooms are filled with antiques and personal touches.

Four rooms. Complimentary breakfast. No children under 12. $61-150

THE BEAUFORT HOUSE VICTORIAN INN

61 N. Liberty St., Asheville, 828-254-8334, 800-261-2221; www.beauforthouse.com

Experience Victorian afternoon tea, gourmet breakfasts and elegant guest rooms in the former home of Charleton Heston. The mansion is surrounded by two acres of landscaped grounds complete with 5,000 flowers.

11 rooms. Complimentary breakfast. No children under 10. $61-150

CEDAR CREST VICTORIAN INN

674 Biltmore Ave., Asheville, 828-252-1389, 877-251-1389; www.cedarcrestinn.com

Dating from 1891, this luxurious mansion has been transformed into a romantic inn that is listed on the National Register of Historic Places. Of particular note is the ornate woodwork on the first floor and the Victorian gardens filled with dogwood and rhododendrons.

12 rooms. Complimentary breakfast. No children under 10. $151-250

LION AND THE ROSE

276 Montford Ave., Asheville, 828-255-7673, 800-546-6988; www.lion-rose.com

This elegantly restored Georgian mansion is nestled in beautifully landscaped gardens in one of Asheville's historic districts and within walking distance of downtown. Decadent complimentary breakfasts are a delightful perk.

5 rooms. Complimentary breakfast. No children under 12. $151-250

THE OLD REYNOLDS MANSION

100 Reynolds Heights, Asheville, 828-254-0496, 800-709-0496;
www.oldreynoldsmansion.com

This antebellum mansion is on a hill overlooking the mountains. There are verandas throughout the home to enjoy the views.

10 rooms. Complimentary breakfast. Closed November-June, Sunday-Thursday. $61-150

OWL'S NEST

2630 Smokey Park Highway, Candler, 828-665-8325, 800-665-8868;
www.engadineinn.com

Located just outside of Asheville, this inn was built in 1885 and has been restored to its original Victorian grandeur. The mountain views from the wraparound porches are exquisite. Enjoy a cozy, romantic dinner by the fireplace.

Five rooms. Complimentary breakfast. No children under 12. $61-150

WHERE TO EAT

★★★FLYING FROG CAFÉ

1 Battery Park Ave., Asheville, 828-254-9411; www.flyingfrogcafe.com

Located in the first floor of the Haywood Park Hotel, the Flying Frog Restaurant is in the center of downtown Asheville, surrounded by shopping, lodging and entertainment venues. Decorated in a modern Indian theme, the restaurant has booths draped with sheer curtains, a display kitchen and private wine room. The variety of menu options changes seasonally.

Continental, Indian. Dinner. Closed Monday-Tuesday. Bar. $36-85

★★★GABRIELLE'S

87 Richmond Hill Drive, Asheville, 828-252-7313, 800-545-9238;
www.richmondhillinn.com

Victorian ambiance and contemporary Southern Cuisine come together at the Richmond Hill Inn. Chef Duane Fernandes offers a choice between a seasonal three-course prix fixe and five-course menu.

American. Dinner. Closed Tuesday. Bar. Jacket required. No children under 8. $86 and up

★★★HORIZONS

290 Macon Ave., Asheville, 828-252-2711, 800-438-5800; www.groveparkinn.com

Located in the Grove Park Inn, this restaurant has elegant décor and innovative classic cuisine. Enjoy views of the mountains and the groomed golf course through large windows while listening to live piano music. House specialties include wild-striped bass and an extensive wine list. A special nine-course meal at the chef's table in the kitchen and wine dinners organized around specific tastes and interests are available.

International. Dinner. Closed Sunday-Monday. Bar. Jacket required. Reservations recommended. $86 and up

★★LA PAZ

10 Biltmore Plaza, Asheville, 828-277-8779; www.lapaz.com

Mexican. Lunch, dinner. Bar. Children's menu. Outdoor seating. $16-35

★★★THE MARKET PLACE RESTAURANT & WINE BAR

20 Wall St., Asheville, 828-252-4162; www.marketplace-restaurant.com

Located in the center of downtown on a side street with quaint shops, this restaurant offers organic cheeses and salads, free-range chickens and local trout. Meat is smoked over hickory and oak.

American, French. Dinner. Closed Sunday. Bar. Outdoor seating. $36-85

★MOOSE CAFÉ AT WESTERN NORTH CAROLINA FARMER'S MARKET

570 Brevard Road, Asheville, 828-255-0920; www.moosecafe.samsbiz.com

Southern, American. Breakfast, lunch, dinner. $15 and under

★★★REZAZ

28 Hendersonville Road, Asheville, 828-277-1510; www.rezaz.com

Rezaz is two restaurants in one: the main dining room has sleek, modern décor and an upscale Mediterranean menu; Enoteca, a wine bar, is the informal side of the restaurant and has display cases of meat, cheeses and decadent desserts. The restaurant is located in the historic Biltmore Village, opposite the entrance to the Biltmore Estate.

Mediterranean. Breakfast, lunch, dinner. Closed Sunday. Bar. Reservations recommended. $16-35

★★★SAVOY

641 Merrimon Ave., Asheville, 828-253-1077; www.savoyasheville.com

A must for those traveling to Asheville, and a favorite of North Carolina locals, Savoy features a Mediterranean-spiced menu that puts a tasty spin on American favorites. The fresh food—the only freezer on the premises is for their homemade ice cream, so we'll let that slide—is 80 percent organic with a "farm to table" lunch and dinner menu that ranges from Carolina bison short ribs to local line-caught trout. Get intimate at the bar with small plates and their diverse wine selection and signature martini list. Yellow cake martini? Make it a double.

American menu. Lunch (Monday-Friday), dinner. $36-85

★★TUPELO HONEY CAFÉ
12 College St., Asheville, 828-255-4404; www.tupelohoneycafe.com
American, Southern. Breakfast, lunch, dinner, late-night. Closed Monday.
Children's menu. Outdoor seating. $16-35

BEAUFORT
See also Morehead City
Beaufort, dating from the colonial era, is a seaport with more than 125 historic houses and sites.

WHAT TO SEE
BEAUFORT HISTORIC SITE
138 Turner St., Beaufort, 252-728-5225; www.historicbeaufort.com
The site includes an old burial ground, a restored old jail, restored houses, a
courthouse dating back to 1796, apothecary shop, art gallery and a gift shop.
Get a self-guided walking tour map from the historical center, 138 Turner
Street, Monday-Saturday.

CAPE LOOKOUT NATIONAL SEASHORE
131 Charles St., Harkers Island, 252-728-2250; www.nps.gov/calo
Part of the National Park System on the outer banks of North Carolina, the
Cape Seashore extends 55 miles south from Ocracoke Inlet and includes
unspoiled barrier islands. There are no roads or bridges; accessible by boat
only. Catch a ferry from Beaufort, Harkers Island, Davis, Atlantic, or Ocracoke (April-November). Excellent fishing and shell collecting; primitive
camping; interpretive programs (seasonal). The lighthouse at Cape Lookout
is still operational.
Visitor center daily 8:30 a.m.-4:30 p.m.

SPECIAL EVENTS
OLD HOMES TOUR AND ANTIQUES SHOW
138 Turner St., Beaufort, 252-728-5225; www.beauforthistoricsite.org
Sponsored by the Beaufort Historical Association, the tour is of private
homes and historic public buildings and the history of the Carteret County
Militia. If you don't feel like walking, take a bus tours instead.
Last weekend in June.

WHERE TO STAY
THE CEDARS INN
305 Front St., Beaufort, 252-728-7036; www.cedarsinn.com
11 rooms. No children under 10. Complimentary breakfast. Restaurant.
Beach. $61-150

PECAN TREE INN
116 Queen St., Beaufort, 252-728-6733; www.pecantree.com
Seven rooms. Restaurant. Complimentary breakfast. No children under 10.
$61-150

BELHAVEN

See also Plymouth, Washington

Along the banks of the Pungo River and Pantego Creek, Belhaven is one of several towns along the Pamlico Sound, the Sailing Capital of North Carolina.

WHERE TO STAY
RIVER FOREST MANOR

738 E. Main St., Belhaven, 252-943-2151, 800-346-2151; www.riverforestmanor.com
Nine rooms. Restaurant. Complimentary breakfast. $61-150

WHERE TO EAT
★★RIVER FOREST MANOR

738 E. Main St., Belhaven, 252-943-2151; www.riverforestmanor.com
American. Dinner, Sunday brunch. Bar. $16-35

BLOWING ROCK

See also Banner Elk, Boone, Linville

On the Blue Ridge Parkway, Blowing Rock was named, based on Native American folklore, for the cliff near town where lightweight objects thrown outward are swept back to their origin by the wind. It has been a mountain resort area for more than 100 years. A wide variety of recreational facilities and shops can be found nearby.

WHAT TO SEE
APPALACHIAN SKI MOUNTAIN

940 Ski Mountain Road, Blowing Rock, 828-295-7828, 800-322-2373;
www.appskimtn.com
The mountain's features include: two quad, double chair lift, rope tow, handle-pull tow; patrol; French-Swiss Ski College, Ski-Wee children's program; equipment rentals; snowmaking; restaurant; and eight runs. The longest run is 2,700 feet, with a vertical drop of 400 feet.
December-mid-March. Night skiing (all slopes lighted); half-day and twilight rates.

BLOWING ROCK

432 Rock Road, Blowing Rock, 828-295-7111; www.blowingrock.com
The cliff hangs over Johns River Gorge 2,000-3,000 feet below. There are scenic views of Grandfather, Grandmother, Table Rock and Hawksbill mountains.
Daily.

MOSES H. CONE MEMORIAL PARK

Blue Ridge Parkway, Blowing Rock, 828-295-7938; www.nps.gov
This was the former summer estate of a textile magnate. There are bridle paths, two lakes, 25 miles of hiking and cross-country skiing trails.
May-October, daily.

PARKWAY CRAFT CENTER

Blue Ridge Parkway, Blowing Rock, 828-295-7938; www.nps.gov

The center holds demonstrations of weaving, wood carving, pottery, jewelry making and other crafts. Many of the handcrafted items are for sale.
May-October, daily.

TWEETSIE RAILROAD

300 Tweetsie Railroad Lane, Blowing Rock, 828-264-9061, 800-526-5740;
www.tweetsierailroad.com

This is a 3-mile excursion, with a mock holdup and raid, on an old narrow-gauge railroad. There is a country fair, petting zoo, amusement park rides, craft village and chair lift to Mouse Mountain Picnic Area.
May-October, limited hours.

WHERE TO STAY
★ALPINE VILLAGE INN

297 Sunset Drive, Blowing Rock, 828-295-7206; www.alpine-village-inn.com

17 rooms. $61-150

★BLOWING ROCK INN

788 N. Main St., Blowing Rock, 828-295-7921; www.blowingrockinn.com

24 rooms. Closed mid-December-March. $61-150

★CLIFF DWELLERS INN

116 Lakeview Terrace, Blowing Rock, 828-295-3121, 800-322-7380;
www.cliffdwellers.com

21 rooms. Complimentary breakfast. $61-150

★★★CHETOLA RESORT AT BLOWING ROCK

North Main St., Blowing Rock, 828-295-5500, 800-243-8652; www.chetola.com

This Blue Ridge Mountains retreat, bordered on one side by a national forest, houses the Highlands Sports and Recreation Center. A conference center, professional tennis courts and other amenities are within the resort's 78-acre property.
104 rooms. Restaurant, bar. $151-250

★★★CRIPPEN'S COUNTRY INN

239 Sunset Drive, Blowing Rock, 828-295-3487, 877-295-3487; www.crippens.com

This mountain inn offers a lively atmosphere and well-rated restaurant.
Eight rooms. Restaurant. Bar. Complimentary breakfast. No children under 12. $61-150

★★★GLENDALE SPRINGS INN

7414 Highway 16, Glendale Springs, 336-982-2103, 800-287-1206;
www.glendalespringsinn.com

Located in a quaint community on the top of the Blue Ridge Mountains, this historic inn is well-known for its dining room and comfortable accommodations.
Nine rooms. Complimentary breakfast. Restaurant. $61-150

★★★HOUND EARS CLUB
328 Shulls Mills Road, Blowing Rock, 828-963-4321; www.houndears.com
Set atop the Blue Ridge Mountains, this small, secluded resort is a relaxing respite. The 18-hole golf course was designed by George Cobb, and the views are gorgeous.
28 rooms. Restaurant, bar. $151-250

ALSO RECOMMENDED
INN AT RAGGED GARDENS
203 Sunset Drive, Blowing Rock, 877-972-4433; www.ragged-gardens.com
The 19th-century inn has original stone pillars and floors, period furnishings, individually decorated rooms and a full acre of beautifully landscaped property.
11 rooms. Complimentary breakfast. No children under 12. $151-250

MAPLE LODGE
152 Sunset Drive, Blowing Rock, 828-295-3331, 866-795-3331; www.maplelodge.net
11 rooms. Complimentary breakfast. No children under 12. Closed January-February. $151-250

WHERE TO EAT
★★THE BEST CELLAR RESTAURANT
203 Sunset Drive, Blowing Rock, 877-972-4433
International. Dinner. Bar. Reservations recommended. Outdoor seating. $36-85

★★★CRIPPEN'S
239 Sunset Drive, Blowing Rock, 828-295-3487, 877-295-3487; www.crippens.com
This spacious, cozy dining room is located in Crippen's Country Inn. Chef James Welch's award-winning seasonal menu features many organic meats, seafood and homemade breads and desserts.
American. Dinner. Bar. Children's menu. Reservations recommended. Outdoor seating. $36-85

BOONE
See also Banner Elk, Blowing Rock, Linville
Boone was named for Daniel Boone, who had a cabin and hunted here in the 1760s. This area sprawls over a long valley, which provides a natural pass through the hills. Watauga County is the location of Appalachian State University. Mountain crafts are featured in a variety of craft fairs, festivals and shops.

WHAT TO SEE
APPALACHIAN CULTURAL MUSEUM
University Hall Drive, Blowing Rock, 828-262-3117; www.museum.appstate.edu
This regional museum presents an overview of the Blue Ridge area. Exhibits include Native American artifacts, mountain music, plus look into the life of Daniel Boone.
Tuesday-Saturday 10 a.m.-5 p.m., Sunday 1-5 p.m.

WHERE TO STAY
★HOLIDAY INN EXPRESS
1943 Blowing Rock Road, Boone, 828-264-2451, 800-315-2621; www.holiday-inn.com
138 rooms. Complimentary breakfast. Pool. $61-150

ALSO RECOMMENDED
LOVILL HOUSE INN
404 Old Bristol Road, Boone, 828-264-4204, 800-849-9466; www.lovillhouseinn.com
Captain E.F. Lovill, a Civil War hero and state senator, built this traditional farmhouse in 1875. The 11-acre, wooded property has a charming wrap-around porch with plenty of rocking chairs.
Six rooms. No children under 12. Complimentary breakfast. Closed March. $151-250

WHERE TO EAT
★DAN'L BOONE INN
130 Hardin St., Boone, 828-264-8657; www.danlbooneinn.com
American. Breakfast, lunch, dinner. No credit cards accepted. $15 and under

★★MAKOTO
2124 Blowing Rock Road, Boone, 828-264-7976; www.makotos-boone.com
Japanese. Lunch, dinner. Bar. Children's menu. Outdoor seating. $16-35

CASHIERS
See also Franklin, Highlands
High in the Blue Ridge Mountains, this well-known summer resort area offers scenic drives on twisting mountain roads, hiking trails, views, waterfalls, lake sports, fishing and other recreational activities.

WHAT TO SEE
FAIRFIELD SAPPHIRE VALLEY SKI AREA
4350 Highway 64 W., Sapphire, 828-743-3441, 800-722-3956; www.skisapphire.com
The ski area offerings include: chair lift, rope tow; patrol, school and snow-making. The longest run is 1,600 feet, with a vertical drop of 200 feet. Mid-December-mid-March, daily. Night skiing. Evenings, half-day rates.

WHERE TO STAY
★★★THE GREYSTONE
Greystone Lane, Lake Toxaway, 828-966-4700, 800-824-5766; www.greystoneinn.com
The main building of this historic inn was built in 1915 and welcomed the Ford and Rockefeller families. The inn offers extra fine touches including individually decorated rooms, a full-service spa and outdoor recreation.
33 rooms. Restaurant. Complimentary breakfast. Beach. $251-350

★★★HIGH HAMPTON INN AND COUNTRY CLUB
1525 Highway 107 S., Cashiers, 828-743-2411, 800-334-2551;
www.highhamptoninn.com
Located in the Blue Ridge Mountains, this 1,400-acre property boasts a pri-

vate lake and a quiet, wooded landscape. Guests of the inn, private cottages or colony homes, stay busy with the scenic 18-hole golf course, six clay tennis courts and hiking trails.

120 rooms. Restaurant, bar. Beach. Closed mid-November-April. $151-250

CHAPEL HILL

See also Durham, Raleigh

The University of North Carolina is the oldest state university in the country. The town of Chapel Hill's mission from its inception has been to support the college. And residents do cheer loudly for the blue and white Tarheels. Most notorious for its basketball fandom and renowned athletic alumni such as Michael Jordan, UNC is also a leading academic institution and part of the "research triangle" with Duke University in Durham and North Carolina State University in Raleigh.

WHAT TO SEE
HORACE WILLIAMS HOUSE

610 E. Rosemary St., Chapel Hill, 919-942-7818; www.chapelhillpreservation.com

This historic house is home to the Chapel Hill Preservation Society. It hosts changing art exhibits and chamber music concerts.

Tuesday-Friday, also Sunday afternoons; closed holidays and the first two weeks in August.

MOREHEAD-PATTERSON MEMORIAL BELL TOWER

Stadium Drive and South Road, Chapel Hill

This 172-foot Italian Renaissance campanile concert chimes 12 bells ranging in weight from 300 pounds to nearly two tons.

Popular tunes ring daily.

NORTH CAROLINA BOTANICAL GARDEN

15501 Old Mason Farm Road, Chapel Hill, 919-962-0522; www.ncbg.unc.edu

The garden is approximately 600 acres with a variety of trees and plants of the southeastern U.S. There are wildflower areas, herb gardens and nature trails.

Daily.

OLD WELL

Cameron Avenue, Chapel Hill

Long the unofficial symbol of the university, this well was the only source of water here for nearly a century. The present Greek temple structure dates from 1897.

SOUTH (MAIN) BUILDING

Cameron Avenue, and Raleigh Street, Chapel Hill

The cornerstone was laid in 1798, but the building was not completed until 1814, during which time students lived inside the roofless walls in little huts. Future President James K. Polk lived here from 1814 to 1818.

UNIVERSITY OF NORTH CAROLINA AT CHAPEL HILL

250 E. Franklin St., Chapel Hill, 919-962-1630; www.unc.edu

Approximately 27,000 students attend the institution, founded in 1795. The 720-acre campus has more than 200 buildings, and is packed with Southern charm.

WHERE TO STAY
★★★THE CAROLINA INN

211 Pittsboro St., Chapel Hill, 919-933-2001, 800-962-8519; www.carolinainn.com

This historic 1924 inn is set in the middle of the University of North Carolina campus and around the corner from the Chapel Hill Medical Center. The entrance, with a high portico and pillars, and its red-brick building echo a Georgian Revival theme. Inside, hardwood floors, Oriental rugs, mahogany tables, palms and fresh flowers add to the beautiful setting. Guest rooms continue the theme and include mahogany two-poster beds and furnishings. Art galleries, museums, charming shops and fine restaurants are all just a short distance away.

184 rooms. Restaurant, bar. $151-250

★★★FRANKLIN HOTEL

311 W. Franklin St., Chapel Hill, 919-442-9000, 866-831-5999;
www.franklinhotelnc.com

The Franklin Hotel combines the intimacy and charm of a bed and breakfast with the services and amenities of a larger hotel. The guest rooms are beautifully done in chocolate brown and celadon, while the seven VIP penthouse suites are the definition of luxury. Breakfast is an elegant affair at Windows Restaurant, while guests and locals mingle over drinks and light fare at Roberts, the lobby and patio bar.

67 rooms. Restaurant, bar. $251-350

★HAMPTON INN CHAPEL HILL

1740 Fordham Blvd., Chapel Hill, 919-968-3000, 800-426-7866; www.hamptoninn.com

120 rooms. Complimentary breakfast. $61-150

★★HOLIDAY INN CHAPEL HILL

1301 N. Fordham Blvd., Chapel Hill, 919-929-2171, 888-452-5765;
www.hichapelhill.com

For the truly school-spirited, this lobby is painted in UNC colors, the front desk staff dress in referee uniforms, all types of sports equipment are displayed on the outside walls leading to the rooms, and the floors have blue foot prints with tar on the heel.

134 rooms. Restaurant, bar. $61-150

★★★SHERATON HOTEL

1 Europa Drive, Chapel Hill, 919-968-4900, 800-325-3535;
www.sheraton.com/chapelhill

This modern hotel is located on the main road and connects the UNC-Chapel Hill campus and the Duke University campus, just a short distance to Interstate 85 and the Research Triangle. The wraparound open lobby features marble floors and floor-to-ceiling windows looking out to the pool and water fountain. Guest rooms are spacious with desks and sofas.

168 rooms. Restaurant, bar. $151-250

★★★SIENA HOTEL

1505 E. Franklin St., Chapel Hill, 919-929-4000, 800-223-7379; www.sienahotel.com

Southern hospitality and grand European styling make the Siena Hotel a favorite in Chapel Hill. The guest rooms and suites are tastefully decorated with fine Italian furnishings and rich fabrics, while modern amenities ensure the highest levels of comfort. Guests receive privileges at the UNC golf course and nearby fitness center. Il Palio Ristorante charms visitors throughout the day with a delicious Northern Italian-influenced menu.

79 rooms. Restaurant, bar. Complimentary breakfast. $151-250

WHERE TO EAT

★ALLEN & SON BARBEQUE

6203 Milhouse Road, Chapel Hill, 919-942-7576

Barbecue. Lunch, dinner. Closed Sunday-Monday. Children's menu. Outdoor seating. $15 and under

★★★BONNE SOIRÉE

431 W. Franklin St., Chapel Hill, 919-928-8388

Smack dab in the middle of Chapel Hill's vibrant Franklin Street, Bonne Soirée is a hit with locals and visitors alike. This intimate restaurant is sophisticated without being stuffy. The menu is handwritten and the wines are handpicked. The chef crafts his country French cooking with precision and pride, at times, making it difficult to believe you're in North Carolina rather than the French countryside.

French. Dinner. $16-35

★★★★CAROLINA CROSSROADS

211 Pittsboro St., Chapel Hill, 919-933-9277, 800-962-8519; www.carolinainn.com

Set in the historic Carolina Inn, the Carolina Crossroads dining room is elegantly classic and delivers a picture-perfect example of Southern hospitality and charm. The menu features regional dishes, from a classic North Carolina pulled pork sandwich to salmon with grilled acorn squash in white-wine butter sauce. Local, seasonal ingredients are incorporated into many of the dishes.

Southern. Breakfast, lunch, dinner, brunch. Bar. Children's menu. Reservations recommended. Outdoor seating. $36-85

★★★ELAINE'S ON FRANKLIN

454 W. Franklin St., Chapel Hill, 919-960-2770; www.elainesonfranklin.com

Elaine's on Franklin promises that each meal is made up of "food for the soul, prepared for the heart." Among a menu of fresh greens and local meat and seafood, you'll see some truly unique dishes such as tuna ceviche and even something for the herbivores: white lasagna with housemade wheat pasta. Your palate will continue the love affair with a selection of organic wines and the definition of soul food: a dessert menu with bread pudding and warm chocolate cake.

American, Southern. Dinner. Closed Sunday-Monday. $36-85

★★★IL PALIO

1505 E. Franklin St., Chapel Hill, 919-929-4000, 800-223-7379; www.sienahotel.com

Located in the Siena Hotel, this Italian restaurant offers guests a fine-dining experience with tasteful interpretations of Italian-Mediterranean classics. A prix fixe Market Tasting Menu offers a chef's choice selection of food made from all local and seasonal ingredients. The restaurant features nightly live piano or guitar music and an impressive wine and martini list.

Northern Italian. Breakfast, lunch, dinner, brunch. Bar. Reservations recommended. $36-85

★★★JUJUBE RESTAURANT

1201-L Raleigh Road, Glen Lennox Shopping Center, Chapel Hill, 919-960-0555; www.jujuberestaurant.com

Jujube proclaims it's "almost Asian," but that doesn't mean it's a copout or a fake. Southern stomachs will delight as they ease their way into exotic cuisine, with North Carolina shrimp lo mein and wontons made of beef short rib and goat cheese. Dates can cuddle at secluded tables along the brightly colored wall or adventurous types can sit chef-side at the open-kitchen bar. Each week the restaurant hosts special dinners and events where food and drink are the main guests. On Wednesdays, the kitchen goes Italian with its specials, and an advanced reservation will get you the Tuesday 20-course chef's table.

Asian. Lunch, dinner. $16-35

★★LA RESIDENCE

202 W. Rosemary St., Chapel Hill, 919-967-2506; www.laresidencedining.com

Continental, French. Dinner, late-night. Bar. Reservations recommended. Outdoor seating. $16-35

★★★LANTERN

423 W. Franklin St., Chapel Hill, 919-969-8846; www.lanternrestaurant.com

Lantern's head chef and owner Andrea Reusing wanted to create authentic Asian food using local, seasonal ingredients in a simply chic setting. Restaurant-goers' taste buds are treated with entrees tickled by curries and ginger, tamarind and lemongrass spices, mingling American cooking with Thai and Vietnamese flavors. Save room for spirits; Lantern's exhaustive wine selection is only to be outdone by the uber-cosmopolitan cocktail list, which features The Red Geisha (muddled fresh organic strawberries with lime, ginger and vodka) and a Saketini worth raising a glass for.

Asian. Dinner. Closed Sunday. $36-85

★SPANKY'S

101 E. Franklin St., Chapel Hill, 919-967-2678; www.spankysrestaurant.com

American. Lunch, dinner. Bar. Children's menu. Casual attire. $16-35

★SQUID'S

1201 N. Fordham Blvd., Chapel Hill, 919-942-8757; www.squidsrestaurant.com

Seafood. Dinner. Bar. Children's menu. $16-35

CHARLOTTE

The Carolinas' largest metropolis, and one of the country's fastest growing areas, Charlotte is a top banking center. British General Cornwallis occupied the town for a short time in 1780, but met such determined resistance that he called it a "hornet's nest," a name that has been applied to the city seal and by sports teams such as the NBA's Carolina Hornets. Gold was discovered here in 1799, and the region around Charlotte was the nation's major gold producer until the California gold rush in 1848. The city had a U.S. Mint between 1837 and 1861. The last Confederate Cabinet meeting was held here in 1865.

Today there is much to see and do, whether it's history (the birthplace of the 11th president, James K. Polk), religion (the birthplace and headquarters for evangelical minister Billy Graham), sports (professional football, baseball, basketball, NASCAR) or the arts (try the free and fabulous public art walking tour).

WHAT TO SEE

THE CHARLOTTE MUSEUM OF HISTORY AND HEZEKIAH ALEXANDER HOMESITE

3500 Shamrock Drive, Charlotte, 704-568-1774; www.charlottemuseum.org

This museum includes the Hezekiah Alexander House, the oldest dwelling still standing in Mecklenburg County. There is a two-story springhouse with a working log kitchen. Tours are avaialble.

Tuesday-Saturday 10 a.m.-5 p.m., Sunday 1-5 p.m.; open Monday in summer.

DISCOVERY PLACE

301 N. Tryon St., Charlotte, 704-372-6261, 800-935-0553; www.discoveryplace.org

A hands-on science museum that gives kids a chance to learn about electricity, weather, rocks, minerals and other scientific wonders. Visit the aquarium, science circus, life center, rain forest, collections gallery and OMNIMAX theater, as well as major traveling exhibits.

Daily.

JAMES K. POLK MEMORIAL STATE HISTORIC SITE

308 S. Polk St., Pineville, 704-889-7145; www.nchistoricsites.org/polk

A replica of the log cabin and outbuildings at the birthplace of the 11th President of the United States can be found here. There is also a visitor center with exhibits and films.

Tuesday-Saturday 9 a.m.-5 p.m.

LEVINE MUSEUM OF THE NEW SOUTH

200 E. Seventh St., Charlotte, 704-333-1887; www.museumofthenewsouth.org

Chronicle the history of the post-Civil War South with an ever-changing series of exhibits featuring industry, ideas, people and historical eras such as the Civil Rights Movement.

Monday-Saturday10 a.m.-5 p.m., Sunday noon-5 p.m.

PARAMOUNT'S CAROWINDS

14523 Carowinds Blvd., Charlotte, 704-588-2600, 800-888-4386; www.carowinds.com
This 100-acre family theme park has more than 40 rides, shows and attractions including a 12-acre water entertainment complex WaterWorks, Nickelodeon Central children's area, Drop Zone stunt tower and roller coasters. The 13,000-seat Paladium amphitheater hosts special events.
June-late August, daily; March-May and September-October, weekends.

U.S. NATIONAL WHITEWATER CENTER

820 Hawfield Road, Charlotte, 704-391-3900; www.usnwc.org
An official Olympic training site and site for World Cup whitewater rafting since 2006, this 307-acre park on the Catawba River was modeled after Olympic rafting courses. Four thousand linear feet of whitewater rafting as well as biking, canoeing, wall climbing, kayaking and more are offered at this playground for serious sports enthusiasts. Mountain bikes are available to rent.

WHERE TO STAY

★★★★THE BALLANTYNE RESORT, A LUXURY COLLECTION HOTEL
10000 Ballantyne Commons Parkway, Charlotte, 704-248-4000, 866-248-4824; www.ballantyneresort.com
This elegant resort within the city limits of Charlotte is a paradise for golf enthusiasts, with one of the state's best 18-hole courses and the renowned Dana Rader Golf school. Rooms are crisply and classically decorated and have lavish finishes, such as marble entrances and bathrooms. The Gallery Restaurant offers creative selections and seasonal ingredients. The Gallery bar serves a tapas menu and lengthy selection of cocktails, whiskeys and after-dinner drinks.
249 rooms. Restaurant, bar. Spa. $151-250

★★COURTYARD CHARLOTTE CITY CENTER
237 S. Tryon St., Charlotte, 704-926-5800, 800-321-2211; www.marriott.com
181 rooms. Bar. Fitness center. $151-250

★★COURTYARD CHARLOTTE UNIVERSITY RESEARCH PARK
333 W. T. Harris Blvd., Charlotte, 704-549-4888, 888-270-8582; www.marriott.com
152 rooms. Business center. Fitness center. $61-150

★★DOUBLETREE HOTEL
895 W. Trade St., Charlotte, 704-347-0070, 800-222-8733; www.doubletree.com
187 rooms. Restaurant, bar. Business center. Fitness center. Pool. $151-250

★★DOUBLETREE HOTEL CHARLOTTE AIRPORT
2600 Yorkmont Road, Charlotte, 704-357-9100, 800-222-8733; www.charlotteairport.doubletree.com
173 rooms. Restaurant, bar. Business center. Pool. Fitness center. $151-250

★★★THE DUKE MANSION

400 Hermitage Road, Charlotte, 704-714-4400, 888-202-1009; www.dukemansion.com

This 1915 Southern estate is a lovely setting for a weekend getaway, and the mansion also serves as a facility for meetings and retreats. The charming Colonial Revival house was once owned by James Buchanan Duke, founder of Duke University. Acres of gardens surround the well-maintained house. Treetop rooms as well as standard guest rooms—some with sleeping porches—are decorated with traditional and antique furniture.

20 rooms. Complimentary breakfast. $151-250

★★★THE DUNHILL HOTEL

237 N. Tryon St., Charlotte, 704-332-4141, 800-354-4141; www.dunhillhotel.com

This was one of the city's first luxury hotels when it opened as the Mayfair Manor in 1929. Guest rooms feature 18th-century furniture, antiques and four-poster beds. The Dunhill's onsite restaurant, the Monticello, is an elegant spot for a special night out.

60 rooms. Restaurant, bar. Business center. $151-250

★★EMBASSY SUITES

4800 S. Tryon St., Charlotte, 704-527-8400, 800-362-2779;
www.embassy-charlotte.com

274 rooms. Restaurant, bar. Complimentary breakfast. Business center. Fitness center. Pool. $151-250

★★★HILTON CHARLOTTE CENTER CITY

222 E. Third St., Charlotte, 704-377-1500, 800-445-8667; www.charlotte.hilton.com

Perfect for business or pleasure, this hotel in the financial district is near shops and restaurants. Also nearby are beaches, golf courses and the Carolina Mountains. Rooms have oversized desks, 42-inch flat-screen TVs and black marble bathrooms.

400 rooms. Restaurant, bar. Business center. Fitness center. Pool. $151-250

★★★HILTON UNIVERSITY PLACE

8629 J. M. Keynes Drive, Charlotte, 704-547-7444, 800-445-8667;
www.charlotteuniversity.hilton.com

A beautiful sunlit atrium lobby anchors the Hilton. Guest rooms and suites feature a contemporary, sleek style and great views of the university area. The Lakefront Restaurant offers a menu of steak and seafood-focused fare.

393 rooms. Restaurant, bar. Business center. Fitness center. Pool. $151-250

★HYATT SUMMERFIELD SUITES

4920 S. Tryon St., Charlotte, 704-525-2600; www.hyatt.com

135 rooms. Complimentary breakfast. Business center. Spa. Pool. $61-150

★LA QUINTA INN AND SUITES CHARLOTTE COLISEUM

4900 S. Tryon St., Charlotte, 704-523-5599, 800-687-6667; www.laquinta.com

131 rooms. Complimentary breakfast. Fitness center. $61-150

★★★MARRIOTT CITY CENTER

100 W. Trade St., Charlotte, 704-333-9000, 800-228-9290; www.marriottcitycenter.com
Located in the central uptown business district, this hotel is only blocks from
the New Charlotte Convention Center and Bank of America Stadium.
438 rooms. Restaurant, bar. Fitness center. $151-250

★★★THE MOREHEAD INN

1122 E. Morehead St., Charlotte, 704-376-3357, 888-667-3432;
www.moreheadinn.com
Meticulously kept gardens can be found at this charming Southern inn, an
historic building listed on the National Register of Historic Places. Hardwood
floors, Oriental rugs, antiques and beautiful tapestries are placed throughout,
while four-poster beds and fireplaces provide cozy touches in guest rooms.
12 rooms. Complimentary breakfast. $151-250

★★★OMNI HOTEL

132 E. Trade St., Charlotte, 704-377-0400, 800-843-6664; www.omnihotels.com
The ultramodern Omni Hotel is located within walking distance of the Charlotte Convention Center and the Overstreet Mall, which offers shopping and
dining. The Charlotte-Douglas Airport is only 15 minutes away. Comfortable
guest rooms have views of the city.
374 rooms. Restaurant, bar. Business center. Fitness center. $151-250

★RAMADA

7900 Nations Ford Road, Charlotte, 704-522-7110, 800-272-6232; www.ramada.com
110 rooms. Complimentary breakfast. Pool. $61-150

★★RENAISSANCE CHARLOTTE SUITES

2800 Coliseum Centre Drive, Charlotte, 704-357-1414, 800-468-3571;
www.renaissancehotels.com
275 rooms. Restaurant, bar. Business center. Fitness center. $151-250

★★VAN LANDINGHAM ESTATE

2010 The Plaza, Charlotte, 704-334-8909, 888-524-2020;
www.vanlandinghamestate.com
Nine rooms. Complimentary breakfast. $151-250

★★★THE WESTIN CHARLOTTE

601 S. College St., Charlotte, 704-375-2600, 800-937-8461; www.westin.com/charlotte
Rooms and suites are modern and comfortable and feature countless amenities from in-room video games to the hotel's signature luxury bedding. Spa
services are available. The Ember Grille serves American fare for breakfast,
lunch and dinner, while Charlotte's Treats and Eats offers light fare during
the day.
700 rooms. Restaurant, bar. Business center. Spa. $151-250

ALSO RECOMMENDED
THE VICTORIAN VILLA
10925 Windy Grove Road, Charlotte, 704-394-5545; www.victorianvillainn.com
Five rooms. Breakfast, dinner. $151-250

WHERE TO EAT
★AMALFI'S
8542 University City Blvd., Charlotte, 704-547-8651; www.amalfi-charlotte.com
Italian. Lunch, dinner. Bar. Closed Monday. Children's menu. Outdoor seating. $16-35

★★★BONTERRA
1829 Cleveland Ave., Charlotte, 704-333-9463; www.bonterradining.com
Bonterra is located close to Uptown Charlotte in the historic Southend District. Choose from an extensive wine list featuring 100 wines by the glass and 300 bottles—wine tastings can be booked for groups of 15 to 50 people. Menu selections include deep-fried lobster tails, braised veal osso bucco, fire-roasted filet mignon and Sonoma County duck breast.
American, California. Dinner. Closed Sunday. Bar. Reservations recommended. Outdoor seating. $36-85

★BRIXX PIZZA
225 E. Sixth St., Charlotte, 704-347-2749; www.brixxpizza.com
Pizza. Lunch, dinner, late-night. Bar. Children's menu. Outdoor seating. $16-35

★FLYING SAUCER DRAFT EMPORIUM
9605 N. Tryon St., Charlotte, 704-568-7253; www.beerknurd.com
American. Lunch, dinner, late-night. Bar. Children's menu. Outdoor seating. $16-35

★FUEL PIZZA CAFÉ
1501 Central Ave., Charlotte, 704-376-3835; www.fuelpizza.com
American. Lunch, dinner. Children's menu. Outdoor seating. $15 and under

★★FUSE BOX
227 W. Trade St., Charlotte, 704-376-8885: www.fuseboxcharlotte.com
Sushi, Thai. Lunch, dinner. Closed Sunday. Bar. Reservations recommended. $16-35

★★★★GALLERY RESTAURANT
10000 Ballantyne Commons Parkway, Charlotte, 704-248-4000, 866-248-4824;
www.gallery-restaurant.com
The setting is relaxing and welcoming at Gallery Restaurant & Bar, located on the ground level of the Ballantyne Resort. Enjoy artfully presented dishes such as cedar plank-roasted sea bass with blue crab, shallots and English pea risotto, and rosemary and citrus-roasted free-range chicken. Fine service makes dining here a delight.
American. Breakfast, lunch, dinner. Bar. Reservations recommended. Outdoor seating. $36-85

★★THE KABOB HOUSE
6432 E. Independence Blvd., Charlotte, 704-531-2500; www.kabobhousenc.com
Persian. Lunch, dinner. Reservations recommended. Outdoor seating. $16-35

★★★LAVECCHIA'S SEAFOOD GRILLE
225 E. Sixth St., Charlotte, 704-370-6776; www.lavecchias.com
LaVecchia's features seafood entrées such as Chilean sea bass and seared yellowfin tuna, as well as prime steaks. To complement the menu, the restaurant is decked out in a modern, urban, marine-themed design. A live jazz band spices things up on Friday and Saturday nights.
Seafood, steak. Dinner. Closed Sunday. Bar. Children's menu. Reservations recommended. Outdoor seating. $36-85

★LUPIE'S CAFÉ
2718 Monroe Road, Charlotte, 704-374-1232; www.lupiescafe.com
American. Lunch, dinner. Closed Sunday. Bar. $15 and under

★MAMA FU'S ASIAN HOUSE
1600 E. Woodlawn, Charlotte, 704-714-5080; www.mamafus.com
Pan-Asian. Lunch, dinner. Children's menu. Reservations recommended. Outdoor seating. $15 and under

★★★MCNINCH HOUSE
511 N. Church St., Charlotte, 704-332-6159; www.mcninchhouserestaurant.com
This restaurant's unique setting, attention to detail and ever-changing but consistently strong French menu are well-suited for special-occasion dinners. Situated in a historic building, McNinch House is in a residential area on the west side of Church Street and within walking distance of downtown hotels and businesses.
French. Dinner. Closed Sunday-Monday. Bar. Jacket required. Reservations recommended. Valet parking. $86 and up

★MERT'S HEART & SOUL
214 N. College St., Charlotte, 704-342-4222; www.mertsuptown.com
American. Lunch, dinner, brunch. Children's menu. Outdoor seating. $16-35

★PRESTO BAR AND GRILL
445 W. Trade St., Charlotte, 704-334-7088; www.prestobarandgrill.com
American. Lunch, dinner. Closed Sunday. Bar. Reservations recommended. Outdoor seating. $16-35

★RAINBOW CAFÉ
201 S. College St., Charlotte, 704-372-2256; www.rainbowcafeuptown.com
American. Lunch, dinner. Closed Saturday-Sunday. Bar. Children's menu. $15 and under

★RANCH HOUSE
5614 Wilkinson Blvd., Charlotte, 704-399-5411; www.ranchhouseofcharlotte.com
Seafood, steak. Dinner. Closed Sunday; first two weeks in July. Bar. Children's menu. Reservations recommended. $16-35

★★★TAVERNA 100
100 N. Tryon St., Charlotte, 704-344-0515; www.taverna100.com
Located in uptown Charlotte, Taverna 100 is housed in Founders Hall in the Bank of America's Corporate Center. Fresh herbs and olive oils accent the flavorful Mediterranean dishes, many of which are prepared on the wood-burning grill or the rotisserie.
Mediterranean. Lunch, dinner. Closed Sunday. Bar. Children's menu. Reservations recommended. Outdoor seating. $36-85

★★★UPSTREAM
6902 Phillips Place, Charlotte, 704-556-7730; www.upstreamit.com
With a wide selection of fresh seafood, a sushi and oyster bar and an extensive wine list, this Charlotte dining spot (near SouthPark Mall) is a local favorite. Start with the lobster bisque or the jumbo lump crab cakes before trying a main entrée such as the mushroom-crusted mahimahi, sake-marinated South American sea bass or the pan-roasted Idaho trout.
Seafood. Lunch, dinner, brunch. Bar. Reservations recommended. Outdoor seating. $36-85

SPAS
★★★★THE SPA AT BALLANTYNE RESORT
1000 Ballantyne Commons Parkway, Charlotte, 704-248-4141;
www.ballantyneresort.com
Tucked inside Charlotte's luxurious Ballantyne Resort, this spa offers a classic pampering experience delivered by an amiable, well-trained staff. With 16 treatment rooms, there's ample space for sampling Swedish massages, rejuvenating facials or moisturizing body wraps. The spa also offers a full range of nail and salon services. Couples can opt for massages delivered in the privacy of a couples' suite.

CHEROKEE
See also Bryson City, Maggie Valley, Waynesville
This is the capital of the Eastern Band of the Cherokee, who live on the Qualla Reservation at the edge of Great Smoky Mountains National Park and the Blue Ridge Parkway. The reservation, the largest east of the Mississippi, is shared by the descendants of members of the tribe who avoided being driven to Oklahoma on the "Trail of Tears."

WHAT TO SEE
CHEROKEE HERITAGE MUSEUM AND GALLERY
Acquoni Road, Cherokee
This is located in Saunooke Village. Interpretive center features Cherokee culture and history. There is a gift shop.
Daily.

MUSEUM OF THE CHEROKEE INDIAN
Highway 441 N., On Cherokee Reservation, Cherokee, 828-497-3481;
www.cherokeemuseum.org

The museum houses arts and crafts, audiovisual displays, portraits and pre-historic artifacts depicting the life of the Cherokee.
Daily.

OCONALUFTEE INDIAN VILLAGE
Highway 441 N., Cherokee, 828-497-2111; www.cherokee-nc.com

A replica of a Native American village dating back more than 250 years ago includes a seven-sided council house, herb garden, craft demonstrations, and lectures.
Guided tours Mid-May-late October, daily.

WHERE TO STAY
★★BEST WESTERN GREAT SMOKIES INN
1636 Acquoni Road, Cherokee, 828-497-2020, 800-937-8376; www.bestwestern.com
152 rooms. Restaurant. Pool. $61-150

★COMFORT INN
44 Tsalagi Road, Cherokee, 828-497-2411, 800-424-6423; www.comfortinn.com
88 rooms. Complimentary breakfast. Pets not accepted. $61-150

★★HOLIDAY INN
Highway 19 S., Cherokee, 828-497-9181, 800-315-2621; www.hicherokeenc.com
154 rooms. Pool. Fitness center. $61-150

CONCORD
See also Charlotte

Concord located in the heart of Carolina NASCAR country. The town boasts several NASCAR teams, Lowe's Motor Speedway and a NASCAR research and development office. For those who need a break from car racing, hit more than 200 stores at Concord Mills outlet mall.

WHAT TO SEE
CONCORD MILLS
8111 Concord Mills Blvd., Concord, 704-979-3000; www.concordmills.com

This outlet mall has more than 200 stores, including factory outlets for popular chains such as Banana Republic and Saks Fifth Avenue. It also houses a movie theater.
Daily.

CONCORD MOTORSPORT PARK
7940 Highway 601 S., Concord, 704-782-4221; www.concordmotorsportpark.com

The NASCAR weekly series runs Saturday nights from April through October at this asphalt tri-oval 30 miles northeast of Charlotte in the heart of NASCAR country. The grandstands seat 8,000, and there are spots for 28 RVs at Turn 3.

DALE EARNHARDT TRIBUTE

3003 Dale Earnhardt Plaza, Kannapolis, 800-848-3740; www.visitcabarrus.com

The people of Kannapolis have preserved the memory of their favorite son, Dale Earnhardt, in 900 pounds of bronze. Nearby are murals depicting Earnhardt's race car driving career.

NASCAR SPEEDPARK, CONCORD MILLS

8461 Concord Mills Blvd., Concord, 704-979-6770; www.nascarspeedpark.com

A 7-acre race-themed amusement park offers five racetracks, a state-of-the-art interactive arcade, an 18-hole miniature golf course, kiddie rides and Lazer Tag.
Daily.

REED GOLD MINE STATE HISTORIC SITE

9621 Reed Mine Road, Midland, 704-721-4653; www.reedmine.com

The Reed Gold Mine State Historic Site boasts the first documented discovery of gold in the United States in 1799. Stop and check out the underground mine tours, history trail, working machinery, demonstrations, exhibits, or enjoy the panning area and see what you find.
Tuesday-Saturday. Panning area: April-October, daily; fee.

RICHARD PETTY DRIVING EXPERIENCE

Lowe's Motor Speedway, 5555 Concord Parkway South, Concord, 800-237-3889; www.1800bepetty.com

Always wanted to rip a stock car around the curves at a NASCAR racetrack? This is the largest of the driving schools that takes fans right onto the track at Lowe's Motor Speedway. For anywhere between $99 for a ride along to almost $3,000 for an advanced racing experience, you can live your racing dream.

CORNELIUS

See also Charlotte, Mooresville, Statesville

Like Concord, Cornelius is close to Lowe's Motor Speedway and steeped in NASCAR culture. Nearby Mooresville is the home of the North Carolina Auto Racing Hall of Fame.

WHAT TO SEE
LAKE NORMAN

www.visitlakenorman.org

Lake Norman is the state's largest freshwater lake at 32,510 acres. It was created by the Cowans Ford Dam, a Duke Power project on the Catawba River. There are nine public access areas, with fishing areas and boating access.

MEMORY LANE MOTORSPORTS & HISTORIC AUTOMOTIVE MUSEUM

769 River Highway, Mooresville, 704-662-3673; www.memorylaneautomuseum.com

One-of-a-kind vehicles from race to vintage cars and motorcycles are on display at the museum, as well as toys, memorabilia and more.
Monday-Saturday 10 a.m.-5 p.m.

NORTH CAROLINA AUTO RACING HALL OF FAME
119 Knob Hill Road, Mooresville, 704-663-5331; www.ncarhof.com
As Mooresville's official visitor's center, the museum offers a large display of more than 35 cars dedicated to all types of auto racing. The gift shop is also the official Race City, USA merchandise headquarters, and carries a wide selection of racing memorabilia.
Monday-Friday 10 a.m.-5 p.m. Saturday-Sunday 10 a.m.-3 p.m.

WHERE TO STAY
★HAMPTON INN
19501 Statesville Road, Cornelius, 704-892-9900, 800-426-7866;
www.hamptoninn.com
116 rooms. Complimentary breakfast. $61-150

ALSO RECOMMENDED
DAVIDSON VILLAGE INN
117 Depot St., Davidson, 704-892-8044, 800-892-0796; www.davidsoninn.com
18 rooms. Complimentary breakfast. $61-150

WHERE TO EAT
★★KOBE JAPANESE HOUSE OF STEAK & SEAFOOD
20465 Chartwell Center Drive, Cornelius, 704-896-7778; www.kobeherolkn.com
Japanese. Lunch, dinner. Bar. Reservations recommended. $16-35

DURHAM
See also Chapel Hill, Raleigh
Durham's sparkle has brought it near-top national ranking in livability studies. Known for excellence in medicine, education, research and industry, Durham is also a recreational and cultural center in the rolling Piedmont region.

In 1924, an endowment from James B. Duke, head of the American Tobacco Company, helped establish Duke University as one of the nation's top universities. North Carolina Central University is located here as well. In the 1950s, Durham County was chosen as the site of Research Triangle Park, a planned scientific research center that includes the Environmental Protection Agency, the National Institute for Environmental Health Sciences, IBM Corporation, the Glaxo Wellcome Company and others.

WHAT TO SEE
BENNETT PLACE STATE HISTORIC SITE
4409 Bennett Memorial Road, Durham, 919-383-4345; www.nchistoricsites.org/bennett
This was the site of the April 26, 1865 surrender of Confederate General Johnston to Union General Sherman. There is a reconstructed Bennett homestead and picnicking onsite, as well as an informative audiovisual display.
Visitor center, exhibits, audiovisual show. Tuesday-Saturday 9 a.m.-5 p.m.

DUKE HOMESTEAD STATE HISTORIC SITE
2828 Duke Homestead Road, Durham, 919-477-5498; www.nchistoricsites.org
This was the ancestral home of the Duke family. The estate houses the first

Duke tobacco factory, curing barn, outbuildings and farm crops. There is a tobacco museum, exhibits, film; and period furnishings. Tours are available. Tuesday-Saturday 9 a.m.-5 p.m.

DUKE UNIVERSITY
2138 Campus Drive, Durham, 919-684-3214; www.duke.edu
Duke University is one of the nation's top private universities, situated on 8,000 acres. It includes original Trinity College. The West Campus, occupied since 1930, is the showplace of the university.

DUKE'S WALLACE WADE STADIUM
290 Frank Bassett Road, Durham, 919-681-2583; www.goduke.com
Home of the Duke Blue Devils, the stadium packs in the crowds during college basketball season. Game tickets are hard to come by.

DURHAM BULL ATHLETIC PARK
409 Blackwell St., Durham, 919-687-6500; www.durhambulls.com
This 10,000-seat stadium is home to the Durham Bulls Triple A baseball team, affiliated with the Tampa Bay Devil Rays.

NORTH CAROLINA MUSEUM OF LIFE AND SCIENCE
433 W. Murray Ave., Durham, 919-220-5429; www.ncmls.org
The museum highlights North Carolina wildlife. Hands-on science exhibits; aerospace, weather and geology collections; train ride; farmyard; science park; discovery rooms; and the Butterfly House round out the property.
Tuesday-Saturday 10 a.m.-5 p.m., Sunday noon-5 p.m.

SARAH P. DUKE GARDENS
426 Anderson St., Durham, 919-684-3698; www.hr.duke.edu/dukegardens
There are 55 acres of landscaped gardens and pine forest, with regional plants on display.
Monday-Saturday 9 a.m.-6 p.m., Sunday noon-5 p.m.

SPECIAL EVENTS
AMERICAN DANCE FESTIVAL
715 Broad St., Durham, 919-684-6402; www.americandancefestival.org
The festival is marked by six weeks of performances by the finest of both major and emerging modern dance companies from the United States and abroad. It is held at the Page Auditorium and Reynolds Industries Theater, Duke University, West Campus.
June-July.

BULL DURHAM BLUES FESTIVAL
804 Old Fayetteville St., Durham, 919-683-1709; www.hayti.org/blues
This acclaimed blues festival, held in early September, has been running for more than 20 years and features performances by blues legends.

WHERE TO STAY

★★ARROWHEAD INN BED & BREAKFAST
106 Mason Road, Durham, 919-477-8430, 800-528-2207; www.arrowheadinn.com
Nine rooms. Complimentary breakfast. $151-250

★BEST WESTERN SKYLAND INN
5400 U.S. Highway, 70 W., Durham, 919-383-2508, 800-937-8376; www.bestwestern.com
31 rooms. Complimentary breakfast. Pool. $61-150

★COURTYARD BY MARRIOTT DURHAM
1815 Front St., Durham, 919-309-1500, 800-321-2211; www.courtyard.com
146 rooms. Restaurant. Business center. $61-150

★★DOUBLETREE GUEST SUITES RALEIGH-DURHAM
2515 Meridian Parkway, Durham, 919-361-4660, 800-365-9876; www.doubletree.com
203 rooms. Restaurant, bar. $151-250

★★HILTON DURHAM
3800 Hillsborough, Durham, 919-383-8033, 800-445-8667; www.hilton.com
195 rooms. Restaurant, bar. $151-250

★★★MARRIOTT DURHAM CIVIC CENTER
201 Foster St., Durham, 919-768-6000, 800-909-8375; www.marriott.com
This hotel is near the theater district, Durham Athletic Park, and Duke University. The elegant charm is enhanced by fountains that flow through the atrium lobby.
187 rooms. Restaurant, bar. $151-250

★★★MARRIOTT RESEARCH TRIANGLE PARK
4700 Guardian Drive, Durham, 919-941-6200, 800-228-9290; www.marriott.com
This ultramodern hotel is only five minutes from Research Triangle Park and the Raleigh-Durham Airport. North Carolina State, University of North Carolina and Duke University campuses are all close by.
223 rooms. Restaurant, bar. $151-250

★★★MILLENNIUM HOTEL
2800 Campus Walk Ave., Durham, 919-383-8575, 866-866-8086;
www.millennium-hotels.com
Conveniently located near Duke University and Medical Center, this hotel caters to business travelers with amenities such as wireless Internet access and a business center. Relax in the lounge, where mahogany bookshelves, overstuffed sofas and wing-backed chairs provide the atmosphere of a private club.
313 rooms. Restaurant, bar. Business center. $61-150

★QUALITY INN & SUITES
3710 Hillsborough Road, Durham, 919-382-3388, 877-424-6423;
www.choicehotels.com
115 rooms. Complimentary breakfast. $61-150

★★★WASHINGTON DUKE INN & GOLF CLUB
3001 Cameron Blvd., Durham, 919-490-0999, 800-443-3853;
www.washingtondukeinn.com

Campus living never looked this elegant, yet the Washington Duke Inn & Golf Club calls Duke University campus home. Rooms and suites reflect English country influences, as does the daily afternoon tea. With four restaurants, dining choices here are terrific. A leading golf course just outside the door and privileges at the university's fitness facilities means there's always plenty to do.

271 rooms. Restaurant, bar. Fitness center. $251-350

WHERE TO EAT
★★★FAIRVIEW
3001 Cameron Blvd., Durham, 919-490-0999, 800-443-3853;
www.washingtondukeinn.com

Located in the Washington Duke Inn & Golf Club, this Southern-influenced restaurant has traditional décor and nightly piano music. Try for a seat by one of the many windows for a beautiful view of the golf course. Weather permitting, the terrace is the perfect spot for outdoor dining.

American. Breakfast, lunch, dinner, Sunday brunch. Bar. Children's menu. Reservations recommended. Outdoor seating. $36-85

★★★FOUR-SQUARE RESTAURANT
2701 Chapel Hill Road, Durham, 919-401-9877; www.foursquarerestaurant.com

The location might throw you off, but once you sidle up to the elegant converted Victorian that houses Four-Square, you'll be in the right place for a romantic meal. Past the wraparound porch await seven dining rooms—easily converted to party space if you're in need of a venue—with fireplaces, and a screened porch for warmer weather use. Dining here will never get old, as the menu changes monthly to make sure the kitchen is always cooking up the freshest tastes, using local produce, cheese and meat each season.

American. Dinner. Closed Sunday. $36-85

★★★MAGNOLIA GRILL
1002 Ninth St., Durham, 919-286-3609; www.magnoliagrill.net

At Magnolia Grill, husband-and-wife chefs and co-owners Ben and Karen Barker exhibit an independent streak in Southern cooking. He handles the savories, taking Southern ingredients beyond regional confines in dishes such as smoked trout with avocado and red pepper slaw and sea bass carpaccio with Thai crab vinaigrette; she creates the sweets that take Southern comforts upscale, including shaker pie and upside-down caramel banana cake with bourbon praline ice cream.

American, Southern. Dinner. Closed Sunday-Monday. Bar. Reservations recommended. $36-85

★★★NANA'S RESTAURANT
2514 University Drive, Durham, 919-493-8545; www.nanasdurham.com

Locals like to frequent the bar for a quick bite and a glass or two off the wine list, but first-timers might want to treat their taste buds to all three courses: pate or peekytoe crab chowder to start, fish or fowl next, and a local

cheese plate or Nana's Crème Brulee for dessert. All of your special occasion needs are covered with space to host big parties or a tasting menu with wine pairings for a more intimate outing. You can also bring home more than the doggy bag—the restaurant offers cooking classes with the chef.
American. Dinner. Closed Sunday. $36-85

★★★PAPA'S GRILLE
1821 Hillandale Road, Durham, 919-383-8502; www.papasgrille.com
Watch the chef's work in the open display kitchen of this restaurant located in a little strip mall near Route 70 and Interstate 85. Bistro tables surround the outside of the room, while dining room tables are set with crisp white tablecloths, dark blue glasses and candles. Executive chef Sam Papanikas is known for his cast-iron pan-seared graviera cheese flambé and lavender-glazed lamb tenderloin.
Mediterranean. Lunch, dinner. Closed Sunday. Bar. Children's menu. Reservations recommended. $36-85

★★PARIZADE
2200 W. Main St., Durham, 919-286-9712; www.parizaderestaurant.com
Mediterranean. Lunch, dinner. Bar. Reservations recommended. Outdoor seating. $16-35

★★WATT'S GROCERY
1116 Broad St., Durham, 919-416-5040; www.wattsgrocery.com
American. Lunch (Tuesday-Friday), dinner, late-night, Sunday brunch. Closed Monday. $16-35

EDENTON
This is one of the oldest communities in North Carolina and was the capital of the colony for more than 22 years. The women of Edenton staged their own Revolutionary tea party on October 25, 1774, signing a resolution protesting British injustice. A bronze teapot, at the west side of the Courthouse Green, commemorates the event. Today Edenton, the seat of Chowan County, is known as the South's prettiest small town because of the large number of original historic homes dating back to the 1700s.

WHAT TO SEE
HISTORIC EDENTON
108 N. Broad St., Edenton, 252-482-2637; www.nchistoricsites.org/iredell/iredell.htm
Tour of historic properties, which may be seen individually or as a group; allow 2 1/2 to 3 hours for the complete tour.
April-October, Monday-Saturday 9 a.m.-5 p.m. Sunday 1-5 p.m. November-March, Monday-Saturday 10 a.m.-4 p.m. Sunday 1-4 p.m.

JAMES IREDELL HOUSE
108 N. Broad St., Edenton, 252-482-2637; www.nchistoricsites.org
Tour the home of early Attorney General of North Carolina, James Iredell, who was appointed by George Washington to the first U.S. Supreme Court.

SOMERSET PLACE STATE HISTORIC SITE

2572 Lake Shore Road, Creswell, 252-797-4560; www.albemarle-nc.com/somerset
Located on Lake Phelps in Pettigrew State Park, the original plantation, one of the largest in North Carolina, encompassed more than 100,000 acres. The first primary crop was rice, which gave way to corn and wheat. The mansion and outbuildings date back to the 1830s.
April-October, Monday-Saturday 9 a.m.-5 p.m.; Sunday 1-5 p.m.; November-March, Tuesday-Saturday 10 a.m.-4 p.m.; Sunday 1-4 p.m.

WHERE TO STAY

CAPTAIN'S QUARTERS INN

202 W. Queen St., Edenton, 252-482-8945, 800-482-8945;
www.captainsquartersinn.com
Eight rooms. Complimentary breakfast. No children under 8. $61-150

LORDS PROPRIETORS INN

300 N. Broad St., Edenton, 252-482-3641, 888-394-6622; www.edentoninn.com
This inn is actually three separate homes set on two acres of land. All 20 rooms are decorated with period antiques and reproductions. The New American dining room is for inn guests only and offers an impressive seasonal menu.
20 rooms. $151-250

ELIZABETH CITY

A town with a freshwater harbor on the Pasquotank River and accessible to the ocean, Elizabeth City has been a busy port since the middle of the 17th century. The Dismal Swamp Canal, dug in 1793, provided a critical north-south transportation route and brought much prosperity to the area. Shipyards, warehouses, fisheries, tanneries, sawmills and other industries flourished alongside commission merchants, artisans and navigators.

Although captured in the Civil War, Elizabeth City sustained minor damage. Today, many antebellum houses still stand alongside the historic homes and commercial buildings of the late 19th and early 20th centuries. The town welcomes boating traffic from the Intracoastal Waterway and is a great location for sportfishing. It serves as a gateway to Nags Head and Cape Hatteras National Seashore.

WHAT TO SEE
HISTORIC DISTRICT

Elizabeth City; www.historicelizabethcity.com
This 30-block area in the city center contains the largest number of antebellum commercial buildings in the state. Tour brochures are available at the Chamber of Commerce.

MUSEUM OF THE ALBEMARLE

501 S. Water St., Elizabeth City, 252-335-1453
The museum houses regional historical displays; Native American exhibits; local artifacts, including decoys, fire engines; and changing exhibits.
Tuesday-Saturday 9 a.m.-5 p.m., Sunday 2-5 p.m.

WHERE TO STAY
★HAMPTON INN
402 Halstead Blvd., Elizabeth City, 252-333-1800, 800-426-7866;
www.hamptoninn.com
100 rooms. Complimentary breakfast. $61-150

★HOLIDAY INN EXPRESS
306 S. Hughes Blvd., Elizabeth City, 252-338-8900, 800-315-2621; www.hiexpress.com
80 rooms. Complimentary breakfast. Fitness center. $61-150

WHERE TO EAT
★MARINA
Camden Causeway, Elizabeth City, 252-335-7307; www.elizcity.com
Seafood, steak. Dinner. Bar. Children's menu. Outdoor seating. $16-35

FAYETTEVILLE
See also Goldsboro
In 1783, the towns of Cross Creek and Campbellton merged and were renamed Fayetteville for the Revolutionary War hero the Marquis de Lafayette.
It was the site of North Carolina's Constitutional Convention in 1787 and
the capital of the state from 1789 to 1793. By 1831 it had become a busy
commercial city.

Fayetteville is the state's farthest inland port, at the head of navigation on
the Cape Fear River, with an eight-foot-deep channel connecting it to the
Intracoastal Waterway. Today, the town is a center for retail, manufacturing
and conventions, and the home of Fort Bragg and Pope Air Force Base.

WHAT TO SEE
CAPE FEAR BOTANICAL GARDEN
536 N. Eastern Blvd., Fayetteville, 910-486-0221; www.capefearbg.org
This garden is on 85 acres overlooking Cross Creek and the Cape Fear River.
The grounds feature wildflowers, oaks and native plants.
Mid-December-mid-February, Monday-Saturday 10 a.m.-5 p.m. March-
mid-December, Monday-Saturday 10 a.m.-5 p.m., Sunday noon-5 p.m.

FIRST PRESBYTERIAN CHURCH
102 Ann St., Fayetteville, 910-483-0121; www.firstprez.com
Classic Southern colonial-style architecture and whale-oil chandeliers are on
display here. Among contributors to the original building (destroyed by fire
in 1831) were James Monroe and John Quincy Adams.
Tours by appointment only.

FORT BRAGG AND POPE AIR FORCE BASE—82ND AIRBORNE -DI-
VISION WAR MEMORIAL MUSEUM
Gela and Ardennes Streets, Fort Bragg, 910-432-3443; www.bragg.army.mil
The museum houses weapons, relics of World War I and II, Vietnam, Korea,
Desert Storm; history of 82nd airborne division; there is also a gift shop.
Tuesday-Saturday.

WHERE TO STAY

★COMFORT INN
735 South Shiloh Drive, Fayetteville, 479-695-2121, 800-621-6596; www.comfortinn.com
60 rooms. Complimentary breakfast. Pool. $61-150

★FAIRFIELD INN
720 E. Millsap Road, Fayetteville, 479-587-8600, 800-228-2800; www.igougo.com
135 rooms. Complimentary breakfast. $61-150

★HAMPTON INN
915 Krupa Drive, Fayetteville, 479-587-8300, 800-426-7866; www.hamptoninn.com
121 rooms. Complimentary breakfast. Business center. Fitness center. Pool. $61-150

★★HOLIDAY INN
1944 Cedar Creek Road, Fayetteville, 910-323-1600, 800-315-2621; www.holiday-inn.com
198 rooms. Restaurant, bar. $61-150

★HOLIDAY INN EXPRESS
1706 Skibo Road, Fayetteville, 910-867-6777, 800-315-2621; www.hiexpress.com
84 rooms. Complimentary breakfast. Fitness center. Pool. $61-150

★★QUALITY INN
2035 S. Eastern Blvd., Fayetteville, 910-485-8135, 800-828-2346; www.qualityinn.com
62 rooms. Restaurant. Pool. $61-150

FRANKLIN
See also Cashiers, Highlands
Home of the Cowee Valley ruby mines, Franklin attracts rock hounds who often find interesting gems in surface mines. Franklin is surrounded by waterfalls, mountain lakes and streams that offer excellent fishing for trout and bass, as well as boating, tubing and swimming. Around the county are 420,000 acres of the Nantahala National Forest, offering hiking trails, camping and fishing. A Ranger District office is located here. The Appalachian Trail bisects the western part of the county through Standing Indian Wildlife Management area and over Wayah Bald Mountain.

WHAT TO SEE
FRANKLIN GEM AND MINERAL MUSEUM
25 Phillips St., Franklin, 828-369-7831; www.fgmm.org
The museum boasts a nice collection of gems and minerals; Native American artifacts, fossils; and a fluorescent mineral display.
May-October, Monday-Friday noon-4 p.m., Saturday 11 a.m.-3 p.m., 6-9 p.m. November-April, Saturday 11 a.m.-3 p.m.

NANTAHALA NATIONAL FOREST

90 Sloan Road, Franklin, 828-524-6441

Nantahala, a Native American name meaning Land of the Noonday Sun, refers to Nantahala Gorge, so deep and narrow that the sun reaches the bottom only at noon. In addition to the gorge, the park offers scenic drives through the southern Appalachians, sparkling waterfalls (including the Whitewater Falls a series of cascades dropping 411 feet) and the 17,013-acre Joyce Kilmer-Slickrock Wilderness, with more than 100 species of trees native to the region. There is on site hiking, camping, swimming, boating, fishing for bass and trout, hunting for deer, wild boar, turkey and ruffed grouse.

SCOTTISH TARTANS MUSEUM

W.C. Burrell Building, 86 E. Main St., Franklin, 828-524-7472; www.scottishtartans.org

An American extension of the Scottish Tartans Society in Edinburgh, Scotland, the museum's exhibits trace heritage of Scottish Tartan and traditional Scottish dress. There is a research library as well.

Monday-Saturday 10 a.m.-5 p.m.

WHERE TO EAT

★★FROG & OWL KITCHEN

46 E. Main St., Franklin, 828-349-4112

French. Lunch, dinner. Children's menu. Reservations recommended. $16-35

★GAZEBO CAFÉ

44 Heritage Hollow, Franklin, 828-524-8783

American. Lunch. Closed mid-November-mid-April. Children's menu. $15 and under

GOLDSBORO

See also Fayetteville

Center of the bright-leaf tobacco belt, Goldsboro is also the seat of Wayne County and home of Seymour Johnson Air Force Base. There are also many food, wood product and textile plants here.

WHAT TO SEE

CLIFFS OF THE NEUSE STATE PARK

345 Park Entrance Road, Seven Springs, 919-778-6234; www.ncparks.gov

With more than 700 acres on the Neuse River, park features include swimming, bathhouse, fishing and boating (rowboat rentals). There are nature trails, picnicking, a museum and interpretive center.

Tent and trailer sites: mid-March-November; fee.

GOVERNOR CHARLES B. AYCOCK BIRTHPLACE STATE HISTORIC SITE

264 Governor Avcock Road, Fremont, 919-242-5581; www.nchistoricsites.org

The site has a mid-1800s farmhouse and outbuildings. There is an audio-visual presentation in 1893 one-room school that is worth seeing as well. Picnicking is allowed.

Monday-Saturday.

WHERE TO STAY

★HOLIDAY INN EXPRESS

909 N. Spence Ave., Goldsboro, 919-751-1999, 800-315-2621;
www.hiexpress.com-goldsboronc
122 rooms. Complimentary breakfast. $61-150

★★QUALITY INN

708 Corporate Drive, Goldsboro, 919-735-7901; www.qualityinn.com
125 room. Restaurant, bar. Complimentary breakfast. $61-150

GREENSBORO

See also High Point
North Carolina's third largest city, Greensboro has historically been an industrial town, manufacturing textiles, cigarettes, machinery and electronic components. Urban redevelopment and a growing population have also brought more cultural, nightlife and recreational activities—from the unique science museum, the numerous high-quality golf courses and even the biggest water park in the Carolinas.

WHAT TO SEE

CHARLOTTE HAWKINS BROWN MEMORIAL STATE HISTORIC SITE

6136 Burlington Road, Sedalia, 336-449-4846; www.nchistoricsites.org/chb/chb.htm
In 1902, C.H. Brown, granddaughter of a former slave, founded Palmer Memorial Institute, which became one of the finest preparatory schools for blacks in the nation. The campus later became the state's first historic site honoring education for African Americans. There are guided tours of the historic campus, visitor center and an audiovisual program. Picnicking is allowed.
April-October, Tuesday-Saturday; rest of year, Tuesday-Sunday; closed holidays.

FIRST HORIZON PARK

408 Bellemeade St., Greensboro, 336-268-2255; www.gsohoppers.com
The Greensboro Grasshoppers, minor league affiliates of the Florida Marlins, play in this new 8,000-seat brick stadium.

GREENSBORO HISTORICAL MUSEUM

130 Summit Ave., Greensboro, 336-373-2043; www.greensborohistory.org
Housed in an 1892 building in the downtown area, the museum features displays on the Revolutionary War, First Lady Dolley Madison and writer O. Henry, among others.
Tuesday-Saturday 10 a.m.-5 p.m., Sunday 2-5 p.m.

GUILFORD COURTHOUSE NATIONAL MILITARY PARK

2332 New Garden Road, Greensboro, 336-288-1776; www.nps.gov/guco
On March 15, 1781, Lord Cornwallis won a costly victory that was one link in a series of events that led to his surrender at Yorktown in October of the same year. After destroying a quarter of the enemy troops, General Nathanael Greene (for whom the city is named) made a successful retreat and then severely hampered the British plan of subduing the Southern colonies. The

220-acre park, established in 1917, has monuments marking important locations and honoring those who fought here. There is a self-guided auto tour and walking trails. The visitor center has a museum housing Revolutionary War weapons, other items and a 20-minute film.
Daily 8:30 a.m.-5 p.m.

NATURAL SCIENCE CENTER OF GREENSBORO
4301 Lawndale Drive, Greensboro, 336-288-3769; www.natsci.org
This natural science museum includes a zoo and indoor exhibits on geology and paleontology. Check out the 36-foot-tall Tyrannosaurus Rex model. Inquire for the schedule of planetarium shows.
Monday-Saturday 9 a.m.-5 p.m., Sunday 12:30-5 p.m.

WHERE TO STAY
★COMFORT INN GREENSBORO
2001 Veasley St., Greensboro, 336-294-6220, 877-424-6423; www.choicehotels.com
121 rooms. Complimentary breakfast. $61-150

★★★GRANDOVER RESORT & CONFERENCE CENTER
1000 Club Road, Greensboro, 336-294-1800, 800-472-6301; www.grandover.com
The Grandover Resort & Conference Center features exceptional, award-winning golf, fine dining, stylish accommodations and Southern hospitality. The Ken Venturi Golf school is located here along with 36 holes. A full-service spa, four clay tennis courts, a state-of-the-art fitness center, indoor-outdoor pool, two racquetball courts and volleyball court also provide fun diversions.
247 rooms. Restaurant, bar. Spa. $151-250

★★EMBASSY SUITES HOTEL GREENSBORO-AIRPORT
204 Centreport Drive, Greensboro, 336-668-4535, 800-362-2779;
www.embassysuitesgreensboro.com
219 rooms, all suites. Restaurant, bar. Complimentary breakfast. Pool. $151-250

★HAMPTON INN GREENSBORO-FOUR SEASONS
2004 Veasley St., Greensboro, 336-854-8600, 800-426-7866; www.hamptoninn.com
120 rooms. Complimentary breakfast. Business center. Pool. $61-150

★★★MARRIOTT GREENSBORO AIRPORT
1 Marriott Drive, Greensboro, 336-852-6450, 800-228-9290; www.marriott.com
This hotel is located at the Piedmont Triad International Airport but offers 17 acres of its own landscaped grounds with a lake and a pavilion. The comfortable guest rooms feature the Marriott Revive bedding. Try dinner at JW's Steakhouse or a nightcap at Pitchers Bar and Grill.
299 rooms. Restaurant, bar. $151-250

★★MARRIOTT GREENSBORO DOWNTOWN
304 N. Greene St., Greensboro, 336-379-8000, 800-228-9290; www.marriott.com
281 rooms. Restaurant, bar. Business center. $151-250

★★★O. HENRY HOTEL

624 Green Valley Road, Greensboro, 336-854-2000; 877-854-2100;
www.ohenryhotel.com

This locally-owned boutique hotel, named for the writer William Sydney Porter (O. Henry), who was born and raised in Greensboro, is decorated with North Carolina pine walls and ceilings, marble floors, Oriental rugs, leather and brocade furniture and large windows that overlook a cloistered courtyard. Spacious guest rooms include separate dressing rooms and soaking tubs.

131 rooms. Restaurant, bar. $151-250

WHERE TO EAT
★★★BISTRO SOFIA

616 Dolley Madison Road, Greensboro, 336-855-1313; www.bistrosofia.com

This restaurant, located northwest of downtown Greensboro, serves dishes created using homegrown organic vegetables, berries and herbs. The early-evening prix fixe menu is $25 for three courses, with bistro favorites such as steak frites making appearances on the ever-changing menu.

American. Dinner. Closed Monday. Bar. Children's menu. Reservations recommended. Outdoor seating. $36-85

★★GATE CITY CHOP HOUSE

106 S. Holden St., Greensboro, 336-294-9977; www.gatecitychophouse.com

The main dining room at this steakhouse features a display kitchen and walls adorned with pictures of Greensboro. Menu selections include grilled peppered salmon, Carolina crab cakes, roasted prime rib and filet mignon.

Seafood, steak. Lunch, dinner. Closed Sunday. Bar. Children's menu. Reservations recommended. Outdoor seating. $36-85

★★★RESTAURANT MUSE

3124 Kathleen Ave., Greensboro, 336-323-1428; www.restaurantmuse.net

Exquisite French cuisine prepared with fresh local ingredients draws diners back to Restaurant Muse time and time again. Chef and owner Mitchell Nicks offers creative plates that include roasted rack of lamb brushed with bergamot and mustard as well as his "untraditional Brutus salad" with pancetta, spicy chile dressing, fried artichoke hearts and a manchego cheese crisp. An à la carte menu is available, as is a chef's tasting menu.

French. Lunch, dinner, brunch. Bar. Reservations recommended. Outdoor seating. $36-85

GREENVILLE

See also Washington, Williamston

An educational, cultural, commercial and medical center, Greenville is one of the towns named for General Nathanael Greene, a hero of the American Revolutionary War.

WHAT TO SEE
GREENVILLE MUSEUM OF ART

802 Evans St., Greenville, 252-758-1946; www.gmoa.org

Collections emphasize North Carolina contemporary fine arts and drawings,

also paintings and prints of the period 1900-1945.
Tuesday-Friday 10 a.m.-4.30 p.m., Saturday 1-4 p.m.

RIVER PARK NORTH SCIENCE AND NATURE CENTER
1000 Mumford Road, Greenville, 252-329-4560; www.greenvillenc.gov
This 309-acre park has four lakes and a mile of Tar River water frontage. The
science center near the park entrance offers hands-on exhibits. Fishing, pedal
boats and picnicking are all allowed onsite.
Tuesday-Sunday.

WHERE TO STAY
★FAIRFIELD INN
821 S. Memorial Drive, Greenville, 252-758-5544, 877-424-6423; www.qualityinn.com
110 rooms. Complimentary breakfast. Pool. $61-150

WHERE TO EAT
★★BEEF BARN
400 St. Andrews Drive, Greenville, 252-756-1161; www.beefbarn.net
Steak, seafood. Lunch, dinner. Bar. Children's menu. Reservations recommended. $16-35

★PARKER'S BAR-B-QUE
3109 S. Memorial Drive, Greenville, 252-756-2388
American. Lunch, dinner. Children's menu. No credit cards accepted. $15
and under

HENDERSONVILLE
See also Asheville
Nestled in the Blue Ridge Mountain area, Hendersonville is well known as a
summer resort and popular retirement community. The nearby town of Flat
Rock is also home to visit-worthy inns and restaurants.

WHAT TO SEE
CARL SANDBURG HOME NATIONAL HISTORIC SITE
81 Carl Sandburg Lane, Flat Rock, 828-693-4178; www.nps.gov-carl.com
The famous poet's 264-acre farm, Connemara, is maintained as it was when
Sandburg and his family lived here from 1945 until his death in 1967. On
the grounds are a house and a historic barn for the three breeds of goats that
Sandburg raised, as well as a visitor center.
Tours daily 9 a.m.-5 p.m.

JUMP-OFF ROCK
Hendersonville, Fifth Ave., www.historichendersonville.org
Enjoy panoramic views of the Blue Ridge Mountains from atop Jump-Off
Mountain.

SPECIAL EVENTS
FLAT ROCK PLAYHOUSE
2661 Greenville Highway, Flat Rock, 828-693-0731; www.flatrockplayhouse.org
This outstanding professional theater has been running since 1939. Vagabond Players offer 10 Broadway and London productions in 15 weeks. Mid-May-mid-December, Wednesday-Saturday evenings; Thursday, Saturday, Sunday matinees.

WHERE TO STAY
★COMFORT INN
206 Mitchell Drive, Hendersonville, 828-693-8800, 800-424-6423; www.comfortinn.com
85 rooms. Complimentary breakfast. $61-150

★★ECHO MOUNTAIN INN
2849 Laurel Park Highway, Hendersonville, 828-693-9626, 800-324-6466;
www.echoinn.com
45 rooms. Complimentary breakfast. $61-150

★HAMPTON INN
155 Sugarloaf Road, Hendersonville, 828-697-2333, 800-426-7866;
www.hamptoninn.com
118 rooms. Complimentary breakfast. Business center. Fitness center. Pool. $61-150

★★★HIGHLAND LAKE INN
86 Lily Pad Lane Highland Lake Road, Flat Rock, 828-693-6812, 800-635-5101;
www.hlinn.com
This hotel is just 25 minutes from Asheville, and sits on 26 acres of woods near a lake. It's a lovely country getaway in the Blue Ridge Mountains.
63 rooms. Restaurant, bar. Beach. $151-250

ALSO RECOMMENDED
LAKE LURE INN
2771 Memorial Highway, Lake Lure, 828-625-2525, 800-277-5873;
www.lakelureinn.com
69 rooms. Restaurant, bar. Complimentary breakfast. $61-150

LODGE ON LAKE LURE BED & BREAKFAST
361 Charlotte Drive, Lake Lure, 828-625-2789, 800-733-2785;
www.lodgeonlakelure.com
This is an elegant bed and breakfast in the countryside. The beauty of the lake adds a wonderful backdrop to this scenic property.
16 rooms. Complimentary breakfast. No children under 8. $151-250

THE WAVERLY INN
783 N. Main St., Hendersonville, 828-693-9193, 800-537-8195; www.waverlyinn.com
15 rooms. Complimentary breakfast. $61-150

WHERE TO EAT
★SEASONS RESTAURANT
Highland Lake Road, Flat Rock, 828-696-9094, 800-762-1376; www.hlinn.com
American. Breakfast, lunch, dinner, brunch. Bar. Children's menu. Outdoor seating. $16-35

★★SINBAD
202 S. Washington St., Hendersonville, 828-696-2039; www.sinbadrestaurant.com
Mediterranean, American. Lunch, dinner. Closed Sunday-Monday. Bar. $16-35

HICKORY
See also Statesville
Hickory is the country's center of furniture making. In a 200-mile radius of the town, 60 percent of the nation's furniture is produced and visitors often come looking for unique and interesting pieces. Golf, car racing and baseball add to the entertainment, along with a number of historical sites and museums.

WHAT TO SEE
20 MILES OF FURNITURE
Hickory, 800-737-0782; www.20milesoffurniture.com
This area offers golf, shopping and dining, but is best known for its nearly 40 furniture stores. Plant tours are available.

CATAWBA COUNTY MUSEUM OF HISTORY
21 E. First St., Newton, 828-465-0383; www.catawbahistory.org
Exhibits include a fire engine, country doctor's office, Waugh Cabin, Barringer Cabin, a blacksmith shop, and an agriculture exhibit.
Wednesday-Saturday 9 a.m.-4 p.m.; Sunday 1.30-4:30 p.m. Closed Monday-Tuesday.

HICKORY FURNITURE MART
2220 Highway 70 S.E., Hickory, 800-462-6278; www.hickoryfurniture.com
More than 1,000 home-furnishing lines are displayed in this 1 million-square-foot complex, which includes 100 factory outlets, stores and galleries, a museum, café, shipping service, visitor center and motel.

HICKORY MUSEUM OF ART
234 Third Ave., Hickory, 828-327-8576; www.hickorymuseumofart.org
American realist 19th- and 20th-century art, including works by Gilbert Stuart, are on display here. European, Oriental and pre-Columbian pieces often rotate in through the changing exhibits.
Tuesday-Sunday 10 a.m.-4 p.m.; Sunday 1-4 p.m. Closed Monday.

WHERE TO STAY
★HAMPTON INN HICKORY
1520 13th Ave., Hickory, 828-323-1150, 800-426-7866; www.hamptoninn.com
119 rooms. Complimentary breakfast. Pool. Fitness center. Business center. $61-150

★★HOLIDAY INN SELECT

1385 Lenoir Rhyne Blvd. S.E., Hickory, 828-323-1000, 800-366-5010;
www.holiday-inn.com

200 rooms. Restaurant, bar. Business center. Fitness center. Pool. $61-150

WHERE TO EAT
★★★1859 CAFÉ

443 Second Ave. S.W., Hickory, 828-322-1859; www.hickoryonline.com/1859cafe

The international cuisine at this restaurant includes options such as pesto-crusted scallops with mushroom risotto, sautéed duck breast with strawberry rhubarb sauce and pork tenderloin stuffed with spiced fruit and walnuts. International. Dinner. Closed Sunday. Bar. Reservations recommended. Outdoor seating. $16-35

★★★VINTAGE HOUSE

271 Third Ave. N.W., Hickory, 828-324-1210

This restaurant is a converted 100-year-old Victorian home located two blocks from the downtown center of Hickory. Dine in one of five dining rooms, two of which are enclosed porch rooms with large windows, over-looking the gardens.

American. Dinner. Closed Sunday. Bar. Reservations recommended. $36-85

HIGH POINT

See also Greensboro

Furniture making has put this North Carolina city on the map. The city rests on the highest point along the North Carolina and Midland Railroad, which the state built in 1853. The plank road (finished in 1854), stretching 130 miles from Salem to Fayetteville, made it a center of trade. Mileposts on this road had carved numbers instead of painted ones so travelers could feel their way at night.

SPECIAL EVENTS
NORTH CAROLINA SHAKESPEARE FESTIVAL

High Point Theatre, 220 E. Commerce Ave., High Point, 336-841-2273;
www.ncshakes.org

Each season includes three productions and A Christmas Carol. August-October and December.

WHERE TO STAY
★★RADISSON HOTEL HIGH POINT

135 S. Main St., High Point, 336-889-8888, 800-201-1718; www.radisson.com

252 rooms. Restaurant, bar. Pool. Fitness center. $61-150

ALSO RECOMMENDED
BOULDIN HOUSE BED AND BREAKFAST

4332 Archdale Road, High Point, 336-431-4909, 800-739-1816;
www.bouldinhouse.com

Five rooms. Complimentary breakfast. No children under 12. $61-150

WHERE TO EAT
★★★J. BASUL NOBLE'S
101 S. Main St., High Point, 336-889-3354; www.noblesrestaurant.com
Creative menu options are prepared in a wood-fired oven, a grill and a rotisserie, enhancing the flavors in dishes such as bacon-wrapped wood-fired grouper, grilled pork tenderloin and rotisserie half chicken. Several pizzas are offered as well as a bistro menu with lighter fare. Live jazz completes the dining experience.
Italian. Lunch, dinner. Closed Sunday. Bar. Outdoor seating. $16-35

HIGHLANDS
See also Cashiers, Franklin
Highlands is a summer resort near the Georgia state line. Many unusual plants are part of the primeval rain forest preserve. Completely encircled by Nantahala National Forest, the area surrounding the town is called "land of the waterfalls." A Ranger District office is located here.

WHERE TO STAY
★HIGHLANDS SUITE HOTEL
200 Main St., Highlands, 828-526-4502, 877-553-3761; www.highlandssuitehotel.com
29 rooms. Complimentary breakfast. $61-150

★★★★OLD EDWARDS INN
445 Main St., Highlands, 828-526-8008; www.oldedwardsinn.com
Nestled in the charming mountain town of Highlands, this historic inn is on the National Register of Historic Places. Each guest room, suite and cottage is filled with period antiques and modern amenities. The luxurious 25,000-square-foot full-service spa uses herbs and botanicals from the spa's garden.
28 rooms. Restaurant, bar. Complimentary breakfast. Fitness center. No children under 11. $351 and up

WHERE TO EAT
★★★MADISON'S RESTAURANT & WINE GARDEN
445 Main St., Highlands, 828-526-5477; www.oldedwardsinn.com
There's something old, something new, something Southern and everything delicious at Madison's Restaurant and Wine Garden at Old Edward's Inn and Spa. The chef uses local ingredients to cook Madison's contemporary Southern cuisine, serving up Southern with a twist to locals and visitors for breakfast, dinner or just dessert and drinks. Weather permitting, pop the cork on a bottle in the Wine Garden and take in views of the lush North Carolina nature. Mountains and countryside not your thing? Dine inside on Carolina mountain trout, with a side of white truffle macaroni and cheese. And definitely save room for the plantation chocolate soufflé.
American, Southern. Breakfast, lunch, dinner. $36-85

★★NICK'S
108 North Main St., Highlands, 828-526-2706; www.nicksfinefoods.com
American. Lunch, dinner. Closed Wednesday; also January-February. Children's menu. Reservations recommended. $16-35

★★ON THE VERANDAH

1536 Franklin Road, Highlands, 828-526-2338; www.ontheverandah.com

American. Dinner, Sunday brunch. Closed January-mid-March; weekdays in December and March. Children's menu. Reservations recommended. Outdoor seating. $36-85

SPAS
★★★★OLD EDWARDS INN SPA

445 Main St., Highlands, 828-526-8008; www.oldedwardsinn.com

Tucked into the mountains of the North Carolina Highlands, the Old Edwards Inn and Spa offers luxury rooms, suites and cottages for those looking to be one with nature, or one with a pedicure. Chilling out is the only task at hand at this 25,000-square-foot spa, which boasts treatments that use native North Carolina herbs and botanicals (some grown in the spa's own garden) for the signature Carolina Cocoon treatments. Or try one of the massages—go exotic with the Balinese massage or bliss out with Hot Spring Stone massage—for a knot-kneading experience. But for the ultimate in relaxation, just book a Spa Suite and let the royal treatments come to you.

JACKSONVILLE

On the edge of the New River Marine Base (Camp Lejeune), Jacksonville has excellent fishing. The surrounding Onslow County has more than 30 miles of beaches.

WHERE TO STAY
★BEST WESTERN COURTYARD RESORT

603 N. Marine Blvd., Jacksonville, 910-455-4100; www.ramada.com

121 rooms. Complimentary breakfast. $61-150

★HAMPTON INN

474 Western Blvd., Jacksonville, 910-347-6500, 800-426-7866; www.hamptoninn.com

122 rooms. Complimentary breakfast. Business center. $61-150

★HOLIDAY INN EXPRESS

2115 Highway 17 N., Jacksonville, 910-347-1900, 800-465-4329; www.hiexpress.com

118 rooms. Complimentary breakfast. Business center. Pool. Fitness center. $61-150

KILL DEVIL HILLS

See also Manteo, Nags Head

Although the name Kitty Hawk is usually associated with the Wright Brothers, their early flying experiments took place on and near these dunes on the Outer Banks.

WHAT TO SEE
WRIGHT BROTHERS NATIONAL MEMORIAL

1401 National Park Drive, Kill Devil Hills, 252-441-7430; www.nps.gov

The field where the first powered flight took place on December 17, 1903 is marked, showing the takeoff point and landing place. The living quarters and hangar buildings used by the Wrights during their experiments have been replicated. The visitor center has reproductions of a 1902 glider and a 1903 flyer, with exhibits on the story of their invention.

Summer daily 9 a.m.-6 p.m., September-May 9 a.m.-5 p.m.

WHERE TO STAY

★BEST WESTERN OCEAN REEF SUITES

107 Virginia Dare Court, Kill Devil Hills, 252-441-1611, 800-528-1234;
www.bestwestern.com

71 rooms. Restaurants. Fitness center. Pool. Spa. Beach. $151-250

★COMFORT INN

401 N. Virginia Dare Trail, Kill Devil Hills, 252-480-2600, 800-424-6423;
www.comfortinn.com

118 rooms. Complimentary breakfast. Beach. Pool. $61-150

★DAYS INN

201 N. Virginia Dare Trail, Kill Devil Hills, 252-441-7211, 800-329-7466;
www.daysinn.com

54 rooms. Complimentary breakfast. Pool. Beach. $61-150

★★RAMADA

1701 S. Virginia Dare Trail, Kill Devil Hills, 252-441-2151, 800-635-1824;
www.ramada.com

171 rooms. Restaurant, bar. Business center. Pool. Fitness center. Beach. $151-250

★★★THE SANDERLING

1461 Duck Road, Duck, 252-261-4111, 877-650-4812; www.sanderlinginn.com

Nestled on the northern reaches of the Outer Banks, the Sanderling is designed to complement the natural setting and includes an eco-center and low-rise, cedar-shingled buildings. Composed of three inns and oceanside villas, the Sanderling offers secluded beaches, conference centers and a full-service spa. The restaurant is housed in a historic U.S. lifesaving station.

88 rooms. Restaurant, bar. $151-250

WHERE TO EAT

★★FLYING FISH CAFÉ

2003 S. Croatan Highway, Kill Devil Hills, 252-441-6894; www.flyingfishcafe.net

Mediterranean. Dinner. Bar. Children's menu. Reservations recommended. $16-35

★JOLLY ROGER

1836 N. Virginia Dare Trail, Kill Devil Hills, 252-441-6530; www.jollyrogerobx.com

American. Breakfast, lunch, dinner. Bar. Children's menu. $16-35

★★PORT O' CALL

504 Virginia Dare Trail, Kill Devil Hills, 252-441-7484; www.outerbanksportocall.com

Seafood, steak. Dinner. Closed January-March. Bar. Children's menu. $16-35

LINVILLE

See also Blowing Rock, Boone, Little Switzerland

Linville is located in a ruggedly beautiful resort area. Several miles to the south, just off the Blue Ridge Parkway, is scenic Linville Falls, which cascade down the steep Linville Gorge. Visible from vantage points in this area are the mysterious Brown Mountain lights, a natural phenomenon observed for hundreds of years.

WHAT TO SEE
GRANDFATHER MOUNTAIN

2050 Blowing Rock Road, Linville, 828-733-4337; www.grandfather.com

The highest peak of the Blue Ridge Mountains offers spectacular views, rugged rock formations, a mile high-swinging bridge, bald eagles, gold eagles, river otters, deer, cougars, black bears, bear cubs and others in natural habitats. Be sure to check out the museum with exhibits on local animals, birds, flowers, geology.

Daily dawn-dusk, weather permitting.

SPECIAL EVENTS
GRANDFATHER MOUNTAIN HIGHLAND GAMES

828-733-1333; www.gmhg.org

This event marks the gathering of members of more than 100 Scottish clans to view or participate in traditional Scottish sports, track-and-field events, dancing, piping and drumming, ceremonies and pageantry. No pets or bicycles allowed.

Mid-July.

WHERE TO STAY
★★★THE ESEEOLA LODGE AT LINVILLE GOLF CLUB

175 Linville Ave., Linville, 828-733-4311, 800-742-6717; www.eseeola.com

The Eseeola Lodge at Linville Golf Club has an historic 18-hole golf course, eight tennis courts, a pool and a croquet lawn to keep guests busy. For children, there is a well-equipped playground and day camp. The chef prepares a daily four-course dinner of international dishes with a Southern bent.

24 rooms. Closed late October-mid-May. Restaurant, bar. Complimentary breakfast. Children's activity center. $251-350

LITTLE SWITZERLAND

See also Linville, Morganton

Named for its sweeping panoramic views, the mountain village of Little Switzerland has been a popular resort since the early 1900s. The Blue Ridge Parkway passes through town.

WHAT TO SEE
EMERALD VILLAGE

McKinney Mine Road and Blue Ridge Parkway, Little Switzerland, 828-765-6463,
828-765-0000; www.emeraldvillage.com

This historical area includes the North Carolina Mining Museum; Main Street 1920s Mining Community Museum; Gemstone Mine, where visitors

can prospect for gems under shaded flumes; Mechanical Music Maker Museum; waterfall and scenic overlook; shops and a deli.
Daily.

MOUNT MITCHELL STATE PARK
2388 State Highway 128, Brunsville Little Switzerland, 828-675-4611; www.ncparks.gov
Adjacent to Pisgah National Forest, a natural national landmark, at 6,684 feet, Mount Mitchell is the highest point east of the Mississippi River. There are trails, picnicking, a restaurant and refreshment stands. There is also a small-tent camping area, observation tower and museum.

WHERE TO STAY
★★SWITZERLAND INN
86 High Ridge Road, Little Switzerland, 828-765-2153, 800-654-4026;
www.switzerlandinn.com
73 rooms. Closed November-mid-April. Restaurant, bar. Complimentary breakfast. Pool. $61-150

MAGGIE VALLEY
See also Asheville, Cherokee, Waynesville
In 1909, Henry Setzer decided the expanding community of Plott needed a post office. He submitted the names of his three daughters to the postmaster general, who selected Maggie, age 14. Lying in the shadow of the Great Smoky Mountains National Park, the town is 4 miles from the Soco Gap entrance to the Blue Ridge Parkway and has become a year-round resort area.

WHAT TO SEE
CATALOOCHEE SKI AREA
1080 Ski Lodge Road, Maggie Valley, 828-926-0285, 800-768-0285;
www.cataloochee.com
The ski area features the following: quad, two double chair lifts, T-bar, rope tow; patrol, school, rentals; snowmaking; half-day and twilight rates; cafeteria and bar. The longest run is 3,800 feet, with a vertical drop of 740 feet. December-mid-March, daily. Monday-Friday, 9 a.m.-4:30 p.m.; Saturday, Sunday and holidays 8:30 a.m.-4:30 p.m.

WHERE TO STAY
★COMFORT INN
3282 Soco Road, Maggie Valley, 828-926-9106, 800-228-5150; www.comfortinn.com
68 rooms. Complimentary breakfast. Pool. $61-150

ALSO RECOMMENDED
CATALOOCHEE SKI AREA
119 Ranch Drive, Maggie Valley, 828-926-0285, 800-768-0285; www.cataloochee.com
Guests can relax in the lodge with a hot toddy and put their feet up around the crackling circular fireplace. Enjoy a hearty home-cooked meal or picnic on the sun-drenched deck overlooking the slopes.
26 rooms. $61-150

WHERE TO EAT
★★J. ARTHUR'S
2843 Soco Road, Maggie Valley, 828-926-1817; www.jarthurs.com
Seafood, steak. Dinner. Closed Sunday-Tuesday in November-April. Bar. Children's menu. Outdoor seating. $16-35

MANTEO
See also Kill Devil Hills, Nags head
Found on the eastern side of Roanoke Island on the Outer Banks, the quaint town of Manteo has more bed and breakfasts than any other Outer Banks village. Fishing in the waters off Manteo is excellent. A large sport fishing fleet is available for booking at Oregon Inlet as well as on Roanoke Island.

WHAT TO SEE
ELIZABETHAN GARDENS
1411 National Park Drive, Manteo, 252-473-3234; www.elizabethangardens.org
These 10.5 acres include the Great Lawn, Sunken Garden, Queen's Rose Garden, an herb garden, a 16th-century gazebo with thatched roof and an ancient garden statuary. Plants bloom all year. The Gate House Reception Center displays period furniture, English portraits and coat of arms. Daily.

ROANOKE ISLAND FESTIVAL PARK
Manteo waterfront, 252-475-1500; www.roanokeisland.com
This park boasts a representative 16th-century sailing vessel similar to those that brought the first English colonists to the New World more than 400 years ago. In summer there is a living history interpretation. There is also a visitor center with exhibits and audiovisual program.
February-December, daily.

SPECIAL EVENTS
THE LOST COLONY OUTDOOR DRAMA
Waterside Theater, Manteo, 800-488-5012
Pulitzer Prize-winner Paul Green's outdoor drama focuses on the first English colony established in the New World whose curious disappearance remains a mystery to this day.
Mid-June-late August. Monday-Saturday evenings. Reservations recommended.

WHERE TO STAY
★★★TRANQUIL HOUSE INN
405 Queen Elizabeth St., Manteo, 252-473-1404, 800-458-7069; www.tranquilinn.com
Built in 1988 in the style of a 19th-century Outer Banks resort, this waterfront property offers a continental breakfast and evening wine and cheese with each of its 25 rooms. Elegant dockside dining overlooking Shallowbag Bay can be found at 1587 Restaurant.
25 rooms. Complimentary breakfast. Restaurant. $151-250

MOREHEAD CITY

See also Beaufort

Just across the Intracoastal Waterway from Beaufort, Morehead City is the largest town in Carteret County and a year-round resort town. The port accommodates oceangoing vessels and charter boats.

WHAT TO SEE
FORT MACON STATE PARK
E. Fort Macon Road, Atlantic Beach, 252-726-3775

This restored fort, built in 1834, was originally used as a harbor defense. The beach has lifeguards in summer as well as a bathhouse; surf fishing; hiking, nature trails. The museum features interpretive program and battle re-enactments.

WHERE TO STAY
★★BUCCANEER INN
2806 Arendell St., Morehead City, 252-726-3115

91 rooms. Restaurant, bar. Complimentary breakfast. $61-150

★HAMPTON INN
4035 Arendell St., Morehead City, 252-240-2300, 800-426-7866; www.hamptoninn.com

119 rooms. Complimentary breakfast. Fitness center. $61-150

★★★SHERATON ATLANTIC BEACH OCEANFRONT HOTEL
2717 W. Fort Macon Road, Atlantic Beach, 252-240-1155, 800-624-8875;
www.sheratonatlanticbeach.com

Each room at this beachfront hotel features a private balcony. There are two restaurants, two lounges and two pools as well as nearby golf and tennis. 200 rooms. Complimentary breakfast. Pool. Restaurant, bar. $151-250

ALSO RECOMMENDED
EMERALD ISLE INN AND BED & BREAKFAST
502 Ocean Drive, Emerald Isle, 252-354-3222; www.emeraldisle.com

Four rooms. Complimentary breakfast. $61-150

HARBOR LIGHT GUEST HOUSE
332 Live Oak Drive, Cape Carteret, 252-393-6868, 800-624-8439;
www.harborlightnc.com

Nine rooms. Complimentary breakfast. No children under 16. $151-250

WHERE TO EAT
★CAPTAIN BILL'S WATERFRONT
701 Evans St., Morehead City, 252-726-2166

Seafood. Lunch, dinner. Children's menu. Outdoor seating. $151-250

★MRS. WILLIS
3114 Bridge St., Morehead City, 252-726-3741

Seafood, steak. Lunch, dinner. Bar. Children's menu. $151-250

★SANITARY FISH MARKET
501 Evans St., Morehead City, 252-247-3111; www.sanitaryfishmarket.com
Seafood. Lunch, dinner. Closed December-January. Children's menu. $151-250

MORGANTON
See also Little Switzerland
Morganton boasts a vibrant, park-filled downtown, beautiful views and access to golf, boating and other recreation, plus a thriving cultural community. It's near the site of some of the earliest evidence of European explorers to North America. In 1893, the county became a haven for the Waldenses, a religious group from the French-Italian Alps who were seeking freedom and space to expand outside their alpine homeland. They settled in nearby Valdese, and their history is part of the area's local lore.

WHERE TO STAY
★★HOLIDAY INN MORGANTON
2400 S. Sterling St., Morganton, 828-437-0171, 800-465-4329; www.holiday-inn.com
133 rooms. Restaurant, bar. Fitness center. Pool. $61-150

NAGS HEAD
See also Kill Devil Hills, Manteo
This is a year-round town on the Outer Banks, just south of Kill Devil Hills and at the north end of Cape Hatteras National Seashore. Swimming is good in summer. The soft sand dunes and Atlantic breezes make this a popular area for hang gliding. Offshore, partly buried in the drifting sand, are many wrecks of both old sailing ships and more modern vessels.

WHERE TO STAY
★NAGS HEAD INN
4701 S. Virginia Dare Trail, Nags Head, 252-441-0454, 800-327-8881;
www.nagsheadinn.com
100 rooms. Beach. $61-150

★SURF SIDE MOTEL
6701 S. Virginia Dare Trail, Nags Head, 252-441-2105, 800-552-7873;
www.surfsideobx.com
76 rooms. Complimentary breakfast. Beach. $61-150

ALSO RECOMMENDED
FIRST COLONY INN
6720 S. Virginia Dare Trail, Nags Head, 252-441-2343, 800-368-9390;
www.firstcolonyinn.com
This beach-style bed and breakfast has welcomed Outer Banks' visitors since 1932 and is on the National Register of Historic Places. Rooms are decorated with English antiques. Wide, two-story verandas wrap around the shingled building and deliver great sunset views.
26 rooms. Complimentary breakfast. $61-150

WHERE TO EAT
★★OWENS' RESTAURANT
7114 S. Virginia Dare Trail, Nags Head, 252-441-7309; www.owensrestaurant.com
American. Dinner. Closed January-mid-March. Bar. Children's menu. $36-85

★★PENGUIN ISLE
6708 S. Croatan Highway, Nags Head, 252-441-2637; www.penguinisle.com
American. Dinner. Closed January-February. Bar. Children's menu. Reservations recommended. Outdoor seating. $16-35

★★WINDMILL POINT
Highway 158, Nags Head, 252-441-1535; www.windmillpointrestaurant.com
American. Dinner, brunch. Bar. Children's menu. $36-85

NEW BERN
This town, originally settled by Swiss and German immigrants, is most famous as the birthplace of Pepsi-Cola, which was first sold at a local drugstore. Many Georgian-style and Federal-style buildings give New Bern an architectural look unique in North Carolina. The Neuse and Trent rivers are ideal for swimming, boating and freshwater and saltwater fishing.

WHAT TO SEE
ATTMORE-OLIVER HOUSE
512 Pollock St., New Bern, 252-638-8558
This house, headquarters for the New Bern Historical Society, exhibits 18th- and 19th-century furnishings and historical objects including Civil War artifacts. Early April-mid-December, Tuesday, Thursday, Saturday; also by appointment.

TRYON PALACE HISTORIC SITES AND GARDENS
610 Pollock St., New Bern, 800-767-1560; www.tryonpalace.org
Built from 1767-1770 by Royal Governor William Tryon, this colonial building burned in 1798 and lay in ruins until it was rebuilt between 1952 and 1959. It served as the colonial and first state capital. Reconstruction furnishings and 18th-century English gardens are beautiful and authentic. Guided tours are available.
Daily.

PEPSI STORE
256 Middle St., New Bern, 252-636-5898; www.pepsistore.com
Site of the pharmacy in which Caleb Bradham first served his invention, "Brad's Drink," in 1858. When orders for the concoction took off, he renamed it Pepsi-Cola. Now the site is a store full of Pepsi memorabilia.

WHERE TO STAY
★★AERIE INN BED & BREAKFAST
509 Pollock St., New Bern, 252-636-5553, 800-849-5553; www.aerieinn.com
Seven rooms. Complimentary breakfast. $61-150

★COMFORT INN
218 E. Front St., New Bern, 252-636-0022, 800-517-4000;
www.comfortsuitesnewbern.com
100 rooms. Complimentary breakfast. Fitness center. $61-150

★HAMPTON INN
200 Hotel Drive, New Bern, 252-637-2111, 800-426-7866; www.hamptoninn.com
101 rooms. Complimentary breakfast. $61-150

★HARMONY HOUSE INN
215 Pollock St., New Bern, 252-636-3810, 800-636-3113; www.harmonyhouseinn.com
10 rooms. Complimentary breakfast. $61-150

★★MEADOWS INN
212 Pollock St., New Bern, 252-634-1776, 877-551-1776; www.meadowsinn-nc.com
Seven rooms. Complimentary breakfast. $61-150

★SHERATON NEW BERN HOTEL AND MARINA
100 Middle St., New Bern, 252-638-3585, 800-326-3745; www.sheraton.com-newber
171 rooms. Restaurant, bar. $61-150

OCRACOKE

Settled in the 17th century, Ocracoke was allegedly once used as headquarters by the pirate Blackbeard. One of the Outer Bank's towns, Ocracoke is accessible only by boat or air, but the trek is worth it for the beautiful beaches. The lighthouse, built in 1823, is still in use. A Cape Hatteras National Seashore visitor center is located here.

WHERE TO STAY

★ANCHORAGE INN
205 Highway 12, Ocracoke, 252-928-1101; www.theanchorageinn.com
37 rooms. Closed December-February. Complimentary breakfast. $61-150

ALSO RECOMMENDED
OCRACOKE ISLAND INN
100 Lighthouse Road, Ocracoke, 252-928-4351, 877-456-3466;
www.ocracokeislandinn.com
29 rooms. Restaurant. $151-250

WHERE TO EAT
★★BACK PORCH
110 Back Road, Ocracoke, 252-928-6401
Seafood. Dinner. Closed mid-November-mid-April. Outdoor seating. $151-250

PINEHURST
See also Southern Pines
A famous year-round resort village, Pinehurst has been named the site of the

2014 U.S. Open. The New England-style resort was designed more than 100 years ago by Frederick Law Olmsted, who also designed New York's Central Park and landscaped Asheville's Biltmore Estate. Handsome estates and other residences, mostly Georgian Colonial, dot the village. The Pinehurst Resort and Country Club has a 200-acre lake, 24 tennis courts and other recreational facilities that are open to members as well as to guests staying there.

WHAT TO SEE
SANDHILLS HORTICULTURAL GARDENS
Sandhills Community College, 3395 Airport Road, Pinehurst, 910-695-3882; www.sandhills.edu
The 25 acres include Ebersole Holly Garden; Rose Garden; Conifer Garden; Hillside Garden with bridges, waterfalls and gazebo; Desmond Native Wetland Trail Garden, a nature conservancy and bird sanctuary; and Sir Walter Raleigh Garden, a formal English garden.
Daily.

WHERE TO STAY
★★★★THE CAROLINA HOTEL
1 Carolina Vista Drive, Pinehurst, 910-295-6811, 800-487-4653; www.pinehurst.com
With eight 18-hole courses designed by the sport's leading names, including Fazio, Jones, Maples and Ross, the 31 miles of golf at this property contain 780 bunkers and the largest number of golf holes in the world at a single resort. This Victorian-era hotel provides guests with handsomely furnished accommodations and first-class service. Two of the resort's nine restaurants as well as a luxurious spa are located here.
220 rooms. Restaurant, bar. Spa. Beach. Golf. Tennis. $251-350

★COMFORT INN
9801 Highway 15-501, Pinehurst, 910-215-5500, 800-831-0541; www.comfortinn.com
77 rooms. Bar. Complimentary breakfast. $61-150

★★★HOLLY INN
155 Cherokee Road, Pinehurst, 910-295-6811, 800-487-4653; www.pinehurst.com
The Holly Inn was the first hotel built in Pinehurst (dating to 1895) and is part of the Pinehurst Resort. The inn has dark wood paneling, fireplaces and antique furniture. The onsite 1895 restaurant features an American-Continental menu with Carolina influences. The Tavern is more casual and serves lunch and dinner. Guests at the Holly Inn have access to all the activities of the Carolina Hotel.
82 rooms. Restaurant, bar. $151-250

★★★MAGNOLIA
65 Magnolia Road, Pinehurst, 910-295-6900, 800-526-5562; www.themagnoliainn.com
This historical 1896 inn is nestled in the quaint New England-style village of Pinehurst and is within walking distance of the Carolina Hotel, golf courses, tennis, dining, and shopping. The rooms feature private baths with claw foot tubs, four-poster beds, cable television, and air conditioning. Two guest

rooms also offer fireplaces, perfect for a romantic getaway.
11 rooms. Restaurant, bar. Complimentary breakfast. $61-150

WHERE TO EAT
★★★1895
155 Cherokee Road, Pinehurst, 910-235-8434, 800-487-4653; www.pinehurst.com
This charming restaurant is located in the historic Holly Inn and is part of the famous Pinehurst Resort. The restaurant features a Continental menu with a Carolina influence and plenty of original preparations for seafood and steak.
American, Continental. Dinner. Closed Monday-Tuesday. Bar. Reservations recommended. $36-85

SPAS
★★★★THE SPA AT PINEHURST
1 Carolina Vista Drive, Pinehurst, 910-235-8320, 800-487-4653; www.pinehurst.com
Featuring more than 40 different treatments, this spa is influenced by its southern location. Pine-inspired treatments dominate the menu, from the pine salt body rub to the exfoliating pine cream of the Pinehurst deluxe body treatment. The spa offers eight different massage therapies, including a special massage designed for golfers.

PITTSBORO
See also Chapel Hill
Just south of Chapel Hill, this small community is host to Fearrington Village, a dairy farm dating back to the 1700s and redeveloped in the 1970s. The owners turned the vast farm into a town with stores, custom real estate and award-winning lodging and restaurants.

WHERE TO STAY
★★★★★THE FEARRINGTON HOUSE COUNTRY INN
2000 Fearrington Village Center, Pittsboro, 919-542-2121; www.fearrington.com
The Fearrington House offers just the right mix of country style and worldly sophistication. Part of a charming village of shops, this country house hotel is located on Colonial-era farmland. The inn's former incarnation as a dairy barn is evident today in the striped Galloway cows that graze the grounds. The rooms and suites feature a country theme with authentic details like salvaged church doors used as headboards. Canopied beds and original art create a stylish look.
33 rooms. Restaurant, bar. Complimentary breakfast. Business center. Fitness center. Pool. Tennis. Children over 6 years only. $251-350

WHERE TO EAT
★★★★THE FEARRINGTON HOUSE RESTAURANT
2000 Fearrington Village Center, Pittsboro, 919-542-2121; www.fearrington.com
This charming Victorian-style country restaurant is located on several rolling acres near Chapel Hill. The property is dotted with flower gardens and lush landscapes, and the restaurant is accented with elegant antique furnishings. The upscale menu is American, with techniques borrowed from France and

robust flavors taken from the surrounding region. The thoughtful, seasonal menu is complemented by a deep international wine list that features close to 500 selections with a focus on California varietals.

American, French. Dinner. Bar. Jacket required. Reservations recommended. Valet parking. Outdoor seating. $36-85

★MARKET CAFÉ
2000 Fearrington Village, Pittsboro, 919-542-2121; www.fearringtonvillage.com
American. Lunch, brunch. Children's menu. Reservations recommended. Outdoor seating. $15 and under

RALEIGH
See also Chapel Hill, Durham
The capital of North Carolina, Raleigh is also known as a center of education and technology research. The Research Triangle Park, a 6,800-acre research and development center with more than 50 companies, is located within 15 miles of Raleigh. Three major universities—North Carolina State University, Duke University in Durham and the University of North Carolina at Chapel Hill—are also here.

Named for Sir Walter Raleigh, the town was laid out in 1792, following a resolution by the North Carolina General Assembly that an "unalterable seat of government" should be established within 10 miles of Isaac Hunter's tavern. Like much of North Carolina, Raleigh was sprinkled with Union sympathizers until Fort Sumter was attacked. Lincoln's call for volunteers was regarded as an insult and North Carolina joined the Confederacy. Raleigh surrendered to General Sherman in April 1865. Legend has it that during Reconstruction, carpetbaggers controlled the Assembly, voted themselves exorbitant salaries, set up a bar in the capitol and left permanent nicks in the capitol steps from the whiskey barrels rolled up for the thirsty legislators.

WHAT TO SEE
MORDECAI HISTORIC PARK
1 Mimosa St., Raleigh, 919-857-4364; www.raleigh-nc.org
This preserved plantation home has many original furnishings and is noted for its neoclassical architecture. Also here is the house in which Andrew Johnson, 17th president of the U.S. was born. Guided tours.
Tuesday-Saturday.

NORTH CAROLINA MUSEUM OF HISTORY
5 E. Edenton St., Raleigh, 919-807-7900; www.ncmuseumofhistory.org
Several innovative exhibits convey the state's history. There is a particularly good exhibit on the role Native Americans played in North Carolina's past.
Tuesday-Sunday.

PULLEN PARK
408 Ashe Ave., Raleigh, 919-831-6468; www.raleigh-nc.org
The scenic 72-acre park in the center of downtown features a 1911 carousel, train ride, paddle boats, indoor aquatic center, ball fields, tennis courts, playground and picnic shelters.
Daily.

STATE CAPITOL

1 E. Edenton St., Raleigh, 919-733-4994; www.ncstatecapitol.com

A simple, stately Greek Revival-style building, the State Capitol is brimming with history. The old legislative chambers, in use until 1963, have been restored to their 1840s appearance, as have the old state library room and the state geologist's office.

Self-guided tours. Daily.

WILLIAM B. UMSTEAD STATE PARK

8801 Glenwood Ave., Raleigh, 919-571-4170; www.ncparks.gov

On 5,480 acres with a 55-acre lake, this park is great for fishing, boating, hiking, riding, picnicking and camping.

Daily.

WHERE TO STAY

★CANDLEWOOD SUITES

4433 Lead Mine Road, Raleigh, 919-789-4840, 888-226-3539;
www.candlewoodsuites.com

122 rooms. Fitness center. $61-150

★★CLARION HOTEL STATE CAPITAL

320 Hillsborough St., Raleigh, 919-832-0501, 800-424-6423; www.clarionhotel.com

202 rooms. Restaurant, bar. $61-150

★COURTYARD RALEIGH NORTH

1041 Wake Towne Drive, Raleigh, 919-821-3400, 800-321-2211; www.courtyard.com

153 rooms. Restaurant. Business center. Fitness center. $61-150

★DAYS INN SOUTH-RALEIGH

3901 S. Wilmington St., Raleigh, 919-772-8900, 800-325-2525; www.daysinn.com

103 rooms. Complimentary breakfast. $61-150

★ECONO LODGE RALEIGH

2641 Appliance Court, Raleigh, 919-856-9800, 800-424-6423; www.choicehotels.com

132 rooms. Complimentary breakfast. $61-150

★★EMBASSY SUITES HOTEL RALEIGH-CRABTREE VALLEY

4700 Creedmoor Road, Raleigh, 919-881-0000, 800-362-2779;
www.embassysuites.com

225 rooms. Restaurant, bar. Complimentary breakfast. $151-250

★FAIRFIELD INN & SUITES RALEIGH CRABTREE VALLEY

2201 Summit Park Lane, Raleigh, 919-881-9800, 800-228-2800; www.marriott.com

125 rooms. Complimentary breakfast. $61-150

★HAMPTON INN

6209 Glenwood Ave., Raleigh, 919-782-1112; www.hamptoninn.com

141 rooms. Complimentary breakfast. $61-150

★★HOLIDAY INN BROWNSTONE

1707 Hillsborough St., Raleigh, 919-828-0811, 800-331-7919;
www.brownstonehotel.com
187 rooms. Restaurant, bar. $61-150

★★★MARRIOTT RALEIGH CRABTREE VALLEY

4500 Marriott Drive, Raleigh, 919-781-7000, 800-909-8289; www.marriott.com-rdunc
Guests will enjoy comfortable accommodations at the Marriott Raleigh
Crabtree Valley, and will appreciate ultramodern features like marble floors,
an atrium lobby and a lush indoor tropical garden. Accessible to Interstate-
440 (I-440) and Highway 70, the hotel is 15 minutes from Research Triangle
Park and the airport and across the street from Crabtree Valley Mall. Nearby
activities include tennis and museums of art, history and natural science.
375 rooms. $151-250

★★★SHERATON RALEIGH CAPITAL CENTER HOTEL

421 S. Salisbury St., Raleigh, 919-834-9900, 800-325-3535; www.sheraton.com-raleigh
The Sheraton Raleigh is located adjacent to the convention center and near
the state capitol, dining, museums and entertainment. Marble floors, high
ceilings and a balcony overlooking the lobby give the hotel a polished look.
Guest rooms offer beds with fluffy duvets and pillows.
355 rooms. Restaurant, bar. $151-250

★★★★★THE UMSTEAD HOTEL AND SPA

100 Woodland Pond, Cary, 919-447-4000, 866-877-4141; www.theumstead.com
Located in wooded suburban Cary, just outside of Raleigh in the Research
Triangle area, this contemporary, elegant hotel offers a full-service stylish
stay. Rooms are decorated in muted neutrals and feature luxury linens, fully
stocked bars and plenty of room to spread out. Enjoy the full-service Umstead Spa offers or its state-of-the-art fitness center. Herons restaurant serving creative New American cuisine is a local favorite.
150 rooms. Restaurant, bar. Spa. Pool. $251-350

WHERE TO EAT

★★42 STREET OYSTER BAR & SEAFOOD GRILL

508 W. Jones St., Raleigh, 919-831-2811; www.42ndstoysterbar.com
Seafood. Lunch, dinner. Bar. Children's menu. Reservations recommended.
$36-85

★ABYSSINIA ETHIOPIAN RESTAURANT

2109-146 Avent Ferry Road, Raleigh, 919-664-8151; www.abyssiniarestaurantnc.com
Middle Eastern. Dinner. Bar. $16-35

★★★ANGUS BARN

9401 Glenwood Ave., Raleigh, 919-787-2444, 800-277-2270; www.angusbarn.com
This steakhouse is one of the few restaurants in the country to age its own
beef before it is hand cut and grilled. Also on the menu are steakhouse classics like oysters Rockefeller and chateaubriand. Two cozy, basement-level
wine cellars can be reserved for private dining and hold extensive collection
of bottles from around the world. A collection of antiques adds charm.

Seafood, steak. Dinner. Bar. Children's menu. Reservations recommended. Valet parking. $36-85

★★CASA CARBONE RISTORANTE
6019-A Glenwood Ave., Raleigh, 919-781-8750; www.casacarbone.com
Southern Italian. Dinner. Closed Monday. Children's menu. $16-35

★★ENOTECA VIN RESTAURANT AND WINE BAR
410 Glenwood Ave., Raleigh, 919-834-3070; www.enotecavin.com
Italian, American. Dinner, Sunday brunch. Closed Monday. $$-$$$

★★★★HERONS RESTAURANT AT THE UMSTEAD HOTEL
100 Woodland Pond, Cary, 919-447-4200; www.theumstead.com/dining
It seems like an oxymoron—gourmet dining in a suburban hotel—but Herons at the Umstead Hotel is an exception. Herons puts a Southern spin on American cuisine in a fashionable setting complete with a 2,500-bottle wine cellar. A spa menu designed for those participating in the hotel's spa program is available. Of course, decadence is too, beginning with the restaurant's homemade cinnamon bun French toast with brown sugar streusel at breakfast and ending with the luscious brownie sundae baked Alaska.
Southern/American. Dinner. $36-85

★★IRREGARDLESS CAFÉ
901 W. Morgan, Raleigh, 919-833-8898; www.irregardless.com
American. Lunch, dinner, Sunday brunch. Closed Monday. Bar. Children's menu. Reservations recommended. $16-35

★★★J. BETSKI'S
10 W. Franklin St., Raleigh, 919-833-7999; www.jbetskis.com
You'll see some schnitzel and some spaetzle at this unique addition to the Raleigh restaurant scene—not to mention a 'wurst or two. Owner John F. Korzekwinski brings together his German and Polish heritage to Southern cuisine, offering up traditional Old World dishes that North Carolina natives can relish in. And what better to pair the seasonal menu's pretzel dumplings and duck confit with than a hefty lager or other bubbly brew off of the beer menu? A glass of wine won't be taking away from your experience, as the list offers selections from Germany and Austria.
German, Polish. Dinner, late-night. Closed Sunday. $36-85

★LAS MARGARITAS
231 Timber Drive, Garner, 919-662-1030
Mexican. Lunch, dinner. Bar. Children's menu. $16-35

★★★SECOND EMPIRE
330 Hillsborough St., Raleigh, 919-829-3663; www.second-empire.com
This restaurant is housed in a renovated Second Empire Victorian home, which was built in 1879. The original heart pine floors, masonry walls and windows add to the elegant atmosphere in the upstairs dining room, which offers fine dining. For a more casual dinner, head downstairs to the Tavern or the Atrium Room, both of which offer seasonal, organic and fresh ingredi-

ents with original presentations.
Contemporary American. Dinner. Closed Sunday. Bar. Reservations recommended. $36-85

★★★SIMPSON'S

5625 Creedmoor Road, Raleigh, 919-783-8818; www.simpsonsrestaurant.com
Enjoy the romantic atmosphere as you dine by candlelight and listen to the pianist who plays here Friday and Saturday evenings. The restaurant, styled after an old English pub, serves an impressive steak and seafood menu. American. Dinner. Closed Sunday. Bar. Reservations recommended. $36-85

★★VINNIE'S STEAKHOUSE

7440 Six Forks Road, Raleigh, 919-847-7319; www.vinniessteakhouse.com
Steak. Dinner. Bar. Reservations recommended. Outdoor seating. $36-85

★★WINSTON'S GRILLE

6401 Falls of Neuse Road, Raleigh, 919-790-0700; www.winstonsgrille.com
American. Dinner, Sunday brunch. Bar. Children's menu. Reservations recommended. Outdoor seating. $16-35

SPA
★★★★THE UMSTEAD SPA

100 Woodland Pond, Cary, 919-447-4170; www.theumsteadspa.com
A tranquil, Asian-inspired space, the spa at the Umstead Hotel offers 14,000 square feet devoted to pampering treatments that range from hot-stone massage to milk hydrotherapy baths. Private spa suites, which accommodate four to six people, are perfect for parties and include access to a massage room, a color therapy tub and more. Guests receive fruit, Evian water and a bottle of champagne. The spa also has a fitness studio and salon services.

ROCKY MOUNT

See also Wilson
This is one of the country's largest bright-leaf tobacco marts. Cotton yarn, bolts of fabric and ready-to-wear clothing are made at the local mills. Factories produce fertilizer, furniture, chemicals, metal products, lumber and pharmaceuticals.

WHAT TO SEE
CHILDREN'S MUSEUM

270 Gay St., Rocky Mount, 252-972-1167; www.rockymountnc.gov/museum
Hands-on exhibits provide children with experiences of the latest technological advances.
Tuesday-Saturday 10 a.m.-5 p.m., Sunday 1-5 p.m.

WHERE TO STAY
★HAMPTON INN

530 N. Winstead Ave., Rocky Mount, 252-937-6333, 800-426-7866; www.hamptoninn.com
124 rooms. Complimentary breakfast. Business center. Fitness room. Pool. $61-150

★★**HOLIDAY INN**

651 Winstead Ave., Rocky Mount, 252-937-6888, 888-543-2255; www.holiday-inn.com
169 rooms. Restaurant, bar. $61-150

SALISBURY

See also Concord, Statesville

Daniel Boone spent his youth here and Andrew Jackson studied law in this town, which has been a trading, cultural and judicial center since 1753. During the Civil War, Salisbury was the site of a Confederate prison where 5,000 Union soldiers died. They are buried here in the National Cemetery. The area has six golf courses as well as the North Carolina Transportation Museum, which is housed in an old roundhouse and rail repair yard.

WHAT TO SEE
DR. JOSEPHUS HALL HOUSE

226 S. Jackson, Salisbury, 704-636-0103; www.learnnc.org
Large antebellum house set amid giant oaks and century-old boxwoods, the Hall House contains most of its original Federal and Victorian furnishings. It was used as the Union commander's headquarters following the Civil War.
Saturday-Sunday afternoons.

WATERWORKS VISUAL ARTS CENTER

East Liberty and North Main streets, Salisbury, 704-636-1882; www.waterworks.org
The former Salisbury Waterworks has been restored and adapted into an arts center. Changing exhibits and art classes are offered.
Daily.

WHERE TO STAY
★HAMPTON INN

1001 Klumac Road, Salisbury, 704-637-8000, 800-426-7866; www.hamptoninn.com
121 rooms. Complimentary breakfast. $61-150

★★HOLIDAY INN

530 Jake Alexander Blvd., Salisbury, 704-637-3100, 800-465-4329;
www.holiday-inn.com
181 rooms. Restaurant, bar. $61-150

SANFORD

This central North Carolina town is known for its production of clay bricks, made possible by its location at the topographical meeting point of coastal sand and Piedmont clay.

WHAT TO SEE
HOUSE IN THE HORSESHOE STATE HISTORIC SITE

324 Alston House Road, Sanford, 910-947-2051; www.nchistoricsites.org
The house was the residence of North Carolina governor Benjamin Williams and the site of a Revolutionary War skirmish.
Tuesday-Sunday.

RAVEN ROCK STATE PARK
3009 Raven Rock Road, Lillington, 910-893-4888; www.ravenrockrumble.com
A 2,990-acre park is characterized by a 152-foot outcrop of rock jutting over Cape Fear River. Fishing, nature trails and interpretive programs are all available.

WHERE TO STAY
★THE WINDS RESORT BEACH CLUB
310 E. First St., Ocean Isle Beach, 910-579-6275, 800-334-3581; www.thewinds.com
86 rooms. Restaurant, bar. Complimentary breakfast. Beach. $61-150

SOUTHERN PINES
See also Pinehurst
The Sandhills are famed for golf and horses. The area first gained popularity as a resort in the 1880s, but the enthusiasm for golf in the 1920s fueled Southern Pines' growth as a resort area. Near Pinehurst and Aberdeen, it boasts more than 40 golf courses.

WHAT TO SEE
WEYMOUTH WOODS-SANDHILLS NATURE PRESERVE
1024 Fort Bragg Road, Southern Pines, 910-692-2167; www.sandhillsonline.com
The preserve has excellent examples of Sandhills ecology. Hiking trails along pine-covered sandridges get very busy in fall. There is also a natural history museum.
April-October, daily 9 a.m.-7 p.m.; November-March, daily 9 a.m.-6 p.m.

WHERE TO STAY
★★DAYS INN
650 U.S. Highway 1, Southern Pines, 910-692-8585, 800-262-5737; www.daysinnsp.com
162 rooms. Restaurant, bar. Business center. Fitness center. $61-150

★HAMPTON INN
1675 Highway 1 S., Southern Pines, 910-692-9266, 800-426-7866; www.hamptoninn.com
126 rooms. Complimentary breakfast. $61-150

★★★MID PINES INN AND GOLF CLUB
1010 Midland Road, Southern Pines, 910-692-2114, 800-290-2334; www.pineneedles-midpines.com
Every hole remains where Donald Ross put it in 1921, when he designed the challenging golf course at this stately inn. The large main building houses a restaurant, lounge and more than 100 nicely appointed rooms.
112 rooms. Restaurant, bar. $61-150

★★★PINE NEEDLES LODGE
1005 Midland Road, Southern Pines, 910-692-7111, 800-747-7272; www.pineneedles-midpines.com
Legendary golfer Peggy Kirk has welcomed guests and players to Pine Nee-

dles for more than three decades. The course was designed by Donald Ross and was host to two recent U.S. Women's Opens. The rustic lodge and elegant restaurant make for a relaxing golf holiday.

78 rooms. Restaurant, bar. $61-150

WHERE TO EAT
★SQUIRE'S PUB
1720 Highway 1 S., Southern Pines, 910-695-1161; www.thesquirespub.com
British. Lunch, dinner. Closed Sunday. Bar. Children's menu. $15 and under

★VITO'S RISTORANTE.
615 S.E. Broad St., Southern Pines, 910-692-7815
Italian. Dinner. Closed Sunday. $16-35

SOUTHPORT
See also Wilmington
This coastal area at the head of the Cape Fear River is a haven for saltwater and freshwater fishing. Deep-sea charter boats are available at Southport, Long Beach and Shallotte Point. There is a good yacht harbor facility for small boats and yachts, a municipal pier, three ocean piers, as well as several beaches and golf courses nearby.

WHAT TO SEE
BRUNSWICK TOWN-FORT ANDERSON STATE HISTORIC SITE
8884 St. Philips Road S.E., Southport, 910-371-6613;
www.southport-oakisland.com/attractions
Brunswick, founded in 1726, thrived as a major port exporting tar and lumber. Fearing a British attack, its citizens fled when the Revolution began. In 1776, the town was burned by British sailors. Twenty-three foundations have been excavated. Built across part of the town are the Civil War earthworks of Fort Anderson, which held out for 30 days after the fall of Fort Fisher in 1865. Tuesday-Saturday 10 a.m.-4 p.m.

FORT FISHER STATE HISTORIC SITE
1610 Fort Fisher Blvd. South, Kure Beach, 910-458-5538; www.nchistoricsites.org
This is the largest earthworks fort in the Confederacy. Until the last few months of the Civil War, it kept Wilmington open to blockade runners. Some of the heaviest naval bombardment of land fortifications took place here on December 24-25, 1864, and on January 13-15, 1865. The visitor center has exhibits and audiovisual shows.
October-March, Tuesday-Saturday 10 a.m.-4 p.m.

WHERE TO STAY
ALSO RECOMMENDED
LOIS JANE'S RIVERVIEW INN
106 W. Bay St., Southport, 910-457-6701; www.loisjanes.com
Five rooms. Complimentary breakfast. $61-150

STATESVILLE
See also Hickory, Salisbury

Statesville is a community of many small, diversified industries, including furniture, apparel, metalworking and textiles. Visitors and locals come to nearby Lake Norman for recreation, and the downtown has several significant historic districts. The biggest event in town is the long-running hot air balloon festival in October.

WHAT TO SEE
FORT DOBBS STATE HISTORIC SITE
438 Fort Dobbs Road, Statesville, 704-873-5866; www.fortdobbs.org

Named for Royal Governor Arthur Dobbs, the now-vanished fort was built during the French and Indian War to protect settlers. Exhibits, nature trails, excavations.

By appointment only.

SPECIAL EVENT
CAROLINA BALLOON FESTIVAL, STATESVILLE REGIONAL AIRPORT
Aviation Drive, Statesville, 704-873-2892; www.carolinaballoonfest.com

This national hot air balloon festival and competition has been running for more than 30 years. Late October.

WHERE TO STAY
★★HOLIDAY INN
1215 Gardner Bagnal Blvd., Statesville, 704-878-9691, 888-465-4329;
www.holiday-inn.com

134 rooms. Restaurant, bar. $61-150

TRYON
See also Hendersonville

A temperate climate and scenic location on the southern slope of the Blue Ridge Mountains have given Tryon a reputation as one of the top places to retire in the U.S. While there are plenty of historic sites and cultural events, Tryon is best known for its equestrian events.

WHAT TO SEE
FOOTHILLS EQUESTRIAN NATURE CENTER
3381 Hunting Country Road, Tryon, 828-859-9021; www.fence.org

This 300-acre nature preserve has 5 miles of riding and hiking trails, wildlife programs and bird and nature walks. It's host to many equestrian events, including the Block House Steeplechase Race in April, which has happened annually for more than 60 years.

Monday-Friday.

WHERE TO STAY
★★★PINE CREST INN
85 Pine Crest Lane, Tryon, 828-859-9135, 800-633-3001; www.pinecrestinn.com

Located in the foothills of the Blue Ridge Mountains, near the Foothills Equestrian Nature Center, this lovely inn evokes an English country manor.

The innkeepers have restored the hardwood floors, stone fireplaces and other historic fixtures.

39 rooms. Complimentary breakfast. Restaurant. $251-350

WHERE TO EAT

★★★PINE CREST INN RESTAURANT

85 Pine Crest Lane, Tryon, 828-859-9135, 800-633-3001; www.pinecrestinn.com

This rustic restaurant serves fusion cuisine and features beamed ceilings, a stone fireplace and heavy pine tables. There's also an award-winning wine list. American. Breakfast, dinner, Sunday brunch. Bar. Children's menu. Reservations recommended. Outdoor seating. $16-35

WASHINGTON

See also Williamston

Washington was rebuilt on the ashes of a town left by evacuating Union troops in April 1864. The rebels lost the town in March 1862, and because it was an important saltwater port on the Pamlico Sound tried to retake it for two years. Evidence of the shelling and burning can be seen in the stone foundations on Water Street. Water sports, including sailing, yachting, fishing and swimming, are popular.

WHAT TO SEE

BATH STATE HISTORIC SITE

207 Carteret St., Bath, 252-923-3971; www.nchistoricsites.org

Washington is the oldest incorporated town in the state and the Bath State site has come of the oldest original structures including Bonner House (circa 1820), Van Der Veer House (circa 1790) and Palmer-Marsh House (circa 1745).

April-October, daily; rest of year, daily except Monday.

WHERE TO STAY

★COMFORT INN

1636 Carolina Ave., Washington, 252-946-4444, 800-228-5150; www.comfortinn.com

56 rooms. Complimentary breakfast. $61-150

ALSO RECOMMENDED

RIVER FOREST MANOR

738 E. Main St., Belhaven, 252-943-2151, 800-346-2151; www.riverforestmanor.com

Nine rooms. Restaurant. Complimentary breakfast. A$61-150

WAYNESVILLE

See also Asheville, Cherokee, Maggie Valley

Popular with tourists, this area offers mountain trails for riding and hiking and golf and fishing in cool mountain streams. Waynesville is 26 miles from the Cherokee Indian Reservation and Great Smoky Mountains National Park. The town of Maggie Valley, about 6 miles northwest, is in a particularly attractive area.

SPECIAL EVENTS
INTERNATIONAL FOLK FESTIVAL
Waynesville, 828-452-2997; www.yoconafestival.org
Premier folk groups from more than 10 countries demonstrate their cultural heritage through lively music and costumed dance.
Eleven days in late July.

WHERE TO STAY
★★★BALSAM MOUNTAIN INN
68 Seven Springs Drive, Balsam, 828-456-9498, 800-224-9498; www.balsaminn.com
This 100-year-old-inn sits in the Blue Ridge Mountains and features an award-winning restaurant as well as a library and access to great hiking trails.
50 rooms. Restaurant. Complimentary breakfast. $61-150

★★★THE SWAG COUNTRY INN
2300 Swag Road, Waynesville, 828-926-0430, 800-789-7672; www.theswag.com
The Swag Country Inn sits atop a 5,000-foot mountain with a private entrance to Great Smoky Mountain National Park. The rooms and suites feature handmade quilts, woven rugs and original artwork. Nature trails cover the property, and picnic baskets and brown-bag lunches are available for hikers.
15 rooms. Closed mid-November-April. Restaurant (public by reservation). Complimentary breakfast. Children over 7 only in main building. $351 and up

ALSO RECOMMENDED
YELLOW HOUSE ON PLOT CREEK ROAD
89 Oakview Drive, Waynesville, 828-452-0991, 800-563-1236;
www.theyellowhouse.com
A fabulous yellow house tucked into the hills at a 3,000-foot elevation, the property has rooms with rustic décor that complements the remarkable landscape.
Six rooms. Complimentary breakfast. $61-150

WILLIAMSTON
See also Washington
Centered in Martin County on the Roanoke River, Williamston is part of a thriving river recreation community, with plenty of rafting, canoeing, fishing and hunting.

WHAT TO SEE
HOPE PLANTATION
132 Hope House Road, Windsor, 252-794-3140; www.hopeplantation.org
The two-hour guided tour of Georgian plantation house (circa 1800) built by Governor David Stone is a great way to experience the history of the region. The house has period furnishings and spectacular gardens. Open Monday-Saturday, Sunday afternoon.

WHERE TO STAY

★ECONO LODGE

100 E. Blvd., Williamston, 252-792-8400; www.econolodge.com
59 rooms. Complimentary breakfast. $61-150

★★HOLIDAY INN

101 E. Blvd., Williamston, 252-792-3184, 800-792-3101; www.holidayinn.com
100 rooms. Restaurant, bar. $61-150

WILMINGTON

See also Southport, Wrightsville Beach
Made famous in recent years as the setting of the TV teen drama Dawson's Creek, Wilmington offers a small town beach atmosphere in a historic area. As the major city on North Carolina's Cape Fear Coast, it was the state's biggest town until 1910 when rail-fed industries outgrew those serviced by the harbor. In 1765, eight years before the Boston Tea Party, the citizens of Wilmington kept the British from unloading their stamps for the Stamp Act. In 1781, Cornwallis held the town as his main base of operation for almost a year. During the Civil War, blockade runners brought fortunes in goods past Federal ships lying off Cape Fear, making Wilmington the Confederacy's chief port until January 1865 when it fell. Today the town offers a steady mix of industry and tourism, with historic sites, a vibrant and historic downtown and access to Cape Fear beaches.

WHAT TO SEE

BATTLESHIP NORTH CAROLINA.

Battleship Road, Wilmington, 910-251-5797; www.battleshipnc.com
All aboard this World War II vessel moored on the west bank of Cape Fear River. Tour the museum, gun turrets, galley, bridge, sick bay, engine room and wheelhouse.
Daily.

BURGWIN-WRIGHT HOUSE

224 Market St., Wilmington, 910-762-0570; burgwinwrighthouse.com
British General Cornwallis had his headquarters at this restored colonial town house built on foundation of an abandoned town jail. Enjoy the 18th century furnishings and gardens.
Tuesday-Saturday.

MOORES CREEK NATIONAL BATTLEFIELD

40 Patriot Paul Drive, Currie, 910-283-5591; www.nps.gov/mocr
In 1776, the loosely knit colonists took sides against each other—patriots versus loyalists. Colonels Moore, Lillington and Caswell, with the blessing of the Continental Congress, broke up the loyalist forces, captured the leaders and seized gold and weapons. The action defeated British hopes of an early invasion through the South and encouraged North Carolina to be the first colony to instruct its delegates to vote for independence in Philadelphia. The 86-acre park has a visitor center near its entrance to explain the battle.
Daily.

CAPTAIN J. N. MAFFITT RIVER CRUISES

Wilmington, 910-343-1611, 800-676-0162; www.cfrboats.com

Located at the foot of Market Street, this five-mile narrated sightseeing cruise covers Wilmington's harbor life and points of interest. There is also a river taxi service (additional fee) from Battleship North Carolina.
May-September, daily.

POPLAR GROVE PLANTATION

10200 Highway, 17, Wilmington, 910-686-9989; www.poplargrove.com

The restored Greek Revival plantation incorporates a manor house, smoke-house, tenant house, blacksmith, loom weaver and basket weaver. Guided tours are available.
Daily.

WHERE TO STAY
★★COURTYARD WILMINGTON

151 Van Campen Blvd., Wilmington, 910-395-8224, 800-321-2211;
www.marriott.com-ilmcy

128 rooms. $61-150

★HAMPTON INN

1989 Eastwood Road, Wilmington, 910-256-9600, 877-256-9600;
www.landfallparkhotel.com

120 rooms. Bar. Complimentary breakfast. $61-150

★★HOLIDAY INN

5032 Market St., Wilmington, 910-392-1101, 800-833-4721; www.holiday-inn.com

124 rooms. Restaurant. Complimentary breakfast. $61-150

★★★HILTON WILMINGTON RIVERSIDE

301 N. Water St., Wilmington, 910-763-5900, 800-445-8667;
www.wilmingtonhilton.com

This hotel is a short walk from shops, restaurants, cultural attractions and the city's riverwalk. Guest rooms are comfortable and offer magnificent views of Cape Fear River.
274 rooms. Restaurant, bar. $61-150

★★★THE WILMINGTONIAN

101 S. Second St., Wilmington, 910-343-1800, 800-525-0909;
www.thewilmingtonian.com

Located in downtown Wilmington, just two blocks from Cape Fear River and a 40-minute drive to the beaches on the Atlantic Coast, this renovated inn caters to both leisure and business travelers with roomy suites and plentiful amenities.
40 rooms. Restaurant, bar. Complimentary breakfast. $61-150

ALSO RECOMMENDED
C. W. WORTH HOUSE

412 S. Third St., Wilmington, 910-762-8562, 800-340-8559; www.worthhouse.com

Seven rooms. Children over 12 years only. Complimentary breakfast. $61-150

DARLINGS BY THE SEA—OCEANFRONT WHIRLPOOL SUITES

329 Atlantic Ave., Kure Beach, 910-458-8887, 800-383-8111;
www.darlingsbythesea.com

Best described as a quaint honeymooners' cottage, each suite has a wonderful terrace overlooking the ocean.

Five rooms. No children allowed. Complimentary breakfast. Beach. $151-250

FRONT STREET INN

215 S. Front St., Wilmington, 910-762-6442, 800-336-8184; www.frontstreetinn.com

12 rooms. Complimentary breakfast. Bar. $151-250

THE GRAYSTONE INN

100 S. Third St., Wilmington, 910-763-2000, 888-763-4773; www.graystoneinn.com

The antique-filled inn includes a music room with a grand piano, a mahogany-paneled library and a chandelier lit dining room. Rooms are decorated in period furnishings, some with claw-foot tubs.

Nine rooms. Complimentary breakfast. Children over 12 years only. $151-250

ROSEHILL INN

114 S. Third St., Wilmington, 910-815-0250, 800-815-0250; www.rosehill.com

This elegant Victorian home was built in 1848. Each of the large, luxurious guest rooms has its own individual charm and is perfect for a romantic retreat.

Six rooms. Children over 14 years only. Complimentary breakfast. $151-250

THE VERANDAS

202 Nun St., Wilmington, 910-251-2212; www.verandas.com

This 8,500-square-foot, Victorian-Italianate mansion sits two blocks from the Cape Fear River. Climb the spiral staircase to the enclosed cupola for a spectacular sunset view.

8 rooms. Complimentary breakfast. Children over 12 years only. $151-250

WHERE TO EAT

★CAFÉ PHOENIX

9 S. Front St., Wilmington, 910-343-1395; www.thecaffephoenix.com

Mediterranean. Lunch, dinner. Bar. Children's menu. Reservations recommended. Outdoor seating. $16-35

★DRAGON GARDEN

341-52 S. College Road, Wilmington, 910-452-0708

Chinese, sushi, Thai. Lunch, dinner. Reservations recommended. $15 and under

★★EDDIE ROMANELLI'S

5400 Oleander Drive, Wilmington, 910-799-7000; www.romanellisrestaurant.com

Italian, American. Lunch, dinner, late-night. Bar. Children's menu. $16-35

★★ELIJAH'S

2 Ann St., Wilmington, 910-343-1448; www.elijahs.com

American. Lunch, dinner, Sunday brunch. Bar. Children's menu. Reservations recommended. Outdoor seating. $16-35

★★FREDDIE'S

111 K Ave., Kure Beach, 910-458-5979; www.freddieskurebeach.com

Italian, American. Dinner. Children's menu. Reservations recommended. $16-35

★HIERONYMUS SEAFOOD

5035 Market St., Wilmington, 910-392-6313; www.hieronymusseafood.com

Seafood. Dinner. Bar. Children's menu. Reservations recommended. Outdoor seating. $36-85

★★PILOT HOUSE

2 Ann St., Wilmington, 910-343-0200; www.pilothouserest.com

American. Lunch, dinner, Sunday brunch. Bar. Children's menu. Outdoor seating. $36-85

★★PORT CITY CHOP HOUSE

1981 Eastwood Road, Wilmington, 910-256-4955; www.chophousesofnc.com

Seafood, steak. Lunch, dinner. Closed Sunday. Bar. Children's menu. Reservations recommended. Outdoor seating. $36-85

★★ROY'S RIVERBOAT LANDING

2 Market St., Wilmington, 910-763-7227; www.theunioncafe.com

International. Lunch, dinner, Sunday brunch. Bar. Reservations recommended. Outdoor seating. $36-85

★WATER STREET

5 S. Water St., Wilmington, 910-343-0042; www.5southwaterstreet.com

American. Lunch, dinner. Bar. Children's menu. Outdoor seating. $16-35

WILSON

See also Rocky Mount

Located just off Interstate 95, midway between New York and Florida, Wilson is most often visited by snowbirds heading south. It is also one of the Southeast's leading antique markets and has one of the nation's largest tobacco markets.

WHERE TO STAY

★BEST WESTERN LA SAMMANA

817 Ward Blvd., Wilson, 252-237-8700, 800-937-8376; www.bestwestern.com

78 rooms. Complimentary breakfast. Pool. $61-150

★COMFORT INN

4941 Highway 264 W., Wilson, 252-291-6400, 800-424-6423; www.choicehotels.com

76 rooms. Complimentary breakfast. $61-150

★HAMPTON INN
5606 Lamm Road, Wilson, 252-291-0330; www.hamptoninn.com
100 rooms. Complimentary breakfast. $61-150

WINSTON-SALEM
See also Greensboro, High Point, Lexington
One of the South's biggest industrial cities, Winston-Salem is a combination of two communities. Salem, with the traditions of its Moravian founders, and Winston, an industrial center, matured together. Tobacco markets, large banks and arts and crafts galleries contribute to this thriving community.

WHAT TO SEE
BOWMAN GRAY STADIUM
1250 S. Martin Luther King Jr. Drive, Winston-Salem, 336-727-2748;
www.bowmangrayracing.com
Bowman Gray Stadium is a multiuse public arena that hosts Winston-Salem State Rams college football games as well as a NASCAR short track. Part of the city's Lawrence Joel Veterans Memorial Coliseum Complex, Bowman Gray has hosted races for more than 50 years, making it the longest operating NASCAR short track in the country.

HISTORIC OLD SALEM
900 Old Salem Road, Winston-Salem, 336-721-7300, 888-653-7253;
www.oldsalem.org
Old Salem is a restoration of a planned community that Moravians, with their old-world skills, turned into the 18th-century trade and cultural center of North Carolina's Piedmont. Many of the sturdy structures built for practical living have been restored and furnished with original or period pieces. Early crafts are demonstrated throughout the town. A number of houses are privately occupied. Nine houses and the outbuildings are open to the public. Tours (self-guided) start at the visitor center on Old Salem Road. Special events are held during the year.
Tuesday-Sunday.

REYNOLDA HOUSE, MUSEUM OF AMERICAN ART
2250 Reynolda Road, Winston-Salem, 336-758-5150; www.reynoldahouse.org
On the estate of the late R. J. Reynolds of the tobacco dynasty, the museum houses American paintings, original furniture, art objects and elaborate costume collections. Adjacent is Reynolda Gardens with 125 acres of open fields and naturalized woodlands, formal gardens and a greenhouse.
Tuesday-Saturday, Sunday afternoon.

WAKE FOREST UNIVERSITY
1834 Wake Forest Road, Winston-Salem, 336-758-5000; www.wfu.edu
Established in 1834, Wake Forest has 5,600 students. Sites to visit on campus include the Fine Arts Center, Museum of Anthropology and Reynolda Village, a complex of shops, offices and restaurants. Bowman Gray School of Medicine is on Medical Center Boulevard.

WHERE TO STAY
★★HOLIDAY INN
5790 University Parkway, Winston-Salem, 336-767-9595, 800-553-9595;
www.holiday-inn.com
150 rooms. Restaurant, bar. Pool. $61-150

★QUALITY INN
5719 University Parkway, Winston-Salem, 336-767-9009, 800-426-7866;
www.qualitywinstonsalem.com
113 rooms. Complimentary breakfast. Pool. $61-150

ALSO RECOMMENDED
AUGUSTUS T. ZEVELY
803 S. Main St., Winston Salem, 336-748-9299, 800-928-9299;
www.winston-salem-inn.com
12 rooms. Children over 12 years only. Complimentary breakfast. $61-150

BROOKSTOWN INN
200 Brookstown Ave., Winston-Salem, 336-725-1120, 800-845-4262;
www.brookstowninn.com
This historic inn was built in 1837 as a textile mill. The conversion preserved
the original handmade brick and exposed beam construction. The romantic
rooms include European-style breakfast.
70 rooms. Complimentary breakfast. $151-250

TANGLEWOOD PARK
4061 Clemmons Road, Clemmons, 336-778-6370; www.forsyth.cc/tanglewood
28 rooms. Complimentary breakfast. Golf. Tennis. $61-150

WHERE TO EAT
★★6TH AND VINE
209 W. Sixth St., Winston-Salem, 336-725-5577; www.6thandvine.com
Mediterranean. Lunch, dinner, late-night, brunch. Closed Monday. Bar. Children's menu. Outdoor seating. $16-35

★★★RYAN'S RESTAURANT
719 Coliseum Drive, Winston-Salem, 336-724-6132; www.ryansrestaurant.com
An inviting brick pathway surrounded by philodendron and with a cascad-
ing waterfall leads guests to Ryan's. The décor here is simple yet elegant,
and tables offer a view of the woods and brook below. The menu features
steakhouse standards, along with a wide selection of seafood dishes such as
pepper seared tuna with red cabbage slaw.
Seafood, steak. Dinner. Closed Sunday. Bar. Reservations recommended.
Outdoor seating. $36-85

★★SWEET POTATOES
529 N. Trade St., Winston-Salem, 336-727-4844; www.sweetpotatoes-arestaurant.com
American, Southern. Lunch, dinner. Closed Sunday. Bar. $16-35

★★VINEYARD

120 Reynolda Village, Winston-Salem, 336-748-0269;
www.thevineyards120restaurant.com

Continental. Dinner. Closed Sunday. Bar. Reservations recommended. Outdoor seating. $36-85

★★ZEVELY HOUSE

901 W. Fourth St., Winston-Salem, 336-725-6666; www.zevelyhouse.com

American, French. Dinner, Sunday brunch. Closed Monday. Bar. Reservations recommended. Outdoor seating. $16-35

WRIGHTSVILLE BEACH

See also Wilmington

A pleasant, family-oriented resort town, Wrightsville Beach offers swimming, surfing, fishing and boating. The public park has facilities for tennis, basketball, soccer, softball, volleyball, shuffleboard and other sports.

WHERE TO STAY
★★HOLIDAY INN SUNSPREE RESORT

1706 N. Lumina Ave., Wrightsville Beach, 910-256-2231, 877-330-5050;
www.holiday-inn.com

184 rooms. Restaurant, bar. Pool. $61-150

WHERE TO EAT
★★BRIDGE TENDER

1414 Airle Road, Wrightsville Beach, 910-256-4519; www.thebridgetender.com

Seafood, steak. Lunch, dinner. Bar. Reservations recommended. Outdoor seating. $36-85

★DOCKSIDE

1308 Airlie Road, Wrightsville Beach, 910-256-2752; www.thedockside.com

American. Lunch, dinner. Bar. Children's menu. Outdoor seating. $16-35

★★KING NEPTUNE

11 N. Lumina Ave., Wrightsville Beach, 910-256-2525; www.kingneptunewb.com

Seafood, steak. Dinner. Bar. Children's menu. $16-35

★★OCEANIC

703 S. Lumina Ave., Wrightsville Beach, 910-256-5551; www.oceanicrestaurant.com

Seafood, steak. Lunch, dinner, Sunday brunch. Bar. Children's menu. Outdoor seating. $16-35

SOUTH CAROLINA

LOVELY BEACHES, A TEMPERATE YEAR-ROUND CLIMATE AND GOLF COURSES TO RIVAL THE world's best have made tourism one of South Carolina's most important industries. Hilton Head resorts are packed with families when the weather is warm, while Myrtle Beach is the town of choice for golf lovers. The surrounding area has more than 100 courses.

This state's turbulent and romantic history tells a story that is deeply rooted in its people and the history of the U.S. During the American Revolution, almost 200 battles and skirmishes were fought in South Carolina. The first overt act of revolution occurred at Fort Charlotte on July 12, 1775, making it the first British property seized by American Revolutionary forces. Less than 100 years later on December 20, 1860, South Carolina became the first state to secede from the Union. And, the clash that started the Civil War began on South Carolina soil when Confederate soldiers bombed and seized Fort Sumter in 1861, holding onto the fort until the evacuation of Charleston in 1865. Impoverished and blackened by the fires of General Sherman's "March to the Sea," South Carolina emerged from the difficult Reconstruction days and was readmitted to the Union in 1868.

Economic problems have plagued South Carolina in the past, but in recent decades, diversified industries have brought greater prosperity. South Carolina is a major producer of tobacco, cotton, pine lumber, corn, oats, sweet potatoes, soybeans, peanuts, peaches, melons, beef cattle and hogs, and power projects have been created by damming the Santee, Saluda, Savannah, and other rivers. Tourism is part of this growing economy, and the state is known for its water sports, deep sea fishing, car racing and, of course, golf.

AIKEN
See also Orangeburg
A popular social and sports center, Aiken is known for its equestrian sports including flat-racing training, steeplechase and harness racing, polo, fox hunts and drag hunts. There is also good tennis and golf. The University of South Carolina-Aiken is located here.

WHAT TO SEE
AIKEN COUNTY HISTORICAL MUSEUM
433 Newberry St., Southwest, Aiken, 803-642-2015; www.aikencountysc.gov
The museum is packed with period room settings and displays of a late 1800s home. A log cabin and one-room schoolhouse are on the grounds. Special features include an archaeology exhibit and a 1950s drug store. There is also a museum store here.
Tuesday-Friday 9:30 a.m.-4:30 p.m., Saturday-Sunday 2-5 p.m.

REDCLIFFE
181 Redcliffe Road, Beech Island, 803-827-1473; www.southcarolinaparks.com
Built in the 1850s, this Greek Revival mansion is furnished with Southern antiques, art collections, historic documents and books.
Thursday-Monday 9 a.m.-6 p.m.

WHERE TO STAY
★★★THE WILLCOX
100 Colleton Ave., Southeast, Aiken, 803-648-1898, 877-648-2200;
www.thewillcox.com

This distinguished mansion set on 2,000 acres of the Hitchcock Woods offers some of the best of South Carolina's horse country. Guest rooms and suites are decorated with antiques, Oriental rugs and feather-topped four-poster beds. Most accommodations have working fireplaces. The onsite spa offers everything from massages to rejuvenating facials.

22 rooms. Complimentary breakfast. Restaurant. Spa. $251-350

BEAUFORT
See also Charleston, Hardeeville, Kiawah Island, Waterboro

The second-oldest town in the state, Beaufort is the unofficial capital of South Carolina's low country and is filled with antebellum homes and churches. The town has rebuilt itself several times, first after Native Americans destroyed it in 1715, then after the British attacked in 1812 and finally after Northern troops forced the evacuation of almost the entire town during the Civil War.

WHAT TO SEE
JOHN MARK VERDIER HOUSE MUSEUM
801 Bay St., Beaufort, 843-524-6335; www.historic-beaufort.org

This Federal period house built in 1790 was once known as the Lafayette Building because the Marquis de Lafayette is said to have spoken here from the piazza in 1825.

Monday-Saturday 11 a.m.-4 p.m.

ST. HELENA'S EPISCOPAL CHURCH
505 Church St., Beaufort, 843-522-1712; www.sthelenas1712.org

Tombstones from the surrounding burial ground became operating tables when the church was used as a hospital during the Civil War.

Tuesday-Friday 10 a.m.-4 p.m., Saturday 10 a.m.-1 p.m.

WHERE TO STAY
★★★BEAUFORT INN
809 Port Republic St., Beaufort, 843-379-4667; www.beaufortinn.com

Built in 1897, this romantic low country inn offers rooms, suites and a private, two-bedroom cottage. The dining room has seasonal, Southern cuisine and an extensive wine list.

21 rooms. Children over 8 years only in the inn. Complimentary breakfast. Restaurant. $251-350

★BEST WESTERN SEA ISLAND INN
1015 Bay St., Beaufort, 843-522-2090, 800-780-7234; www.bestwestern.com

43 rooms. Complimentary breakfast. Fitness room. Pool. $61-150

★★★THE RHETT HOUSE INN
1009 Craven St., Beaufort, 843-524-9030, 888-480-9530; www.rhetthouseinn.com

One block from the Intracoastal Waterway, the Rhett House Inn, a plantation

dating back to 1820, has rooms decorated with floral fabrics, fireplaces, four-poster beds and antiques.
Children over 5 years only. Complimentary breakfast. $151-250

WHERE TO EAT
★★BEAUFORT INN
809 Port Republic St., Beaufort, 843-379-4667; www.beaufortinn.com
American. Breakfast, lunch, dinner, Sunday brunch. Bar. Outdoor seating. Reservation recommended. $36-85

★★BREAKWATER RESTAURANT & BAR
205 W. St., Beaufort, 843-379-0052; www.breakwaterrestaurantandbar.com
French. Dinner. Closed Sunday. Bar. Outdoor seating. Reservation recommended. $16-35

★★BRITISH OPEN PUB OF BEAUFORT
8 Waveland Cat Island, Beaufort, 843-524-4653; www.britishopenpub.net
American. Lunch, dinner, Sunday brunch. Bar. Outdoor seating. $16-35

★★PLUMS
904 Bay St., Beaufort, 843-525-1946; www.plumsrestaurant.com
American. Lunch, dinner. Bar. Children's menu. Outdoor seating. $16-35

CAMDEN
See also Columbia, Sumter
During the Revolution, General Cornwallis occupied Camden, the oldest inland town in the state, and made it the principal British garrison and the interior command post for the South. Although several battles were fought in and near the town, including the Battle of Camden, the town was never recaptured by Americans. Instead, it was evacuated and burned by the British in 1781. Today, Camden is famous for its horseback riding, horse shows, hunt meets, polo and steeplechase races. There are 200 miles of bridle paths in the area and three race tracks. Springdale Course is an extremely difficult and exciting steeplechase run.

WHAT TO SEE
BETHESDA PRESBYTERIAN CHURCH
502 DeKalb St., Camden, 803-432-4593; www.bethesdapresbyterianchurch.org
Designed by the architect of the Washington Monument, Robert Mills, the church is considered a masterpiece.
Monday-Friday 9 a.m.-4 p.m.

HISTORIC CAMDEN REVOLUTIONARY WAR SITE
222 S. Broad St., Camden, 803-432-9841; www.historic-camden.net
Archaeological site of South Carolina's oldest inland town, there is a visitor area with two early 19th-century log cabins and a restored 18th-century townhouse. Trails lead to the reconstructed foundation of a pre-Revolutionary War powder magazine, the Kershaw-Cornwallis House and two reconstructed British fortifications. The site of the Battle of Camden, a National

Historic Landmark, is 5 miles north of town.

Self-guided and guided tours, Tuesday-Saturday 10 a.m.-5 p.m., Sunday 2-5 p.m.

SPECIAL EVENTS
CAROLINA CUP STEEPLECHASE

Springdale Race Course, 200 Knights Hill Road, Camden, 803-432-6513, 800-780-8117; www.carolina-cup.org

This annual 'rites of spring' draws more than 70,000 fans every year to enjoy the sport of steeplechase horse racing alongside spring fashions and elaborate tailgate parties.

Early April.

COLONIAL CUP INTERNATIONAL STEEPLECHASE

Springdale Race Course, 200 Knights Hill Road, Camden, 803-432-6513, 800-780-8117; www.carolina-cup.org

The Colonial Cup draws more than 15,000 fans and horsemen from around the world and provides the season's grand finale—often deciding all the national titles including jockey of the year, trainer of the year and horse of the year. Mid-November.

WHERE TO STAY
ALSO RECOMMENDED
GREENLEAF INN

1308 Broad St., Camden, 803-425-1806, 800-437-5874;

www.greenleafinnofcamden.com

Located in the historic district, its guesthouses were built in 1805 and 1890 and are decorated in the Victorian style.

10 rooms. Complimentary breakfast. Restaurant. $61-150

CHARLESTON

See also Beaufort, Kiawah Island, Summerville, Waterboro

This aristocratic and storied American city lives up to its reputation for cultivated manners. Charleston's homes, historic shrines, old churches, lovely gardens, winding streets and intricate iron-laced gateways exude charm.

The Charleston of today is a survivor of siege, flood, hurricane and epidemic. Capital of the province until 1786 and the first permanent settlement in the Carolinas, Charles Towne, as it was first called, was established as a tiny colony by Anthony Ashley Cooper, Earl of Shaftesbury. At the same time, he established the only American nobility in history, with barons, landgraves (dukes) and caciques (earls), each owning great plantations.

This nobility lasted less than 50 years, but it was the foundation for an aristocratic tradition that still exists. Although many of the colonists moved to the Carolina low country and established plantations, every year on May 10 the planters and their families moved back to Charleston to escape the mosquitoes and malarial heat. From spring to frost, these planters created a season of sport, theater and socials. Charleston had the first playhouse, the first museum, the first public school in the colony, the first municipal college in America and the first fire insurance company on the continent. (It was a victim the next year of a fire that destroyed half the city.)

In 1780, Charleston was captured and occupied by the British for two and a half years. The city was almost the last point in the state to be cleared of British troops. With peace came prosperity, but rivalry between the small farmers of the interior and the merchants and plantation owners of the lowlands resulted in the capital's creation in Columbia.

The Ordinance of Secession was passed by convention in Charleston in 1860, and the bombing at Fort Sumter began the Civil War. Today, the beautiful city retains outstanding architecture in its large historic downtown. With a rich mix of styles from early Colonial, Georgian, Federal, Greek Revival and Italianate to Victorian as well as ample historic artifacts, Charleston is a wonderful place to explore on foot.

WHAT TO SEE
AIKEN-RHETT HOUSE
48 Elizabeth St., Charleston, 843-723-1159; www.historiccharleston.org
Built around 1818, this palatial residence was added onto and redecorated by Governor and Mrs. William Aiken Jr. in the mid-1800s. The house remained in the family until 1975, and many original pieces of furniture are still in the rooms for which they were purchased.
Daily.

BOONE HALL PLANTATION
1235 Long Point Road, Mount Pleasant, 843-884-4371; www.boonehallplantation.com
This 738-acre estate has a 1935 Georgian-style house similar to the original plantation house that fell into ruin, a cotton gin house, a pecan grove, nine slave cabins and gardens of antique roses. The property has been used to film many TV shows and movies. Battle reenactments are held during the summer and draw Civil War buffs.
April-Labor Day, Monday-Saturday 8:30 a.m.-6:30 p.m., Sunday 1-5 p.m.; Labor Day-March, Monday-Saturday 9 a.m.-5 p.m., Sunday 1-4 p.m.

CHARLESTON MUSEUM
360 Meeting St., Charleston, 843-722-2996; www.charlestonmuseum.org
Founded in 1773 and first opened to the public in 1824, the Charleston Museum is America's oldest museum. Key artifacts in the collection include an impressive early silver display (George Washington's christening cup is among the pieces), an Egyptian mummy, South Carolina ceramics, a skeleton of a primitive toothed whale, the chairs that delegates sat in to sign South Carolina's Ordinance of Secession and firearms used in the Civil War.
Monday-Saturday 9 a.m.-5 p.m., Sunday 1-5 p.m.

CHARLES TOWNE LANDING
1500 Old Town Road, Charleston, 843-852-4200; www.southcarolinaparks.com
In 1670, colonists established the first permanent English settlement in the Carolinas at this location. Today, visitors find archaeological investigations, reconstructed fortifications, formal gardens, as well as nature trails, a colonial village and a replica of Adventure, a 17th-century trading ketch. Tram tours are available, and there also is a natural habitat zoo of indigenous animals onsite.
Daily 8:30 a.m.-5 p.m.

THE CITADEL, MILITARY COLLEGE OF SOUTH CAROLINA

171 Moultrie St., Charleston, 843-225-3294; www.citadel.edu

Established in 1842 by an act of the South Carolina General Assembly, the Citadel was originally located on Marion Square in downtown Charleston near the Revolutionary War rampart. In 1922, the college was moved to a picturesque setting on the bank of the Ashley River. The site houses 24 major buildings, including Summerall Chapel, a shrine of patriotism and remembrance. Citadel parades on Friday afternoons are said to be the best free show in Charleston. Visitors may take self-guided campus tours.

Cadet-led tours for groups of eight or more are available through the Public Affairs Office, 843-953-6779. Closed Saturday-Sunday.

DOCK STREET THEATRE

135 Church St., Charleston, 843-577-7183, 800-454-7093; www.charlestonstage.com

In 1736, a building on this site opened as the very first in America constructed specifically for theatrical productions. Later, the street name changed to Queen, but the Dock Street Theatre name stuck. Today's theater is on the site of the original and presents productions of the Charleston Stage Company during the spring and fall. Dock Street Theatre is a performance venue for Charleston's Spoleto Festival.

DRAYTON HALL

3380 Ashley River Road, Charleston, 843-769-2600; www.draytonhall.org

One of the oldest surviving pre-American Revolution plantation houses in the area, this Georgian Palladian house is surrounded by live oaks and is located on the Ashley River. Held in the Drayton family for seven generations before its donation to the National Trust, the mansion has been maintained in near original condition.

Tours daily. November-February. Main Gates: 8:30 a.m.-4 p.m.; Museum Shop: 8:30 a.m.-5 p.m.

EDMONDSTON-ALSTON HOUSE

4300 Ashley River Road, Charleston, 843-556-6020, 800-782-3608;
www.middletonplace.org

This Greek Revival style house has an uninterrupted view across the harbor. Guided tours are offered daily.

Tuesday-Saturday 10 a.m.-4:30 p.m., Sunday-Monday 1:30-4:30 p.m.

FRENCH HUGUENOT CHURCH

44 Queen St., Charleston, 843-722-4385; www.frenchhuguenotchurch.org

As early as 1687, French Huguenots were worshipping in a church on this site. The current church is a National Historic Landmark. Completed in 1845, it was the first Gothic Revival building in Charleston. The church features distinctive windows, buttresses and unusual ironwork.

Daily.

GIBBES MUSEUM OF ART

135 Meeting St., Charleston, 843-722-2706; www.gibbesmuseum.org

The more than 100-year-old museum houses an eclectic collection that includes Japanese woodblock prints as well as miniature rooms depicting traditional American and French architecture, decorative arts and design. This museum is also known for its portraits of famous South Carolinians by notable artists, including Thomas Sully, Benjamin West and Rembrandt Peale. Don't miss the Charleston Renaissance Gallery, which showcases works by Charleston artists responsible for the city's cultural renaissance in the 1920s and 1930s.

Tours available. Tuesday-Saturday 10 a.m.-5 p.m., Sunday 1-5 p.m.

HEYWARD-WASHINGTON HOUSE

360 Meeting St., Charleston, 843-722-2996; www.charlestonmuseum.org

This brick double house, noteworthy for its collection of Charleston-made furniture, was built in 1772 during the Revolutionary era. Rice planter Daniel Heyward gave the house to his son Thomas Heyward Jr., a signer of the Declaration of Independence. George Washington stayed here during his weeklong visit to the city in 1791. Dubose Heyward used the neighborhood in which the house stands as the setting for Porgy and Bess.

Monday-Saturday 10 a.m.-5 p.m., Sunday 1-5 p.m.

JOSEPH MANIGAULT HOUSE

360 Meeting St., Charleston, 843-722-2996; www.charlestonmuseum.org

This home was designed by Gabriel Manigault for his brother Joseph. The brothers were descendants of a French Huguenot family. This elegant neoclassical three-story brick town house, a National Historic Landmark, reflects the wealthy lifestyle of the Manigault family, as well as living conditions of the slaves who worked there.

Monday-Saturday 10 a.m.-5 p.m., Sunday 1-5 p.m.

MAGNOLIA PLANTATION AND GARDENS

3550 Ashley River Road, Charleston, 843-571-1266, 800-367-3517; www.magnolia-plantation.com

These internationally famous gardens are America's oldest (circa 1676). They now cover 50 acres with camellias, azaleas, magnolias and hundreds of other flowering species. Also on the grounds are a 125-acre waterfowl refuge, a tri-level observation tower, a 16th-century maze, an 18th-century herb garden, nature trails and a petting zoo. Canoe and bicycle rentals are available.

March-October, 8 a.m.-dusk; November-February, call for hours.

MIDDLETON PLACE PLANTATION

4300 Ashley River Road, Charleston, 843-556-6020, 800-782-3608; www.middleton-place.org

Once the home of Arthur Middleton, a signer of the Declaration of Independence, Middleton Place has America's oldest landscaped gardens and a restored House Museum. Laid out in 1741, the gardens feature ornamental butterfly lakes, sweeping terraces and a wide variety of flora and fauna. Daily.

NATHANIEL RUSSELL HOUSE

51 Meeting St., Charleston, 843-724-8481; www.historiccharleston.org
Regarded as Charleston's grandest neoclassical house museum, this house (circa 1808) features period antiques, lavish plasterwork, oval drawing rooms and a magnificent "free-flying" staircase.
Daily Monday-Saturday 10 a.m.-5 p.m., Sunday 2-5 p.m.

OLD EXCHANGE AND PROVOST DUNGEON

122 E. Bay St., Charleston, 843-727-2165, 1-888-763-0448; www.oldexchange.com
Completed in 1771, the Royal Exchange and Custom House is one of the most historically significant buildings of Colonial and Revolutionary America. The upper levels were designed to accommodate heavy export and import trade and as a place to conduct business, and the lower level held common prisoners, pirates and suspected rebels. In 1788, South Carolina delegates gathered in the building to ratify the U.S. Constitution. George Washington was a guest of honor here at a grand ball in 1791.
Daily 9 a.m.-5 p.m.

ST. PHILIP'S EPISCOPAL CHURCH

142 Church St., Charleston, 843-722-7734; www.stphilipschurchsc.org
Established in 1670, this is the oldest congregation in Charleston and the first Episcopal Church in the Carolinas. Today's building was completed in 1838. During the Civil War, its bells were removed and converted into cannons for the Confederacy. New bells were placed in the steeple on July 4, 1976.
Daily.

SPECIAL EVENTS
FALL HOUSE AND GARDEN CANDLELIGHT TOURS

147 King St., Charleston, 843-722-4630, 800-968-8175; www.preservationsociety.org
The annual Candlelight Tours of Homes and Gardens allows visitors a peek at some of the city's best residential architecture of the 18th, 19th and 20th centuries. Tours are self-paced and self-guided (although there are volunteer guides at each site).
Late September-late October.

FESTIVAL OF HOUSES AND GARDENS

40 E. Bay St., Charleston, 843-722-3405; www.historiccharleston.org
The welcome mats are out at 150-historic private homes in 11 colonial and antebellum neighborhoods during this annual festival. Also available are lectures, luncheons featuring low-country foods, afternoon teas, wine tastings and book signings. Early reservations are essential—most events sell out well in advance.
Mid-March-Mid-April.

SPOLETO FESTIVAL USA

Gaillard Municipal Auditorium, 77 Calhoun St., Charleston, 843-579-3100;
www.spoletousa.org
One of the best arts festivals in the country, Spoleto USA is a counterpart to the arts festival held in Spoleto, Italy, which was founded by composer Gian

Carlo Menotti. The Charleston festival offers opera, dance, chamber music, theater, symphonic music, jazz, solo voice, choral performance, visual arts and special events, including conversations with the artists—more than 120 offerings in total. Venues include the Gaillard Auditorium and historic Dock Street Theatre in Charleston, as well as less-conventional locales such as Middleton Place and Mepkin Abbey Monastery.
Late May-early June.

WHERE TO STAY

★★★ANCHORAGE INN
26 Vendue Range, Charleston, 843-723-8300, 800-421-2952;
www.anchoragencharleston.com
Afternoon tea, English toiletries and period furnishings make for a sophisticated stay at this inn in the downtown historic district.
19 rooms. Complimentary breakfast. Business center. $61-150

★BEST WESTERN KING CHARLES INN
237 Meeting St., Charleston, 843-723-7451, 866-546-4700; www.kingcharlesinn.com
91 rooms. Restaurant. Pool. Business center. Fitness center. $61-150

★BEST WESTERN SWEETGRASS INN
1540 Savannah Highway, Charleston, 843-571-6100, 800-937-8376;
www.bestwestern.com
87 rooms. Complimentary breakfast. Pool. Fitness center. Business center. $61-150

★★★★CHARLESTON PLACE
205 Meeting St., Charleston, 888-635-2350; www.charlestonplace.com
Located in Charleston's historic district, this hotel is within an easy stroll to antebellum mansions, luscious gardens and colonial markets. Guest rooms are traditional and attractively appointed with colonial furnishings. A fitness center, pool with retractable roof and shops such as Godiva and Gucci make this a perfect base for travelers who appreciate modern luxuries.
440 rooms. Restaurant, bar. Fitness center. Spa. Business center. $251-350

★★★CHARLESTON'S VENDUE INN
19 Vendue Range, Charleston, 843-577-7970, 800-845-7900; www.vendueinn.com
With its polished pine floors, Oriental rugs, period furniture and other historic accents, this romantic inn offers a memorable Charleston stay. Many of the individually decorated rooms overlook the Charleston Harbor and Waterfront Park.
65 rooms. Complimentary breakfast. Restaurant, bar. Fitness center. $61-150

★★★FRANCIS MARION HOTEL
387 King St., Charleston, 843-722-0600, 877-756-2121;
www.francismarioncharleston.com
Originally opened in 1924, this European-style hotel was named for an American Revolution war hero who evaded British troops by winding through

swampland. Rooms are cozy, but the hotel's amenities and its prompt, courteous service make for a comfortable stay.

230 rooms. Restaurant, bar. Spa. Fitness center. $151-250

★HAMPTON INN CHARLESTON-HISTORIC DISTRICT

345 Meeting St., Charleston, 843-723-4000, 888-759-4001; www.hamptoninn.com

171 rooms. Complimentary breakfast. $61-150

★★★HARBOUR VIEW INN

2 Vendue Range, Charleston, 843-853-8439, 888-853-8439;
www.harbourviewcharleston.com

Enjoy spectacular vistas of Charleston's East Harbor from this historic inn. Located near some of the city's best restaurants, rooms have four-poster beds, flat-screen TVs and plush beds with luxury bedding.

57 rooms. Business center. $151-250

★★★HILTON CHARLESTON HARBOR RESORT AND MARINA

20 Patriot's Point Road, Charleston, 843-856-0028, 888-856-01028;
www.charlestonharborresort.com

This luxurious resort sits on an 18-hole private championship golf course, private beach and 450-slip marina. Beautiful sunsets across the Charleston Harbor and historic skyline, with many antebellum buildings and churches, are visible from most rooms. Water sports from charter fishing to parasailing are available.

129 rooms. Restaurant, bar. Pool. $151-250

★THE INN AT MIDDLETON PLACE

4290 Ashley River Road, Charleston, 843-556-0500, 800-543-4774;
www.theinnatmiddletonplace.com

53 rooms. Complimentary breakfast. Restaurant, bar. Pool. $151-250

★★★MARKET PAVILION HOTEL

225 E. Bay St., Charleston, 843-723-0500, 877-440-2250; www.marketpavilion.com

Luxury meets Southern hospitality at this downtown Charleston hotel. Guest rooms feature cashmere blankets, four-poster beds, marble baths and fluffy bathrobes. As Charleston's only USDA Prime steakhouse, Grill 225, the hotel's signature restaurant, is a popular setting for lunch and dinner. Afterward, everyone heads upstairs to the rooftop bar for drinks.

66 rooms. Complimentary continental breakfast. Restaurant, bar. $251-350

★★★PLANTERS INN

112 N. Market St., Charleston, 843-722-2345, 800-845-7082; www.plantersinn.com

This delightful inn, located right on the Market, carefully blends historic references with modern amenities. The spacious rooms and suites feature period furnishings, whirlpool baths and fireplaces. The Inn's Peninsula Grill gets kudos from locals and guests alike for its artfully presented and palate-pleasing food.

64 rooms. Complimentary breakfast. Restaurant. $151-250

★★★RENAISSANCE CHARLESTON HOTEL HISTORIC DISTRICT

68 Wentworth St., Charleston, 843-534-0300; www.renaissancehotels.com

The Renaissance Charleston offers luxury in the middle of the city's historic district. Guest accommodations feature baths with granite vanities, beds with plush down comforters and fluffy pillows, plus extras like wireless Internet access and PlayStation. The hotel's signature restaurant, Wentworth Grill, serves fresh, seasonal Southern-influenced cuisine perfect for business meetings or a dinner.

166 rooms. Restaurant, bar. Pool. Spa. Fitness center. $151-250

★★★WENTWORTH MANSION

149 Wentworth St., Charleston, 843-853-1886, 888-466-1886;
www.wentworthmansion.com

Once a private home, this stunning mansion in the city's historic center has hand-carved marble fireplaces, ornate plasterwork and Tiffany stained-glass windows. Guest rooms offer gas fireplaces and charming views. The full European breakfast is served on the sun porch each morning, and the Rodgers Library is a great spot for evening drinks.

21 rooms. Complimentary breakfast. Restaurant. $251-350

ALSO RECOMMENDED
ANSONBOROUGH INN

21 Hasell St., Charleston, 843-723-1655, 800-522-2073; www.ansonboroughinn.com

37 rooms. Complimentary breakfast. Bar. $151-250

BARKSDALE HOUSE INN

27 George St., Charleston, 843-577-4800, 888-577-4980; www.barksdalehouse.com

Built as a town house in 1778 by wealthy Charlestonian George Barksdale, this stately bed and breakfast is filled with period furnishings and modern conveniences.

14 rooms. Children over 10 years only. Complimentary breakfast. $61-150

BATTERY CARRIAGE HOUSE INN

20 S. Battery, Charleston, 843-727-3100, 800-775-5575;
www.batterycarriagehouse.com

Hidden within the flowering gardens of the Steven-Lathers Mansion, an exquisite private home, this 1843 bed and breakfast offers private entrances, romantic décor and a view of Charleston Harbor.

11 rooms. Children over 12 years only. Complimentary breakfast. $61-150

THE GOVERNOR'S HOUSE INN

117 Broad St., Charleston, 843-720-2070, 800-720-9812; www.governorshouse.com

A National Landmark, this inn is the former home of Edward Rutledge, national statesman, patriot and youngest signer of the Declaration of Independence who later served as U.S. Senator and governor of South Carolina. Rooms and common areas are exquisitely detailed.

11 rooms. Bar. $251-350

INDIGO INN

1 Maiden Lane, Charleston, 843-577-5900, 800-845-7639; www.indigoinn.com

Housed in an 1850 warehouse once used to store indigo for dying textiles, this colorful inn is located in the middle of the historic district, just one block from City Market.

40 rooms. Complimentary breakfast. $61-150

JOHN RUTLEDGE HOUSE INN

116 Broad St., Charleston, 843-723-7999, 866-720-2609;
www.johnrutledgehouseinn.com

19 rooms. Complimentary breakfast. $151-250

KINGS COURTYARD INN

198 King St., Charleston, 843-723-7000, 866-720-2949; www.kingscourtyardinn.com

This three-story, antebellum, Greek Revival structure was built in 1854 and remains one of the gems of Charleston's historic district.

44 rooms. Complimentary breakfast. Restaurant, bar. $61-150

MAISON DU PRE

317 E. Bay St., Charleston, 843-723-8691, 800-844-4667; www.maisondupre.com

The main house dates to 1804. Located in historic downtown, adjacent to the Gaillard Auditorium, this inn is decorated in period furniture and art made by the family that runs it.

15 rooms. Complimentary continental breakfast. $61-150

MEETING STREET INN

173 Meeting St., Charleston, 843-723-1882, 800-842-8022; www.meetingstreetinn.com

Each room in this classic, single-house inn opens onto the piazza and court-yard. Rooms are individually decorated with period furniture.

56 rooms. Complimentary breakfast. Bar. $61-150

VICTORIA HOUSE INN

208 King St., Charleston, 843-720-2946, 866-720-2946; www.thevictoriahouseinn.com

Built in the late 1880s, this Romanesque-style Victorian house now serves as a lovely inn. Located in the downtown historic district, the inn offers ameni-ties such as a bedside champagne breakfast.

22 rooms. Complimentary breakfast. $61-150

WHERE TO EAT

★★82 QUEEN

82 Queen St., Charleston, 843-723-7591, 800-849-0082; www.82queen.com

Southern. Lunch, dinner, Sunday brunch. Bar. Children's menu. Reserva-tions recommended. Outdoor seating. $36-85

★★ANSON

12 Anson St., Charleston, 843-577-0551; www.ansonrestaurant.com

Southern. Dinner. Bar. Children's menu. Reservations recommended. $36-85

★★AW SHUCKS

70 State St., Charleston, 843-723-1151; www.a-w-shucks.com
American, seafood. Lunch, dinner. $36-85

★★BASIL

460 King St., Charleston, 843-724-3490;www.basilthairestaurant.com
Charlestonians consider Basil restaurant the finest place to get their Thai food fixes. They praise Basil's deep-fried duck and zesty pad thai. And we're not talking mere take-out Thai here. Basil serves up sophisticated Thai fare that stays true to its roots, thanks to chef Suntorn Cherdchoongarm, who insists on cooking everything from scratch and using freshly made sauces. At Basil, you'll find traditional curries, both green and red, along with savory chicken satay and spicy volcano shrimp. Don't forget to start off with the fresh Basil Roll, wrapped in light, soft rice paper and filled with crisp lettuce, bean sprouts, shrimp and of course, tender leaves of fragrant basil.
Thai. Lunch (Monday-Friday), dinner. $36-85

★★BLOSSOM CAFÉ

171 E. Bay St., Charleston, 843-722-9200; www.magnolias-blossom-cypress.com
Seafood. Lunch, dinner, Sunday brunch. Bar. Children's menu. Outdoor seating. $16-35

★★★CAROLINA'S

10 Exchange St., Charleston, 843-724-3800, 888-486-7673;
www.carolinasrestaurant.com
Located on a quiet, sleepy stretch of Exchange Street, Carolina's is the place to go for honest, straightforward low country cuisine. The restaurant is divided into three distinct dining areas: the romantic Sidewalk Room, the relaxed Bar Room and the Perditas Room, an homage to the restaurant that used to occupy this space. Perditas' famous Fruits de Mer dish is always on the menu, alongside standout items such as the jumbo lump crab cake and the pan-roasted lamb rack.
American. Lunch, dinner. Bar. Reservations recommended. C $36-85

★★★★CHARLESTON GRILL

224 King St., Charleston, 843-577-4522; www.charlestongrill.com
The Charleston Grill is a clubby spot located in the Charleston Place Hotel. Stained-glass French doors, dark wood-paneled walls and marble floors create a classy, old-world atmosphere. Rich dishes like shrimp and catfish hoecakes with fried oysters and tartar remoulade provide a hint of the kind of low country fare served at this sophisticated restaurant. Live jazz draws locals.
American. Dinner. Bar. Children's menu. Reservations recommended. Valet parking. Outdoor seating. $86 and up

★★★★CIRCA 1886

149 Wentworth St., Charleston, 843-853-7828; www.circa1886.com
Located behind the historic Wentworth Mansion, this restaurant offers classic Charleston charm. The 280-bottle wine list complements the local cuisine on the menu, which is created by talented chef Marc Collins using regional ingredients. Try the Carolina crabcake soufflé, a cheese course made from

Appalachian raw cow milk's cheese or the catfish with lobster and white cheddar grits. Desserts are traditional and rich, from gingerbread pudding with orange blossom honey ice cream to sweet potato butterscotch soufflé. The classic presentation of each dish adds an elegant flourish to the meal. The staff is also polished and friendly.

American. Dinner. Closed Sunday. Bar. Reservations recommended. $36-85

★★★CYPRESS: A LOWCOUNTRY GRILLE
167 E. Bay St., Charleston, 843-727-0111;www.magnolias-blossom-cypress.com

This restaurant offers a daring take on classic low-country food (traditionally defined by hearty dishes with plenty of rice, shrimp and unique seasonings). The wood-burning grill adds additional flavor to entrées like reconstruction lamb T-bone.

American. Dinner. Bar. Children's menu. Reservations recommended. $36-85

★★FULTON FIVE
5 Fulton St., Charleston, 843-853-5555

Italian. Dinner. Closed Sunday. Bar. Reservations recommended. Outdoor seating. $16-35

★★GAULART & MALICLET FRENCH CAFÉ
98 Broad St., Charleston, 843-577-9797; www.fastandfrench.org

French. Breakfast, lunch (Monday-Saturday), dinner (Tuesday-Saturday). Closed Sunday. $16-35

★★HANK'S SEAFOOD RESTAURANT
10 Hayne St., Charleston, 843-723-3474; www.hanksseafoodrestaurant.com

Seafood. Dinner. Bar. Children's menu. $16-35

★★★HIGH COTTON
199 E. Bay St., Charleston, 843-724-3815; www.high-cotton.net

"High cotton" is an old Southern saying that means living large. The menu at this casually elegant restaurant echoes that sentiment with boldly flavored dishes such as cornbread-crusted flounder with sweet pea and corn succotash, or bourbon-glazed pork with white cheddar jalapeno grits.

American. Lunch (Saturday), dinner, Sunday brunch. Bar. Children's menu. $16-35

★★HOMINY GRILL
207 Rutledge Ave., Charleston, 843-937-0930; www.hominygrill.com

Low country Southern. Breakfast, lunch, dinner, brunch. Outdoor seating. $16-35

★★LA FOURCHETTE
432 King St., Charleston, 843-722-6261; www.lafourchettecharleston.com

Totally French and utterly divine, this bistro on Upper King has locals pouring in for their signature pommes frites fried twice in duck fat. This method transforms ordinary hand-cut fries into perfectly delectable, crispy frites that are served with housemade mayonnaise for dipping. Cozy, dimly lit and convincingly Parisian, La Fourchette keeps it charmingly modest with a 40-seat dining room and a simple, authentically French menu. Start with a classic salade vert made of Boston lettuce to whet your appetite before the fries and finish off a steaming bowl of mussels cooked in white wine or the coquilles St. Jacques, a dish of rich chopped scallops in baked cream. C'est magnifique!

French. Dinner. $16-35

★★★MAGNOLIA'S

185 E. Bay St., Charleston, 843-577-7771; www.magnolias-blossom-cypress.com

This smart, uptown restaurant specializes in updated Southern food. Chef Donald Barickman uses Southern ingredients in mouth-watering combinations.

American. Lunch, dinner, Sunday brunch. Bar. $16-35

★★★MCCRADY'S

2 Unity Alley, Charleston, 843-577-0025; www.mccradysrestaurant.com

Housed in a beautifully restored building opened and operated as a tavern since 1778, this restaurant is the playground of young rising star chef Sean Brock. Brock's love for fresh, first-rate ingredients shines in dishes such as the spice-roasted rack of lamb with cauliflower, bok choy and huckleberries. The dessert menu features unusual combinations like peanut butter cake with popcorn ice cream and salted caramel.

International. Dinner. Bar. Reservations recommended. $36-85

★★★★PENINSULA GRILL

112 N. Market St., Charleston, 843-723-0700; www.peninsulagrill.com

Located in the Planter's Inn, this restaurant has the sophisticated feel of an urban eatery without losing sight of its Southern charm. The menu is inventive, offering boldly flavored dishes spiced up with low-country accents like collards, hushpuppies, grits and black-eyed peas. Chef Robert Carter's famous coconut layer cake is worth the splurge. There's also a champagne bar menu of decadent little treats like oysters, lobster, foie gras, caviar and duck pâté.

American. Dinner. Bar. Reservations recommended. Outdoor seating. $36-85

★★SERMET'S CORNER

276 King St., Charleston, 843-853-7775

Mediterranean. Lunch, dinner. Bar. Children's menu. $16-35

★★SLIGHTLY NORTH OF BROAD

192 E. Bay St., Charleston, 843-723-3424; www.slightlynorthofbroad.net

Low country. Lunch, dinner. Bar. Children's menu. $16-35

★★★SOCIAL WINE BAR

188 E. Bay St., Charleston, 843-577-5665; www.socialwinebar.com

Social Wine Bar's collection of wine extends beyond wine titans Napa Valley and Burgundy, France. Here, you'll find bottles from Spain and Italy to pinots from Oregon's Willamette Valley and syrahs from France's Cotes du Rhone. Why go to West Coast vineyards when they can come to you? Social Wine

Bar even offers a selection of choice sake, Japan's rice wine. With such a diz-zying array of wine to choose from, any vino lover in Charleston will have to make a stop at this popular venue that serves not only wine but also sophisti-cated, tapas-style small plates. Try the warm spinach salad with grilled pears or the rich, oxtail rillette napoleon from the "hot" menu to start.
American. Dinner, late-night. $36-85

CLEMSON
See also Greenville
Home of Clemson University, this community also hosts vacationers attract-ed to the huge lake formed by the Hartwell Dam on the Savannah River.

WHAT TO SEE
CLEMSON UNIVERSITY
109 Daniel Drive, Clemson, 864-656-3311; www.clemson.edu
Named for Thomas G. Clemson, son-in-law of John C. Calhoun, who be-queathed the bulk of his estate Fort Hill for establishment of a scientific col-lege. Clemson University was founded in 1889 and has 17,000 students.
Guided tours: Monday-Saturday 9:45 a.m. and 1:45 p.m., Sunday 1:45 p.m.

FORT HILL
Clemson University, Fort Hill Street and Calhoun Drive, Clemson, 864-656-2475;
www.clemson.edu
The 1803 mansion sits on 1,100 acres acquired by John C. Calhoun during his first term as vice president. The house has many original furnishings be-longing to Calhoun.
Daily.

HANOVER HOUSE
South Carolina Botanical Garden, Clemson University, 102 Garden Trail, 864-656-2475;
www.clemson.edu
This French Huguenot house was relocated here from its original site in Berkeley County to prevent submersion by Lake Moultrie.
Saturday-Sunday by appointment only.

SOUTH CAROLINA BOTANICAL GARDEN
150 Discovery Lane, Clemson, 864-656-3405; www.clemson.edu
This 250-acre area includes azalea and camelia trails, ornamental plantings, large collection of shrubs, dwarf conifer flower and turf display gardens and a wildflower garden labeled in Braille.
Daily.

WHERE TO STAY
★COMFORT INN
1305 Tiger Blvd., Clemson, 864-653-3600, 877-424-6423; www.comfortinn.com
122 rooms. Complimentary breakfast. Fitness center. Pool. $61-150

ALSO RECOMMENDED
SUNRISE FARM BED & BREAKFAST INN
325 Sunrise Drive, Salem, 864-944-0121, 888-991-0121;
www.bbonline.com/sc/sunrisefarm/
Eight rooms. Complimentary breakfast. Golf. $61-150

COLUMBIA
See also Camden, Orangeburg, Sumter
Located within three miles of the geographic center of the state, Columbia was laid out as the capital in a compromise between the contending up-country and low-country farmers. One of the nation's first planned cities, Columbia rarely departs from a checkerboard pattern. The streets are sometimes 150 feet wide, planned that way originally to discourage malaria.

The University of South Carolina, founded in 1801 as South Carolina College, is based here and is a leading influence in the city. Historical sites abound, as Columbia has a rich revolutionary and Civil War history. In 1865, General William T. Sherman's troops reduced Columbia to ashes, destroying 84 blocks and 1,386 buildings. Today, a city of stately buildings, a rejuvenated downtown and a thriving economy based on government, higher education and a mix of industries make South Carolina's biggest city a popular place to visit and a great town to live in.

WHAT TO SEE
COLUMBIA MUSEUM OF ART
Main and Hampton streets, Columbia, 803-799-2810; www.columbiamuseum.org
Galleries house Renaissance paintings, 19th- and 20th-century American, emphasizing Southeast and European paintings. There are concerts, films, lectures and special events accenting the exhibitions.
Wednesday-Thursday, Saturday 10 a.m.-5 p.m.; -Friday 10 a.m.-5 p.m. in December; Sunday 1-5 p.m.

CONFEDERATE RELIC ROOM AND MUSEUM
Columbia Mills Building, 301 Gervais St., Columbia, 803-737-8095; www.crr.sc.gov
This relic collection from the Colonial period through the space age gives special emphasis on South Carolina's Confederate period.
Tuesday-Saturday 10 a.m-5 p.m. First Sunday of the Month 1-5 p.m.

FIRST BAPTIST CHURCH
1306 Hampton St., Columbia, 803-256-4251; www.fbccola.com
The church is the site of the first Secession Convention, which marked the beginning of the Civil War, on December 17, 1860.
Monday-Friday, Sunday.

FIRST PRESBYTERIAN CHURCH
1324 Marion St., Columbia, 803-799-9062; www.firstprescolumbia.org
First congregation organized in Columbia took place here. President Woodrow Wilson's parents are buried in the churchyard.
Daily.

FORT JACKSON

Fort Jackson, 4394 Strom Thurmond Blvd., Columbia, 803-751-1742;
www.jackson.army.mil

Fort Jackson is the most active initial entry training center for the U.S. Army, with 16,000 soldiers assigned. The museum on Jackson Boulevard has displays on the history of the fort and today's army.

Monday-Friday 8:30 a.m.-4:30 p.m.

GOVERNOR'S MANSION

800 Richland St., Columbia, 803-737-1710; www.scgovernorsmansion.org

This impressive edifice was built in 1855 as the officers' quarters for Arsenal Academy. Tours run every half-hour.

Tuesday-Wednesday 10-11 a.m. Reservations required.

HAMPTON-PRESTON MANSION

1615 Blanding St., Columbia, 803-252-7742; www.historiccolumbia.org

Purchased by Wade Hampton I, the mansion was occupied by the Hamptons and the family of his daughter, Mrs. John Preston. In February 1865, the house served as headquarters for Union General J. A. Logan. Many Hampton surviving family furnishings and decorative arts are on display.

Tours on the hour. Tuesday-Sunday.

RIVERBANKS ZOO AND GARDEN

500 Wildlife Parkway, Columbia, 803-779-8717; www.riverbanks.org

Exhibits of animals in natural habitat areas will entice the whole family. The aquarium-reptile complex has diving demonstrations. Check the schedule for penguin and sea lion feeding times.

Daily 9 a.m.-5 p.m. April-September, Saturday-Sunday to 6 p.m.

ROBERT MILLS HISTORIC HOUSE AND PARK

1616 Blanding St., Columbia, 803-252-7442; www.historiccolumbia.org

One of a few residences designed by Robert Mills, Federal architect and designer of the Washington Monument, the house contains art and furnishings from the Regency period.

Tours on the hour. Tuesday-Saturday 10 a.m.-4 p.m., Sunday 1-5 p.m.

TRINITY CATHEDRAL

1100 Sumter St., Columbia, 803-771-7300; www.trinityepiscopalcathedral.org

A reproduction of Yorkminster, England, Trinity is the oldest church building in Columbia and one of the largest Episcopal congregations in the U.S. Hiram Powers baptismal font, box pews, English stained glass are highlights. Three Wade Hamptons (a politically prominent South Carolina family) are buried in the churchyard; graves of seven governors and six bishops are also here.

Daily.

UNIVERSITY OF SOUTH CAROLINA

McKissick Visitor Center, 816 Bull St., Columbia, 803-777-0169, 800-922-9755;
www.sc.edu/visitorcenter

USC is located downtown. For campus tour information, stop at the Univer-

sity of South Carolina Visitor Center.
Monday-Friday, select weekends.

WHERE TO STAY
★★EMBASSY SUITES HOTEL COLUMBIA-GREYSTONE
200 Stoneridge Drive, Columbia, 803-252-8700, 800-362-2779;
www.embassysuites.com
214 rooms. Complimentary breakfast. Restaurant, bar. Business center. Fitness center. $151-25-

★HAMPTON INN-DOWNTOWN HISTORIC DISTRICT
822 Gervais St., Columbia, 803-231-2000, 800-426-7866;
www.hamptoninncolumbia.com
122 rooms. Complimentary breakfast. Business center. Fitness center. Pool. $61-150

★★RAMADA COLUMBIA
7510 Two Notch Road, Columbia, 803-736-3000, 877-308-4986; www.ramada.com
251 rooms. Restaurant, bar. Fitness center. Pool. $61-150

WHERE TO EAT
★★HAMPTON STREET VINEYARD
1201 Hampton St., Columbia, 803-252-0850; www.hamptonstreetvineyard.com
American. Lunch, dinner. Closed Sunday. Bar. Reservations recommended. Outdoor seating. $36-85

★★HENNESSY'S
1649 Main St., Columbia, 803-799-8280; www.hennessyssc.com
American. Lunch, dinner. Closed Sunday. Bar. Reservations recommended. $16-35

★★★RISTORANTE DIVINO
803 Gervais St., Columbia, 803-799-4550; www.ristorantedivino.com
Ristorante Divino is located in Columbia's historic downtown district. The wine cellar features more than 3,000 bottles of wine and includes 400 varieties to complement the classic Italian dishes on the menu.
Northern Italian. Dinner. Closed Sunday. Bar. Reservations recommended. $36-85

DARLINGTON
See also Florence
Any true fan of stock car racing knows Darlington. It is the state's stock car racing center and home to the Stock Car Hall of Fame as well as what is said to be the nation's largest automobile auction market.

WHAT TO SEE
DARLINGTON RACEWAY
1301 Harry Byrd Highway, Darlington, 866-459-7223; www.darlingtonraceway.com
Remembered as the original "Super Speedway," the track first opened in

1950 and is famous for its unique egg shape. Hundreds of miles raced, millions of fans and numerous legends have left their mark here. Major races in May; check for ongoing events and racing schools on Web site.
Monday-Friday 9 a.m.-5 p.m.

JOE WEATHERLY STOCK CAR MUSEUM AND NATIONAL MOTORSPORTS PRESS ASSOCIATION STOCK CAR HALL OF FAME

1301 Harry Byrd Highway, Darlington, 843-395-8499; www.darlingtonraceway.com

Darlington Raceway, the oldest super-speedway in the country, also houses the sport's hall of fame. The museum details NASCAR's storied Darlington history and features everyone from NASCAR's first champion, Red Byron, to David Pearson and Dale Earnhardt. Several rooms are filled with stock cars that once sped across the raceway, including the blue Plymouth that Richard Petty drove to victory in 10 races back in 1967.
Daily 9 a.m.-5 p.m.

FLORENCE

See also Darlington

This community has grown from a sparsely settled crossroads into a major retail and wholesale distribution center. The economy is no longer dependent on agriculture. Florence is also the home of Francis Marion College and Florence-Darlington Technical College.

WHAT TO SEE
FLORENCE STOCKADE

Stockade and National Cemetery roads, Florence

The stockade was a Civil War prison that housed Union soldiers transferred from the notorious Andersonville prison. Roughly 2,800 soldiers died there, including Florena Budwin, whom Friends of the Florence Stockade say is the only female Civil War prisoner to die in captivity. The site is a Civil War Heritage Site.
Daily.

WAR BETWEEN THE STATES MUSEUM

107 S. Guerry St., Florence, 843-669-1266; www.florenceweb.com/warmuseum.htm

Explore artifacts, pictures and stories from the Civil War.
Wednesday, Saturday 10 a.m.-5 p.m.

WHERE TO STAY
★★★ABINGDON MANOR

307 Church St., Latta, 843-752-5090, 888-752-5090; www.abingdonmanor.com

This opulent Greek Revival building is listed on the National Register of Historic Places. The grand entry hall and luxurious guest rooms are only part of the charm. An excellent restaurant, full breakfast and nightly cocktails make this hotel a true luxury.
Seven rooms. Children over 10 years only. Complimentary breakfast. Restaurant, bar. $151-250

WHERE TO EAT
★★★ABINGDON MANOR RESTAURANT

307 Church St., Latta, 843-752-5090, 888-752-5090; www.abingdonmanor.com

This elegant restaurant, located inside a charming inn of the same name, offers a creative menu of American fare using fresh ingredients from the onsite garden.

American. Dinner. Closed Sunday. Bar. Reservations recommended. $36-85

GAFFNEY

See also Rock Hill

On I-85, just outside of town, stands the Gaffney Peachoid, an elevated tank that resembles a gigantic peach and holds a million-gallon water supply. Gaffney is home to textile and metal working centers and is also a center for agriculture, particularly peaches.

WHAT TO SEE
COWPENS NATIONAL BATTLEFIELD

4001 Chesnee Highway, Gaffney, 864-461-2828; www.nps.gov/cowp

This was the scene of the victory of General Daniel Morgan's American Army over superior British forces on January 17, 1781. The battle wounded the British Army substantially enough to help set the stage for Cornwallis' surrender. It features an 843-acre tract with exhibits, an information and visitor center, a self-guided tour road and a walking trail with audio stations and a restored 1830 historic house.

Daily 9 a.m.-5 p.m.

PRIME OUTLETS GAFFNEY

1 Factory Shops Blvd., Gaffney, 864-902-9900, 888-545-7194; www.primeoutlets.com

This open-air, village-style manufacturers' outlet features 65 outlet shops. Daily.

SPECIAL EVENT
SOUTH CAROLINA PEACH FESTIVAL

225 S. Limestone St., Gaffney, 864-489-5716; www.scpeachfestival.org

Enjoy arts and crafts, sports events and entertainment at this annual festival. July.

GEORGETOWN

See also Myrtle Beach

Georgetown sits on the shore of Winyah Bay, the site of the first European settlement on the North American mainland outside of Mexico. In 1526, a group of Spaniards settled here, only to be driven out within a year by disease and Native American attacks. Rice and indigo plantations were established along nearby rivers around 1700, helping Georgetown thrive as a seaport. Known as a sawmill city during the first three decades of this century, Georgetown currently boasts several manufacturing industries as well as a booming tourist industry anchored by its historic plantations, gardens and beaches.

WHAT TO SEE
HAMPTON PLANTATION STATE PARK
1950 Rutledge Road, McClellanville, 843-546-9361; www.discoversouthcarolina.com
This restored 18th-century mansion was the center of a large rice plantation. Guided tours go on the hour.
Grounds: Memorial Day-Labor Day, daily 9 a.m-6 p.m.; rest of the year, Thursday-Monday 9 a.m.-6 p.m.; mansion: Memorial Day-Labor Day, daily 11 a.m.-4 p.m.; rest of the year, Thursday-Monday 1-4 p.m.

HOPSEWEE PLANTATION
494 Hopsewee Road, Georgetown, 803-546-7891; www.hopsewee.com
This preserved 1740 rice plantation house on the North Santee River marks the birthplace of Thomas Lynch Jr., a signer of the Declaration of Independence.
March-October, Monday-Friday 10 a.m.-4 p.m.; rest of year, Thursday-Friday 10 a.m.-4 p.m.; and by appointment.

PRINCE GEORGE WINYAH CHURCH
708 Broad St., Georgetown, 843-546-4358; www.pgwinyah.org
The English stained-glass window behind the altar was originally a part of St. Mary's Chapel for Negroes at Hagley Plantation on Waccamaw. The church has been in continuous use since it was constructed, except during the American Revolution and the Civil War.
Memorial Day-October, Monday-Friday 11:30 a.m.-4:30 p.m.

TOWN CLOCK BUILDING
633 Front St., Georgetown
Tablet marks the landing of Lafayette at North Island in 1777. Federal troops came ashore on the dock at the rear of the building in an attempt to capture the town.

WHERE TO STAY
★CAROLINIAN INN
706 Church St., Georgetown, 843-546-5191, 800-722-4667; www.carolinianinn.com
89 rooms. Complimentary breakfast. $61-150

WHERE TO EAT
★★RICE PADDY
732 Front St., Georgetown, 843-546-2021; www.ricepaddyrestaurant.com
American. Lunch, dinner. Closed Sunday. Bar. Children's menu. $16-35

★★RIVER ROOM
801 Front St., Georgetown, 843-527-4110; www.riverroomgeorgetown.com
Seafood. Lunch, dinner. Closed Sunday. Bar. Children's menu. $16-35

GREENVILLE
See also Clemson
Best known for its textile industry, Greenville has several hundred manu-

facturing plants producing clothing, nylon, chemicals, plastic film and machinery. Beautiful trees line the streets and there are many forested parks in the area. The Reedy River, passing over falls in the heart of Greenville, originally provided the city's power. Pleasant streets now border the twisting Sylvan Stream. Furman University, a small liberal arts college, is located in Greenville.

WHAT TO SEE
CAESARS HEAD STATE PARK
8155 Geer Highway, Cleveland, 864-836-6115; www.southcarolinaparks.com
Hiking trails abound in approximately 7,000 acres overlooking a valley of almost impenetrable brush and dense forest. One side of the mountain resembles Caesar's head.
Daily.

GREENVILLE COUNTY MUSEUM
420 College St., Greenville, 864-271-7570; www.greenvillemuseum.org
This permanent collection of American art features historical and contemporary works. Rotating exhibits include painting, sculpture and photography.
Tuesday-Sunday.

GREENVILLE ZOO
150 Cleveland Park Drive, Greenville, 864-467-4300; www.greenvillezoo.com
Wildlife from around the world is on display in natural, open-air exhibits. There are also lighted tennis courts, nature, jogging, hiking and bicycle trails, and a park.
Daily. Children under 13 years must be accompanied by an adult.

TABLE ROCK STATE PARK
158 E. Ellison Lane, Pickens, 864-878-9813; www.southcarolinaparks.com
Approximately 3,000 acres, the park extends over Table Rock Mountain (elevation 3,124 feet) and valleys. Enjoy lake swimming; fishing; boating; canoeing (rentals), as well as hiking trail and carpet golf.
Daily 7 a.m.-9 p.m.

WHERE TO STAY
★★COURTYARD GREENVILLE HAYWORD MALL
70 Orchard Park Drive, Greenville, 864-234-0300, 800-321-2211;www.courtyard.com
146 rooms. Restaurant. $61-150

★DAYS INN
60 Roper Mountain Road, Greenville, 864-297-9996, 800-329-7466; www.daysinn.com
121 rooms. Complimentary breakfast. $61-150

★★EMBASSY SUITES HOTEL GREENVILLE GOLF RESORT AND CONFERENCE CENTER
670 Verdae Blvd., Greenville, 864-676-9090, 800-362-2779; www.embassysuites.com
268 rooms. Complimentary breakfast. Restaurant, bar. Golf, 18 holes. Business center. $61-150

★★★GREENVILLE MARRIOTT

1 Parkway East, Greenville, 864-297-0300, 800-833-2221; www.marriott.com

This Marriott has a contemporary theme with marble floors and leather chairs in the lobby and yellow-striped wall coverings and light wood furniture in guest rooms.

204 rooms. Restaurant, bar. Spa. $151-250

★HAMPTON INN

246 Congaree Road, Greenville, 864-288-1200, 800-426-7866; www.hamptoninn.com

123 rooms. Complimentary breakfast. $61-150

★★★HILTON GREENVILLE

45 W. Orchard Park Drive, Greenville, 864-232-4747, 800-445-8667; www.hilton.com

This modern hotel, located on Greenville's suburban East side, has been updated with comfortable beds with luxury bedding and instated a new smoke-free policy. Upscale touches in rooms include Cuisinart coffeemakers with Lavazza coffee, alarm clocks with CD players and MP3 hookups and Crabtree & Evelyn bath products.

256 rooms. Restaurant, bar. $151-250

★★★HYATT REGENCY GREENVILLE

220 N. Main St., Greenville, 864-235-1234, 800-233-1234; www.hyatt.com

Nestled in the heart of downtown Greenville, this Hyatt property is within walking distance of the Bi-Lo Center. Also nearby are the Peace Center for the Performing Arts and Furman University. Spacious rooms feature desks and other amenities designed for business travelers.

328 rooms. Restaurant, bar. $151-250

★★★THE WESTIN POINSETT

120 Main St., Greenville, 864-421-9700, 800-937-8461; www.westin.com

This historic hotel, built in 1925, is located among many of Greenville's boutique shops and dining spots and is near Furman University. The lobby features plaster ceilings, crystal chandeliers and terrazzo floors. Guest rooms are decorated in warm beige hues and feature the chain's signature Heavenly beds.

200 rooms. Restaurant, bar. $151-250

WHERE TO EAT
★★★STAX'S PEPPERMILL

30 Orchard Park Drive, Greenville, 864-288-9320; www.staxs.com

This contemporary restaurant features a wine room, an enclosed porch with window views, and a lounge with inviting soft sofas and plush booths. Features a continental menu with steak and seafood options, as well as sushi. International. Dinner. Closed Sunday. Bar. Reservations recommended. $36-85

GREENWOOD

Located at the junction of highways and railways, Greenwood was originally the plantation of Green Wood. The city later became known as the community of Woodville before adopting its present name. Greenwood's Main

Street is one of the widest (316 feet) in the nation. The area has historic sites related to the Revolutionary War, but the city is best known for its sports and recreation. Rolling hills, year-round temperate climate and lots of undeveloped wooded land have made this a haven for golfers.

WHAT TO SEE
BAKER CREEK STATE PARK
863 Baker Creek Road, McCormick, 864-443-2457; www.discoversouthcarolina.com
This state park occupies approximately 1,300 acres and is ideal for lake swimming, boating and fishing. There are also multiple bridle trails.
Daily 6 a.m.-6 p.m.

NINETY SIX NATIONAL HISTORIC SITE
1103 Highway 248 S., Ninety Six, 864-543-4068; www.nps.gov/nisi
Site of old Ninety Six, an early village in South Carolina backcountry, so named because it is 96 miles away from the Cherokee Village of Keowee on the Cherokee Path. The South's first land battle of the American Revolution in 1775 and the 28-day siege of Ninety Six in 1781 occurred here. The earthworks of the British-built Star Fort remain, along with reconstructed siege works and other fortifications of the period. Also here are subsurface remains of two village complexes, a trading post-plantation complex and a network of 18th-century roads.
Daily 8 a.m.-5 p.m.

HARDEEVILLE
See also Beaufort, Hilton Head
This small low country town is located 15 miles from Savannah and Hilton Head and 20 miles from historic Beaufort. The Savannah River runs through Hardeeville, providing a scenic spot for fishing and angling.

WHAT TO SEE
SAVANNAH NATIONAL WILDLIFE REFUGE
1000 Business Center Drive, Hardeeville, 912-652-4415; www.fws.gov/savannah
More than half of the 25,6000 acres consists of bottomland hardwoods reminiscent of the great cypress and tupelo swamps that once extended along the Carolina and Georgia low country. Argent Swamp can only be reached by boat; wild azaleas, iris, spider lilies and other flowers bloom in succession, beginning in spring. Laurel Hill Wildlife Drive is open to cars and allows viewing of wildlife, especially waterfowl from December to February. Migrating songbirds are abundant in spring and fall. The Tupelo-Swamp Walk (mid-March-September) is best for bird-watchers and photographers.
Daily.

HILTON HEAD
See also Beaufort, Hardeeville
This year-round resort island attracts all travelers from families who want an easy, kid-friendly atmosphere to high-end vacationers. Hilton Head, reached by a bridge on Highway 278, is bordered by one of the few remaining unpolluted marine estuaries on the East Coast and is the largest sea island between

New Jersey and Florida. The island has 12 miles of beaches, numerous golf courses and tennis courts, swimming, miles of bicycle paths, horseback riding, four nature preserves and deep-sea, sound and dockside fishing. There are also nine marinas and a paved 3,700-foot airstrip, 3,000 hotel and motel rooms, more than 200 restaurants and 28 shopping centers, plus many art galleries and numerous sporting and cultural events.

WHAT TO SEE
DAUFUSKIE ISLAND RESORT GOLF
421 Squire Pope Road, Hilton Head, 843-341-4810, 800-648-6778;
www.daufuskieresort.com
Rates for both resort guests and day players are relatively low for the two 18-hole courses on the property (the Melrose, designed by Jack Nicklaus, and the Bloody Point, designed by Tom Weiskopf and Jay Morrish), both of which offer challenging holes and great views of the Atlantic Ocean.

HARBOUR TOWN GOLF LINKS
Sea Pines Resort, 32 Greenwood Drive, Hilton Head Island, 888-807-6873;
www.seapines.com
Pete Dye designed the courses, featuring the designer's signature red-and-white-striped lighthouse, which serves as a backdrop for the course's 18th hole. The par-71 layout is less than 7,000 yards from the back tees, but the fairways can be narrow and the greens small. Two other courses at the resort, Ocean and Sea Pines, add 36 more holes to the offerings.

WHERE TO STAY
★★★CROWNE PLAZA
130 Shipyard Drive, Hilton Head Island, 843-842-2400, 800-334-1881;
www.cphiltonhead.com
Located in Shipyard Plantation, this 11-acre resort is a paradise for golfers and tennis players. The beachfront location is set on miles of sandy oceanfront great for trying sailboats, boogie boards and beach trikes.
340 rooms. Restaurant, bar. Children's activity center. Beach. $151-250

★★★DAUFUSKIE ISLAND RESORT AND BREATHE SPA
421 Squire Pope Road, Hilton Head Island, 843-341-4820, 800-648-6778;
www.daufuskieresort.com
The full-service resort, which has vacation cottages and villas, offers a range of activities from 36 holes of golf to horseback riding, croquet and tennis.
192 rooms. Restaurant, bar. Children's activity center. Spa. Beach. Pool.
$151-250

★HAMPTON INN
1 Dillon Road, Hilton Head Island, 843-681-7900, 800-426-7866; www.hamptoninn.com
115 rooms. Complimentary breakfast. $61-150

★★★HILTON HEAD MARRIOTT BEACH AND GOLF RESORT
1 Hotel Circle at Palmetto Dunes, Hilton Head Island, 843-686-8400, 800-228-9290;
www.hiltonheadmarriott.com
This beachfront Marriott is located at Palmetto Dunes, within walking dis-

tance of the Shelter Cove Marina shops and attractions. Nicely appointed rooms plus beach access and several pools provide reasons to stay within the resort's walls.

513 rooms. Restaurant, bar. Pool. Beach. $61-150

★★★HILTON OCEANFRONT RESORT HILTON HEAD ISLAND
23 Ocean Lane, Hilton Head Island, 843-842-8000, 800-845-8001;
www.hiltonheadhilton.com

Enjoy the widest beach on the island at this luxe, self-contained resort. Manicured gardens and lagoons adorn the property.

324 rooms. Restaurant, bar. Beach. Pool. $251-350

★★★★THE INN AT HARBOUR TOWN
32 Greenwood Drive, Hilton Head Island, 866-561-8802; www.seapines.com

With 5,000 acres of pristine coastal expanse at your disposal, there's little reason to stay inside. That is, until you enter the understated elegance of the Inn at Harbour Town at The Sea Pines Resort. This boutique-style inn mixes southern sophistication—a personal butler to cater to your every whim—with casual charm to ensure a restful and pleasure-packed stay. The tastefully decorated guest rooms are surprisingly spacious with in-room refrigerators, work desks and balconies overlooking the racquet club or sprawling golf course. Active sorts can fill their day with a tennis match on one of the 23 courts or a bike ride over more than 15 miles of paved trails (bike rentals are complimentary). Getting off the plantation is equally sweet with the historic Harbour Town lighthouse and numerous independent boutiques and restaurants only a short walk from the inn. Don't be surprised if the staff remembers your name throughout your visit; it's simply considered good old southern hospitality here.

60 rooms. Restaurant, bar. Fitness center. Pool. Tennis. Golf. Business center. $151-250

★★★★THE INN AT PALMETTO BLUFF
476 Mount Pilla Road, Bluffton, 843-706-6500, 866-706-6565;
www.palmettobluffresort.com

This low country inn, a sister to California's famed Auberge du Soleil, delivers luxury accommodations, fine dining and pure relaxation in a riverfront setting. Rooms offer plenty of luxury touches such as plasma televisions, wet bars with Sub-Zero refrigerators and deep soaking tubs. Enjoy the Jack Nicklaus-designed golf course or full-service spa. The River House restaurant serves Southern-influenced recipes such as she-crab bisque laced with aged sherry and cast-iron fried quail with bacon, eggs, arugula and warm ricotta pudding.

50 rooms. Restaurant, bar. $351 and up

★★★MAIN STREET INN
2200 Main St., Hilton Head Island, 843-681-3001, 800-471-3001;
www.mainstreetinn.com

The Main Street Inn is a beacon of sophistication. The 32 rooms are individually designed, yet all feature luxurious velvet and silk linens, unique artwork

and distinctive furnishings. Afternoon tea is a daily tradition.
33 rooms. Children over 12 years only. Complimentary breakfast. $61-150

★★QUALITY INN & SUITES
200 Museum St., Hilton Head Island, 843-681-3655, 800-784-1180; www.qualityinn.com
127 rooms. Restaurant, bar. $61-150

★★★THE WESTIN RESORT, HILTON HEAD ISLAND
2A Grasslawn Ave., Hilton Head Island, 843-681-4000; www.westin.com/hiltonhead
This self-contained beachfront resort is a standout with its roster of leisure activities from golf, tennis and swimming to a fully stocked Reebok gym with yoga, Pilates and fitness machines. Rooms have plush beds with fluffy duvets, soaking tubs and balconies.
412 rooms. Restaurant, bar. Children's activity center. Spa. Pool. Beach. $151-250

WHERE TO EAT
★★ALEXANDER'S
76 Queens Folly Road, Hilton Head Island, 843-785-4999; www.alexandersrestaurant.com
American, seafood. Dinner. Bar. Children's menu. $16-35

★AUNT CHILADAS EASY STREET CAFÉ
69 Pope Ave., Hilton Head, 843-785-7700; www.auntchiladashhi.com
Mexican, seafood, steak. Lunch, dinner, late-night, brunch. Bar. Children's menu. $15 and under

★★CHARLIE'S L'ETOILE VERTE
8 New Orleans Road, Hilton Head Island, 843-785-9277; www.charliesofhiltonhead.com
French. Lunch Tuesday-Saturday, dinner. Closed Sunday. Bar. Reservations recommended. $16-35

★★★HARBOURMASTER'S OCEAN GRILL
1 Shelter Cove Lane, Hilton Head Island, 843-785-3030; www.oceangrillrestaurant.com
Located on the waterway entrance to Shelter Cove Harbour, this restaurant offers creative and sumptuous seafood cuisine, along with exceptional service, unmatched ambience and dramatic views.
Seafood. Dinner. Closed January. Bar. Children's menu. Reservations recommended. Outdoor seating. $36-85

★★LITTLE VENICE
2 Shelter Cove Lane, Hilton Head Island, 843-785-3300
Italian. Dinner. Bar. Reservations recommended. Outdoor seating. $16-35

★★OLD OYSTER FACTORY
101 Marshland Road, Hilton Head Island, 843-681-6040; www.oldoysterfactory.com
Seafood. Dinner. Bar. Children's menu. Outdoor seating. $16-35

★★PRESTO KITCHEN

45 Pembroke Drive, Hilton Head Island, 843-342-2400

International. Dinner. Closed Sunday-Monday. Bar. Reservations recommended. $36-85

★★★RED FISH

8 Archer Road, Hilton Head Island, 843-686-3388; www.redfishofhiltonhead.com

Red Fish offers a menu of unique Caribbean dishes made with creatively blended house-made seasonings, vegetables and tropical fruits. Grilled grouper, Latin ribs and crispy Ashley Farms free-range brick chicken are among many enticing menu choices. An extensive wine list has more than 1,000 bottles. Warm, terra-cotta walls accented with framed pictures and dark wood chairs set around white-clothed tables add to the casual atmosphere. Caribbean. Lunch, dinner. Bar. Children's menu. Reservations recommended. Outdoor seating. $16-35

★SCOTT'S FISH MARKET

1 Shelter Cove Lane, Hilton Head Island, 843-785-7575

Seafood. Dinner. Closed January. Bar. Children's menu. Outdoor seating. $16-35

★STEAMERS SEAFOOD COMPANY

28 Coligny Plaza, Hilton Head, 843-785-2070; www.steamerseafood.com

Seafood. Lunch, dinner. Bar. Children's menu. Outdoor seating. $16-35

SPA

★★★★SPA AT PALMETTO BLUFF

476 Mount Pilla Road, Bluffton, 843-706-6500, 866-706-6565;

www.palmettobluffresort.com

Plantation shutters, willowing white drapery and the surrounding verdant countryside heighten the serenity of true Southern hospitality. Treatments for golfers include the Masters (hydrating massage and facial for sun-damaged skin) and the 20th Hole (private steam and sports massage). Everyone— not just golfers—will de-stress with treatments such as the Aromatherapy massage, which uses a personalized mix of flower-, herb- and root-based essential oils.

ISLE OF PALMS

This coastal barrier island just north of Charleston and only 20 minutes from downtown was originally home to the Seewee tribe of Native Americans. It's now a popular resort destination.

WHERE TO STAY

★★★BOARDWALK INN AT WILD DUNES RESORT

5757 Palm Blvd., Isle of Palms, 843-886-6000, 888-778-1876; www.wilddunes.com

Beachy elegance defines the atmosphere at this resort. The property includes two 18-hole Tom Fazio-designed golf courses, a 17-court tennis center, a marina and a fitness center. The Sea Island Grill specializes in Low Country cooking.

93 rooms. Restaurant, bar. Children's activity center. $151-250

WHERE TO EAT
★★THE BOATHOUSE RESTAURANT
101 Palm Blvd., Isle of Palms, 843-886-8000; www.boathouserestaurants.com
Seafood. Dinner, Sunday brunch. Bar. Children's menu. Outdoor seating.
$36-85

KIAWAH ISLAND
See also Beaufort, Charleston
Kiawah Island is one of the richest natural environments on the eastern sea-
board. Named for the Native Americans who once hunted and fished here,
the island is separated from the mainland by the Kiawah River and a mile-
wide salt marsh. Separate resort areas and private residential neighborhoods
ensure a minimum of automobile traffic and leave much of the island untouched. The Kiawah Island Resort offers activities such as golf, tennis and
nature programs that take advantage of the island's natural beauty.

WHERE TO STAY
★★★★★THE SANCTUARY AT KIAWAH ISLAND
1 Sanctuary Beach Drive, Kiawah Island, 843-768-6000, 877-683-1234;
www.thesanctuary.com
With five championship courses just outside its door, the Sanctuary hotel at
Kiawah Island is a natural choice for golfers. This elegant resort also offers
fine dining, a first-class spa and a beautiful setting. Rooms blend traditional
early-American furnishings with a crisp coastal ambience and offer ocean
views. Service is spectacular, with a friendly staff attending to every need.
255 rooms. Restaurant, bar. Spa. Beach. Pool. $351 and up

WHERE TO EAT
★★★★THE OCEAN ROOM
1 Sanctuary Beach Drive, Kiawah Island, 843-768-6253, 877-683-1234;
www.thesanctuary.com
Plates sparkle at this fine-dining steakhouse with starters such as lobster
bisque and foie gras torchon with brioche French toast; and entrees such as a
14-ounce rib eye; and Scottish salmon with baby spinach, baby potatoes, and
house-cured pancetta. Or enjoy a five-course tasting menu with wine pairings. If you're feeling especially indulgent, order a side of the black truffle
pommes frites (you won't be disappointed).
Seafood. Dinner. Bar. Jacket recommended. Reservations recommended.
$36-85

SPAS
★★★★★SPA AT THE SANCTUARY
1 Sanctuary Beach Drive, Kiawah Island, 843-768-6340; www.thesanctuary.com
Located inside the Sanctuary at Kiawah Island, the Spa resembles a grand
Southern seaside mansion. Inside, the hospitable staff greets guests with
herbal tea and fresh fruit before leading the way to one of 12 rooms for na-
ture-based treatments, which feature botanical extracts, natural enzymes and
a signature Southern touch. If exercise is on your mind, head downstairs to
the fitness center, which features latest cardiovascular and resistance equipment, a 65-foot-long indoor pool and Pilates and yoga studios.

MOUNT PLEASANT

See also Charleston

Founded 1680, Mount Pleasant is now part of suburban Charleston, and its main point of interest is the U.S.S. Yorktown.

WHAT TO SEE
PATRIOTS POINT NAVAL AND MARITIME MUSEUM

40 Patriots Point Road, Mount Pleasant, 843-884-2727; www.patriotspoint.org

This is an amazing assemblage of naval equipment and lore, appropriately located in Charleston Harbor. The star is the famed World War II aircraft carrier, the *U.S.S. Yorktown*. Onboard the *Yorktown* are numerous displays, including the Congressional Medal of Honor Society's museum and head-quarters, the World War II Fast Carrier exhibit, the Battle of Midway Torpedo Squadrons memorial and a World War II cruiser room. Other vessels include the *Savannah*, the world's first nuclear-powered merchant ship; the *Laffey*, a World War II destroyer; the *Clamagore*, a World War II submarine; and the *Ingham*, a Coast Guard cutter.

April-September 9 a.m.-7:30 p.m.; October-March 9 a.m.-6:30 p.m.

WHERE TO EAT
★THE WRECK

106 Haddrell St., Mount Pleasant, 843-884-0052; www.wreckrc.com

Seafood. Dinner. Outdoor seating. Closed Sunday. No credit cards accepted. $15 and under

MURRELLS INLET

See also Myrtle Beach

Located just 10 miles south of Myrtle Beach, Murrells Inlet calls itself the seafood capital of South Carolina. Besides restaurants, there is a beautiful stretch of beach in the area known as the Grand Strand with amazingly well-preserved marshland and coastline.

WHAT TO SEE
BROOKGREEN GARDENS

1931 Brookgreen Drive, Murrells Inlet, 843-235-6000, 800-849-1931; www.brookgreen. org

On the site of former rice and indigo plantations, these gardens contain more than 500 pieces of American sculpture, boxwood, massive moss-hung oaks and native plants, as well as a wildlife park with native animals. Creek and all-terrain vehicle excursions take visitors through forests, creeks, old planta-tion homes and rice fields.

Daily 9:30 a.m.-5 p.m.; until 9 p.m. Wednesday-Friday in summer; closed Monday in December.

HUNTINGTON BEACH STATE PARK

16148 Ocean Highway, Georgetown, 803-237-4440; www.southcarolinaparks.com

The marsh boardwalk lets you get close to nature in this 2,500 acre parkland. There is fishing and surfing, along with numerous hiking trails. Daily.

SPECIAL EVENTS
ANNUAL ATALAYA ARTS AND CRAFTS FESTIVAL, HUNTINGTON BEACH STATE PARK

16148 Ocean Highway, Murrells Inlet, 843-237-4440; www.atalayafestival.com

This juried art show has been running annually for more than three decades. Fine art, quality crafts and low country food, along with live music. Mid-late September.

WHERE TO EAT
★★CAPTAIN DAVE'S DOCKSIDE

4037A Highway 17 Business, Murrells Inlet, 843-651-5850; www.captdavesdockside.com

Seafood. Lunch, dinner. Bar. Children's menu. Reservations recommended. Outdoor seating. $16-35

★★HOT FISH CLUB

4911 Highway 17 Business, Murrells Inlet, 843-357-9175; www.hotfishclub.com

American. Dinner. Closed Monday-Tuesday. $16-35

MYRTLE BEACH

See also Georgetown

With the warm Gulf Stream only a few miles offshore and dunes to shelter the miles of white sand, Myrtle Beach is one of the most popular seaside resorts on the Atlantic Coast. Named for the many myrtle trees in the area it lures millions of vacationers each summer with swimming, fishing, golf, tennis and its boardwalk.

WHAT TO SEE
BAREFOOT LANDING

4898 Highway 17 S., Myrtle Beach, 843-272-8349, 800-272-2320; www.bflanding.com

With a mixture of specialty shops and factory stores, Barefoot Landing appeals to a variety of shoppers. There are also more than a dozen eateries and a variety of entertainment options, including the House of Blues and a video arcade.

Daily, hours vary by season.

BAREFOOT RESORT

4980 Barefoot Resort Bridge Road, North Myrtle Beach, 843-390-3200, 800-320-6536; www.barefootgolf.com

Maybe the best place in Myrtle Beach to play golf, Barefoot Resort features four courses designed by some of the sport's biggest names—Davis Love III, Tom Fazio, Greg Norman and Pete Dye all took a piece of the land and crafted courses.

BROADWAY AT THE BEACH

1325 Celebrity Circle, Myrtle Beach, 843-444-3200, 800-386-4662; www.broadwayatthebeach.com

This 350-acre complex, billed as the largest venue of its kind in South Carolina, features a wide variety of shops, dining and nightclubs. Also onsite are a 16-screen movie theater, an IMAX theater, a NASCAR SpeedPark, a miniature golf course, a water park and an aquarium. Broadway at the Beach is also home to the Myrtle Beach Pelicans, a Class A affiliate of the Atlanta Braves.

Daily.

WHERE TO STAY

★★BEACH COVE RESORT

4800 S. Ocean Blvd., North Myrtle Beach, 843-918-9000, 800-369-7043;
www.beachcove.com

330 rooms. Restaurant, bar. Children's activity center. Beach. Pool. $61-150

★★COMPASS COVE OCEANFRONT RESORT

2311 S. Ocean Blvd., Myrtle Beach, 843-448-8373, 800-331-0934;
www.compasscove.com

532 rooms. Restaurant, bar. Children's activity center. Beach. Pool. $151-250

★★COURTYARD MYRTLE BEACH BAREFOOT LANDING

1000 Commons Blvd., Myrtle Beach, 843-361-1730, 877-502-4653;
www.courtyard.com

157 rooms. Restaurant. Pool. $61-150

★★★THE CYPRESS INN

16 Elm St., Conway, 843-248-8199, 800-575-5307;www.acypressinn.com

This 12-room bed and breakfast in the quiet town of Conway is located alongside a quaint marina. Go deep-sea fishing or simply walk the beautiful stretches of South Carolina beaches, located only 15 minutes away.

12 rooms. Complimentary breakfast. Spa. $61-150

★★★EMBASSY SUITES

9800 Queensway Blvd., Myrtle Beach, 843-449-0006, 800-876-0010;
www.kingstonplantation.com

Modern and inviting, this Embassy Suites is located close to Myrtle Beach's best theaters, restaurants, water parks and shopping. The hotel itself has six outdoor pools, golf and tennis.

385 rooms. Complimentary breakfast. Restaurant, bar. Children's activity center. Pool. $151-250

★FAIRFIELD INN

1350 Paradise Circle, Myrtle Beach, 843-444-8097, 800-217-1511;
www.fairfieldinn.com

111 rooms. Complimentary breakfast. Pool. Business center. $61-150

★HAMPTON INN

1140 Celebrity Circle, Myrtle Beach, 843-916-0600, 800-426-7866;
www.hamptoninn.com

141 rooms. Complimentary breakfast. Children's activity center. Pool. $61-150

★HAMPTON INN & SUITES OCEANFRONT

1803 S. Ocean Blvd., Myrtle Beach, 843-946-6400, 877-946-6400;
www.hamptoninnoceanfront.com
116 rooms. Complimentary breakfast. Beach. Pool. $151-250

★★★HILTON MYRTLE BEACH RESORT

10000 Beach Club Drive, Myrtle Beach, 843-449-5000, 877-887-9549; www.hilton.com
This oceanfront hotel has great views of the Atlantic Ocean and inviting guest rooms decorated in bright hues of gold, blue, green and terracotta. Nearby activities include the shops at Broadway at the Beach, the NASCAR Speedway, the Palace Theater, as well as many dining options.
385 rooms. Restaurant, bar. Beach. Pool. Golf, 18 holes. $251-350

★LA QUINTA INN

1561 21st Ave. N., Myrtle Beach, 843-916-8801, 800-687-6667; www.laquinta.com
128 rooms. Complimentary breakfast. $61-150

★★OCEAN CREEK RESORT

10600 N. Kings Highway, Myrtle Beach, 843-272-7724, 877-844-3800;
www.oceancreek.com
410 rooms. Restaurant, bar. Beach. $61-150

★★★SHERATON MYRTLE BEACH CONVENTION CENTER HOTEL

2101 N. Oak St., Myrtle Beach, 843-918-5000;www.starwoodhotels.com/sheraton
Situated in the center of Myrtle Beach, within walking distance to the Broadway at the Beach shopping area, this contemporary Sheraton offers an ideal location. The hotel's signature beds come decked out with down comforters and pillow-top mattresses, which are also available in a version designed for canine travelers.
402 rooms. Restaurant, bar. Fitness center. Pool. Business center. $151-250

ALSO RECOMMENDED
SERENDIPITY INN

407 71st Ave., N., Myrtle Beach, 843-449-5268, 800-762-3229;
www.serendipityinn.com
This quaint inn located near the beach offers rooms decorated with country quilts and four poster beds.
15 rooms. Complimentary breakfast. $61-150

WHERE TO EAT
★CAGNEY'S OLD PLACE

9911 N. Kings Highway, Myrtle Beach, 843-449-3824;www.cagneysoldplace.com
American. Dinner. Closed Sunday. Bar. Children's menu. Reservations recommended. $16-35

★CAPTAIN GEORGE'S SEAFOOD

1401 29th Ave., Myrtle Beach, 843-916-2278; www.captaingeorges.com
Seafood. Lunch Sunday, dinner. Bar. Children's menu. $16-35

★★CHESTNUT HILL RESTAURANT

9922 Highway 17 N., Myrtle Beach, 843-449-3984; www.chestnuthilldining.com

American. Dinner, Sunday brunch. Bar. Children's menu. $16-35

★★COLLECTORS CAFÉ

7726 N. Kings Highway, Myrtle Beach, 843-449-9370;
www.collectorscafeandgallery.com

Mediterranean. Lunch, dinner. Closed Sunday. Bar. Reservations recommended. $36-85

★DIRTY DON'S OYSTER BAR & GRILL

408 21st Ave. N., Myrtle Beach, 843-448-4881; www.dirtydonsoysterbar.com

American, seafood. Lunch, dinner, late-night. Bar. Children's menu. Outdoor seating. $16-35

★★JOE'S BAR AND GRILL

810 Conway Ave., North Myrtle Beach, 843-272-4666; www.dinejoes.com

American. Dinner. Bar. Children's menu. Outdoor seating. $16-35

★★★THE PARSON'S TABLE

4305 McCorsley Ave., Little River, 843-249-3702;www.parsonstable.com

Not only can you get a juicy roast prime rib at The Parson's Table, but you can eat it inside a church, too. The location remains very much the same structure that it was in 1885, when Little River Methodist Church was built. The cherished establishment first opened its church doors as a restaurant in the late 1970s and has been serving exquisite American steakhouse fare ever since. The restaurant's décor is positively Southern-charm antique, complete with dark wooden walls, stained glass windows and an original Tiffany glass lamp in the main dining room. A thorough wine list graces The Parson's Table as well as a good seafood selection on top of the traditional beef. American, steakhouse. Dinner. Closed Sunday. $36-85

★★SEA CAPTAIN'S HOUSE

3002 N. Ocean Blvd., Myrtle Beach, 843-448-8082; www.seacaptains.com

Seafood. Breakfast, lunch, dinner. Bar. Children's menu. $36-85

★★★SEABLUE TAPAS

503 Highway 17 North, North Myrtle Beach, 843-249-8800;www.seablueonline.com

SeaBlue Tapas is located in a shopping center across the street from a Home Depot and a TGIF, but step inside its doors and you're suddenly and quite literally transported into ultra chic, impossibly cool blues. The bar, the walls and the glowing aquarium all emanate blue light. At times, you'll feel like you're in an underwater lounge instead of a restaurant. As for the tapas, try the SeaBlue shrimp and grits, sizzling in a garlicky sauce, or the braised baby-back ribs. If you need a break from all that blue, try the Raspberry Flirtini.

American. Dinner. Closed Sunday $36-85

ORANGEBURG

See also Aiken, Columbia

Named for the Prince of Orange, this town is the seat of Orangeburg County, one of the most prosperous farm areas in the state. Manufacturing plants for wood products, ball bearings, textiles, textile equipment, chemicals, hand tools, and lawn mowers are all located within the county.

WHAT TO SEE
EDISTO MEMORIAL GARDENS

367 Green St., Orangeburg, 803-533-6020, 800-545-6153; www.orangeburgsc.net

Thic city-owned 110-acre site has seasonal flowers blooming all year including more than 3,200 rose bushes, camellias, azaleas. Don't miss the many flowering trees.

Gardens daily, dawn-dusk.

PAWLEYS ISLAND

See also Georgetown, Myrtle Beach

A beach community halfway between Myrtle Beach and Georgetown, Pawleys Island has less than 500 year-round residents but thousands of visitors who come for its easy-going atmosphere and beach and golf access.

WHERE TO STAY
★★★LITCHFIELD PLANTATION

King's River Road, Pawleys Island, 843-237-9121, 800-869-1410;
www.litchfieldplantation.com

This former plantation house from the 1750s has been beautifully restored and converted into an elegant country inn. Guests will find uniquely decorated rooms with private baths and suites with antique sleigh beds, fireplaces and double Jacuzzis. The resort has direct beach access via Litchfield Plantation's beach club on Pawleys Island, plus onsite dining at the Carriage House Club.

38 rooms. Complimentary breakfast. Restaurant, bar. Pool. $151-250

ALSO RECOMMENDED
SEAVIEW INN

414 Myrtle Ave., Pawleys Island, 843-237-4253; www.seaviewinn.com

20 rooms. Closed November-mid-April. Children over three years only. Beach. $151-250

WHERE TO EAT
★★CARRIAGE HOUSE CLUB

Kings River Road, Litchfield Plantation, Pawleys Island,843-237-9322;
www.litchfieldplantation.com

Set in the serene backdrop of the Litchfield Plantation, the brick structure that houses the Carriage House Club restaurant is a Southern jewel to be sure. The former English carriage house is now a choice establishment for classic gourmet cuisine with a Southern twist. Must-orders are two chef specialties: the Carriage House grouper, lightly battered and served with a beurre blanc sauce and the goat cheese-Dijon mustard crusted rack of lamb.

If that doesn't do you in, take a look at the dessert list, which features good ol' pecan and key lime pies.

American. Breakfast, dinner. Closed Sunday-Monday. $36-85

ROCK HILL

Both a college and an industrial town, Rock Hill takes its name from the flint rock that had to be cut when a railroad was built through town. Today it is home to Winthrop University and flanked by state parks.

WHAT TO SEE
ANDREW JACKSON STATE PARK

196 Andrew Jackson Park Road, Lancaster, 803-285-3344;
www.southcarolinaparks.com

This 360 acre park is sprinkled with nature trails, camp sites and boat docks. The log house museum contains documents and exhibits of Jackson lore.

CATAWBA CULTURAL CENTER

1536 Tom Steven Road, Rock Hill, 803-328-2427;www.ccppcrafts.com

Located on the Catawba Indian Reservation, this center strives to preserve the heritage of the Catawbas' culture. Tours and programs are available by appointment.

Monday-Saturday 9 a.m.-5 p.m.

HISTORIC BRATTONSVILLE

1444 Brattonsville Road, McConnells, 803-684-2327; www.chmuseums.org

Learn about local history in this restored village of more than two dozen structures, including Backwoodsman Cabin, Colonel Bratton Home, Homestead House and Brick Kitchen. Gift shop. Guided tours (by appointment). Self-guided audio tour. Monday-Saturday 10 a.m.-5 p.m., Sunday 1-5 p.m.

MUSEUM OF YORK COUNTY

4621 Mount Gallant Road, Rock Hill, 803-329-2121; www.chmuseums.org

This intimate museum contains a large collection of mounted African hoofed mammals and a large African artifacts collection. The Hall of Western Hemisphere has mounted animals from North and South America. If you're looking for a souvenir, the gift shop sells Catawba pottery.

Monday-Saturday 10 a.m.-5 p.m., Sunday 1-5 p.m.

WHERE TO STAY
★HAMPTON INN

2111 Tabor Drive, Rock Hill, 803-325-1100, 800-426-7866; www.hamptoninn.com

162 rooms. Complimentary breakfast. $61-150

★MICROTEL INN & SUITES CHARLOTTE-ROCK HILL

1047 Riverview Road, Rock Hill, 803-817-7700; www.microtelinn.com

77 rooms. Business center. $61-150

WHERE TO EAT
★TAM'S TAVERN
1027 Oakland Ave., Rock Hill, 803-329-2226
Cajun, seafood. Lunch, dinner. Closed Sunday. Bar. Reservations recommended. $16-35

SANTEE
See also Orangeburg
This community serves as the gateway to the Santee-Cooper lakes recreation area, created by the Pinopolis and Santee dams on the Santee and Cooper rivers. There are numerous marinas and campgrounds on the Santee-Cooper lakes.

WHAT TO SEE
EUTAW SPRINGS BATTLEFIELD SITE
Santee, 12 miles Southeast off Highway 6
The site marks the spot where ragged colonials fought the British on September 8, 1781 in what is considered to be the last major engagement in South Carolina. Both sides claimed victory.

FORT WATSON BATTLE SITE AND INDIAN MOUND
Santee, 803-478-2217; www.discoversouthcarolina.com
Climb this 48-foot-high mound that is the site of an American Revolution battle on April 15-23, 1781, during which General Francis Marion attacked and captured a British fortification, its garrison, supplies and ammunition. The summit awards you with a view of the Santee-Cooper waters.

SANTEE NATIONAL WILDLIFE REFUGE
Secondary State Road, Summerton, 803-478-2217; www.discoversouthcarolina.com
A great destination for birds (and bird-watchers) in winter, the refuge has an observation tower and nature trails.
Tuesday-Sunday 8 a.m.-4 p.m.

WHERE TO STAY
★★BEST WESTERN
Highway 95, Santee, 803-854-3089; www.bestwestern.com
108 rooms. Complimentary breakfast. Restaurant. Pool. $61-150

SUMMERVILLE
See also Charleston
Long a resort escape for wealthy plantation owners fleeing the mosquitoes of the Low Country, Summerville has a quintessentially Southern charm and history. More than 700 homes and buildings are on the National Register of Historic Places.

WHAT TO SEE
FRANCIS BEIDLER FOREST

336 Sanctuary Road, Summerville, 843-462-2150;
www.audubon.org/local/sanctuary/beidler

Located in the heart of the Low Country, this 11,000-acre site in Four Holes Swamp encompasses the largest remaining virgin stand of bald cypress and tupelo gum trees in the world. Oak, ash and blackgum also grow here, as do 300 varieties of wildlife and numerous flowers, ferns, vines and other plants. A National Audubon Society sanctuary, the forest is named for a lumberman who championed conservation on both public and private lands. A 6,500-foot boardwalk into the swamp leads out from and back to the visitor center. Tuesday-Sunday 9 a.m.-5 p.m.

OLD DORCHESTER STATE HISTORIC SITE

300 State Park Road, Summerville, 843-873-1740; www.southcarolinaparks.com

This 325-acre park is on the site of a colonial village founded in 1697 by a group representing the Congregational Church of Dorchester, Massachusetts. By the time the war was over, the town had been abandoned. Overlooking the Ashley River, the site today includes remnants of a fort, a cemetery and the bell tower of St. Georges Parish Church. Archaeological excavations are ongoing.
Thursday-Monday 9 a.m.-6 p.m.

WHERE TO STAY
★★★★★WOODLANDS RESORT & INN

125 Parsons Road, Summerville, 843-875-2600, 800-774-9999;
www.woodlandsinn.com

The 1906 Greek Revival Main House has casual, refined and lavishly appointed guest rooms designed by interior designer David Eskell-Briggs. Guests can dip their toes in the pool, volley on the two clay tennis courts, play croquet matches on the lawn and ride bikes to the nearby town of Summerville. Sandalwoods Day Spa features Aveda products in all of its treatments. The Dining Room turns out delicious dishes in a cozy space.
19 rooms. Restaurant, bar. Children's activity center. Pool. Tennis. Business center. Spa. $251-350

WHERE TO EAT
★★★★★THE DINING ROOM AT THE WOODLANDS

125 Parsons Road, Summerville, 843-308-2115, 800-774-9999;
www.woodlandsinn.com

Perfecting the atmosphere of Southern charm, the Dining Room offers menus that change daily and feature flavorful, regional American dishes. Chef Tarver King and his staff showcase local ingredients. Standout dishes include hay-smoked duckling with crispy pomme darphin and Maine lobster with morels and English pea-acquerello risotto. With wine pairings by sommelier Stephane Peltier and desserts like chocolate napoleon with fleur de sel caramel, the end of a meal is as memorable as the beginning.
American. Breakfast, lunch, dinner, Sunday brunch. Bar. Jacket required at dinner. Reservations recommended. Valet parking. Outdoor seating. $351 and up

SUMTER

See also Camden, Columbia

Once the center of a prosperous agricultural area, Sumter has in recent years become an industrial center. Both the city and county are named for General Thomas Sumter, the "fighting gamecock" of the American Revolution. As a tourism spot, Sumter offers a unique contrast of antebellum mansions and modern facilities. Shaw Air Force Base, headquarters of the 9th Air Force and the 363rd Tactical Fighter Wing, is nearby.

WHAT TO SEE
CHURCH OF THE HOLY CROSS
335 N. Kings Highway, Stateburg, 803-494-8101, 800-688-4748;
www.discoversouthcarolina.com
Boasting unusual architectural design and construction, the church is built from pise de terre (rammed earth). The structure is also noted for stained-glass windows set to catch the rays of the rising sun. Many notable South Carolinians from the 1700s are buried in the old church cemetery, including Joel R. Poinsett.

OPERA HOUSE
21 N. Main St., Sumter, 803-436-2500, 888-688-4748; www.sumter-sc.com
Today the 1893 Opera House stands not only as a symbol of the past but also as an active sign of the ongoing progressive spirit of the people of Sumter. The 600-seat auditorium is used for concerts, school events and other local happenings. Many performances are free.

POINSETT STATE PARK
6660 Poinsett Park Road, Wedgefield, 803-494-8177; www.southcarolinaparks.com
Visit the approximately 1,000 acres of mountains and swamps named for Joel R. Poinsett, who introduced the poinsettia (which originated in Mexico) to the U.S. Spanish moss, mountain laurel, rhododendron. Enjoy fishing, boating and the onsite nature center.
Daily.

SUMTER COUNTY MUSEUM
122 N. Washington St., Sumter, 803-775-0908; www.sumtercountymuseum.org
This two-story Edwardian house depicting Victorian lifestyle with period rooms, historical exhibits, war memorabilia, economic and cultural artifacts, artwork and archives (genealogical research). There is a museum is surrounded by formal gardens designed by Robert Marvin.
Tuesday-Saturday 10 a.m.-5 p.m.

SUMTER GALLERY OF ART
200 Hasel St., Sumter, 803-775-0543; www.sumtergallery.org
Located in the 24,000-square-foot facility at the Sumter County Cultural Center, regional artwork features paintings, drawings, sculpture, photography and pottery. There is a permanent collection of touchable works for the blind as well.
Tuesday-Saturday 11 a.m.-5 p.m., Sunday 1:30-5 p.m.

SWAN LAKE IRIS GARDENS

822 W. Liberty St., Sumter, 803-436-2640; www.sumter-sc.com

Hosting one of the country's premier Iris festivals, held every May, the 150-acre garde is home to Kaempferi and Japanese iris, seasonal plantings, nature trails, ancient cypress, oak and pine trees. There is a 45-acre lake with all eight species of swan.

Daily 7:30 a.m.-dusk.

WHERE TO STAY
★FAIRFIELD INN

2390 Broad St., Sumter, 803-469-9001, 800-228-2800; www.qualityinn.com

124 rooms. Complimentary breakfast. Pool. $61-150

WALTERBORO

See also Beaufort, Charleston

Settled in 1784 by Charleston plantation owners as a summer resort area, Walterboro has retained its charm of yesterday despite its growth. The town boasts a casual pace and rural lifestyle where people can enjoy fishing and hunting, early 19th-century architectural designs, plantations and beach and recreational facilities.

WHAT TO SEE
COLLETON COUNTY COURTHOUSE

101 Hampton St., Walterboro

The building was designed by Robert Mills. It is the site of the first public nullification meeting in the state in 1828.

OLD COLLETON COUNTY JAIL

239 N. Jefferies Blvd., Walterboro, 843-549-2303; www.southcarolinamuseums.org

This Neo-Gothic 1855 structure resembles a castle and is home to the Colleton Museum and the Chamber of Commerce. It served as the Walterboro jail until 1937.

SOUTH CAROLINA ARTISANS CENTER

334 Wichman St., Walterboro, 843-549-0011; www.southcarolinaartisanscenter.org

Regional artists show their wares and demonstrate their skills here. Check the Web site for special educational programs and classes.

Monday-Saturday 9 a.m.-6 p.m., Sunday 1-6 p.m.

WHERE TO STAY
★★COMFORT INN & SUITES

97 Downs Lane, Walterboro, 843-538-5911, 877-424-6423; www.comfortinn.com

96 rooms. Complimentary breakfast. Restaurant. $61-150

INDEX

B

Babette's Café (Atlanta), *23*

Bacchanalia (Atlanta), *23*

Back Porch (Ocracoke), *120*

Baker Creek State Park (Greenwood), *165*

The Ballantyne Resort, A Luxury Collection Hotel (Charlotte), *87*

Ballastone Inn & Townhouse (Savannah), *63*

Balsam Mountain Inn (Waynesville), *133*

Barber House (Valdosta), *68*

Barefoot Landing (Myrtle Beach), *172*

Barefoot Resort (Myrtle Beach), *172*

Barksdale House Inn (Charleston), *151*

Barnsley Gardens Resort (Calhoun), *40*

Basil (Charleston), *153*

Basil's Mediterranean Café (Atlanta), *24*

Bath State Historic Site (Washington), *132*

Battery Carriage House Inn (Charleston), *151*

Battleship North Carolina. (Wilmington), *134*

Beach Cove Resort (Myrtle Beach), *173*

Beaufort Historic Site (Beaufort), *77*

The Beaufort House Victorian Inn (Asheville), *74*

Beaufort Inn (Beaufort), *142*

Bed & Breakfast Inn (Savannah), *63*

Beef Barn (Greenville), *107*

Belford's (Savannah), *64*

Bennett Place State Historic Site (Durham), *95*

Bennie's Red Barn (Saint Simons Island), *58*

Berry College (Rome), *56*

The Best Cellar Restaurant (Blowing Rock), *80*

Best Western Brunswick Inn (Brunswick), *39*

Best Western Colonial Inn (Athens), *11*

Best Western Columbus (Columbus), *43*

Best Western Courtyard Resort (Jacksonville), *112*

Best Western Great Smokies Inn (Cherokee), *93*

Best Western Hilltop Inn (Forsyth), *47*

Best Western Inn Of Dalton (Dalton), *46*

Best Western Island Inn (Saint Simons Island), *57*

Best Western King Charles Inn (Charleston), *149*

Best Western King Of The Road (Valdosta), *68*

Best Western La Sammana (Wilson), *137*

Best Western Ocean Reef Suites (Kill Devil Hills), *113*

Best Western Riverside Inn (Macon), *53*

Best Western Sea Island Inn (Beaufort), *142*

Best Western Skyland Inn (Durham), *97*

Best Western Sweetgrass Inn (Charleston), *149*

Best Western (Santee), *178*

Bethesda Presbyterian Church (Camden), *143*

Biltmore Estate (Asheville), *72*

Bistro Savannah (Savannah), *64*

Bistro Sofia (Greensboro), *106*

Bistro Vg (Greater Atlanta Area), *33*

Blackbeard's (Jekyll Island), *51*

Blossom Café (Charleston), *153*

Blowing Rock Inn (Blowing Rock), *79*

Blowing Rock (Blowing Rock), *78*

Bludau's Goetchius House (Columbus), *43*

Bluepointe (Atlanta), *24*

Boardwalk Inn At Wild Dunes Resort (Isle Of Palms), *169*

The Boathouse Restaurant (Isle Of Palms), *170*

Bone's Restaurant (Atlanta), *24*

C

ATLANTA

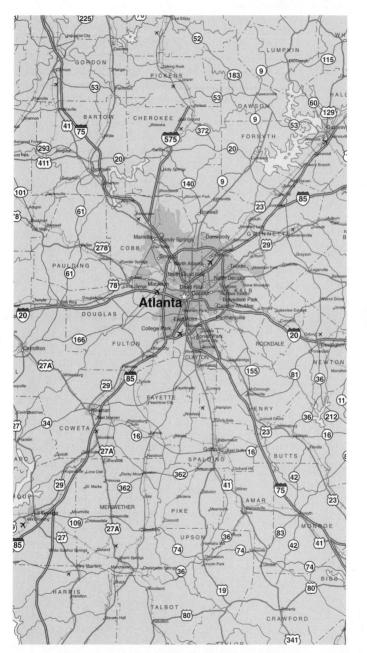

GEORGIA

NORTH CAROLINA

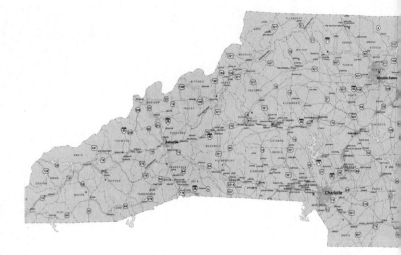

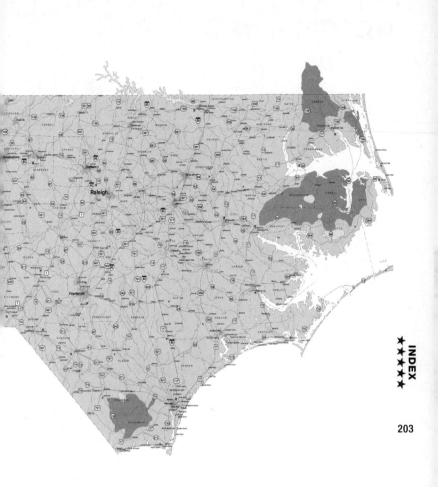

RALEIGH, NC

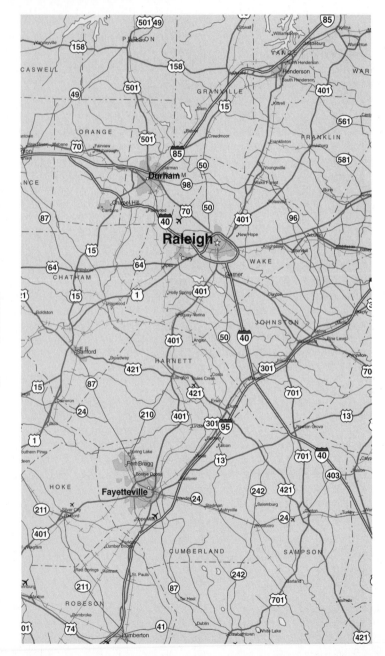

CHARLESTON, SC

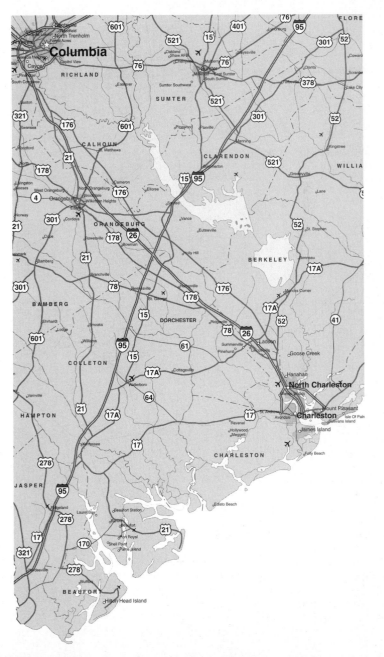

SOUTH CAROLINA

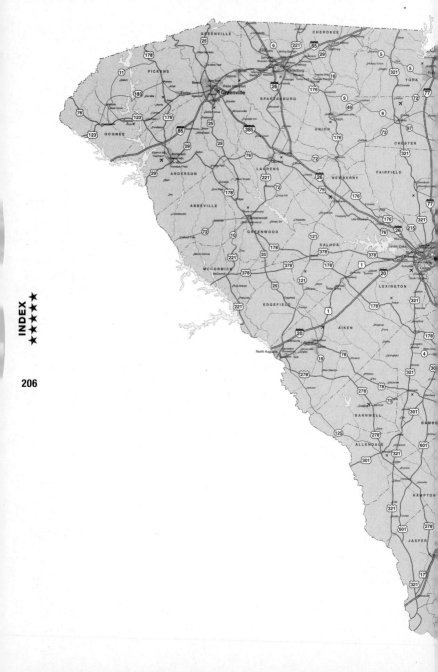